THE
LIVING WELLS
OF WALES

THE LIVING WELLS OF WALES

new photographs and old tales
of our sacred springs, holy wells and spas

PHIL COPE

with the poetry of
Dylan Thomas, Gillian Clarke, RS Thomas, Tony Curtis, TS Eliot, Waldo Williams, Philip Larkin, Ruth Bidgood, William Wordsworth, Susan Richardson, AG Prys-Jones, Lewis Glyn Cothi, Dafydd Benwyn, Matthew Arnold, Dafydd Llwyd ap Llywelyn ap Gruffudd, Lewis Morris, Felicia Hemans, Charlotte Wardle, Valerie Gillies, Seamus Heaney, Lemn Sissay, Maura Dooley and Cathal Ó Searcaigh

SEREN

is the book imprint of
Poetry Wales Press Ltd
Nolton Street, Bridgend, Wales

www.serenbooks.com
facebook.com/SerenBooks
twitter: @SerenBooks

Text and Photographs
© Phil Cope 2019

The right of Phil Cope to be identified as the Author of this Work has been asserted in accordance with the Copyright, Designs and Patents Act, 1988.

ISBN 978-178172-496-5

A CIP record for this title is available from the British Library.

All rights reserved.
No part of this publication may be reproduced, stored in a retrieval system, or transmitted at any time or by any means electronic, mechanical, photocopying, recording or otherwise without the prior permission of the copyright holders.

The publisher works with the financial assistance of the Welsh Books Council.

**Designed for Seren
by Phil Cope**
phil.cope66@gmail.com

Original map designs by George Manley
georgemanley1993@gmail.com

Printed in the Czech Republic
by Akcent Media Ltd.

page 2:
Ffynnon Fair / Mary's Well, Penrhys [8.1]

Keep Wales Tidy is pleased to have contributed to the development of this important new book for Wales, as part of its **Living Wells Project**. It gratefully acknowledges the many hidden stories shared by individuals across the country, and the support of the Heritage Lottery Fund, the Welsh Government, Llŷn Area of Outstanding Natural Beauty, Pembrokeshire Coast National Park, Brecon Beacons National Park and the Sustainable Development Fund.

acknowledgements

The following poems, or excerpts from them are published with our thanks: Ruth Bidgood's 'Ffynnon Gybi' and 'Patricio 2001' (*Scintilla* vol 8); Gillian Clarke's 'Healers' (*Making Beds for the Dead*, Carcanet 2004); Tony Curtis' 'At Gumfreston Church' (*Crossing Over*, Seren 2007); TS Eliot's 'Usk' (*Complete Poems*, Faber 2004); Philip Larkin's 'Water' (*Whitsun Weddings*, Faber 1964); A.G. Prys-Jones' 'St Govan' (*Collected Poems*, Gomer 1988); Susan Richardson's 'Ffynnon Fair' (*Creatures of the Intertidal Zone*, Cinnamon Press, 2009); Cathal Ó Searcaigh's 'The Well' (*Out in the Open*, Cló Iar-Chonnachta, 1997); Dylan Thomas' 'The force that through the green fuse drove the flower' (*Collected Poems*, Dent 1964); RS Thomas' 'A Thicket in Lleyn' (*Experimenting With an Amen*, Macmillan 1986) and 'Ffynnon Fair' (*Laboratories of the Spirit*, Macmillan 1975).

contents

Map of Wales 5
Introduction: *Water That Plays The Oldest Music* 11

1. YNYS MÔN / ANGLESEY: a meeting of opposites 28

1.1 Ffynnon Sant Seiriol / St Seiriol's Well, Penmon, nr Rhosybol 30
1.2 Ffynnon Dwynwen / St Dwynwen's Well, Llanddwyn Island 32
1.3 Ffynnon Wenfaen / St Gwenfaen's Well, nr Rhoscolyn 34
1.4 Ffynnon Eilian / St Eilian's Well, Llaneilian 37
1.5 Ffynnon Llanfihangel Dinsylwy, nr Llanddona 38
1.6 Ffynnon Badrig / Patrick's Well, Llanbadrig 39
1.7 Ffynnon Goch / The Red Spring / Lord Boston's Sulphur Well, Penrhoslligwy 40
1.8 Ffynnon Allgo / St Gallgo's Well 41
1.9 Ffynnon Sant Cyngar / St Cyngar's Well, Llangefni 41
1.10 Ffynnon Gwrachod / Witches Well, Holyhead 41
1.11 Ffynnon Gybi / St Cybi's Well, Clorach Fawr 41
1.12 Ffynnon Ceinwen / St Ceinwen's Well, Cerrigceinwen 41

2. GWYNEDD: walls and bridges 42

2.1 Caer Rufeinig *Segontium* / *Segontium* Roman Fort, Caernarfon 44
2.2 Ffynhonnau Castell Caernarfon / Caernarfon Castle wells 46
2.3 Ffynhonnau Castell Harlech / Harlech Castle wells 47
2.4 Ffynnon Fair / St Mary's Well, Maentwrog 48
2.5 Ffynnon Gwyfil / Gwyfil's Well, Plas Brondanw 50
2.6 Ffynnon Faglan / Baglan's Well, Llanfaglan 50
2.7 Ffynnon Beris / St Peris' Well, nr Llanberis 53
2.8 Ffynnon Enddwyn / Enddwyn's Well, nr Dyffryn Ardudwy 56
2.9 Ffynnon Cegin Arthur / The Well of Arthur's Kitchen, Llanddeiniolen 57
2.10 Ffynnon Eidda / Eidda's Well, nr Blaenau Ffestiniog 57
2.11 Ffynnon-y-Capel / Chapel Well, nr Dolgellau 57
2.12 Ffynnon Bedydd Sgotaidd / Scotch Baptism Well, Harlech 57
2.13 Cafn i geffylau / horse trough, Harlech 57

3. PEN LLŶN / THE LLŶN PENINSULA: to be a pilgrim 58

3.1 Ffynnon Gybi / St Cybi's Well, Llangybi 61
3.2 Ffynnon Beuno / St Beuno's Well, Clynnog Fawr 65
3.3 Ffynnon Fyw (or Dduw) / The Living (or God's) Well, Mynytho 68
3.4 Ffynnon Arian / The Money (or Silver) Well 69
3.5 Ffynnon Sarff / The Serpent Well, Mynytho 71
3.6 Ffynnon Aelrhiw / Aelrhiw Well, Plas yn Rhiw 72
3.7 Ffynnon Saint / Saint's Well, Plas yn Rhiw 75
3.8 Ffynnon Pant / Pant Well, Plas yn Rhiw 77
3.9 Ffynnon Plas yn Rhiw / Plas yn Rhiw Well 78
3.10 Ffynnon y Saint / Saint's Well, nr Aberdaron 79
3.11 Ffynnon Pen-y-Groes, Pen Cilan 79
3.12 Amphitheatre well, Plas Glyn-y-Weddw Arts Centre 81
3.13 Ffynnon Engan / St Engan's Well, Llanengan 82
3.14 Ffynnon Fair / Mary's Well, Uwchymynydd 83

3.15	Ffynnon Barfau / The Well of the Beards, Ynys Enlli	86
3.16	Ffynnon Baglau / Ffynnon Bryn Baglau / Ffynnon Dalar, Ynys Enlli	86
3.17	Ffynnon Dolysgwydd / Dolysgwydd Well, Ynys Enlli	87
3.18	Ffynnon Gwynhoedl / Gwynhoedl Well, Ynys Enlli	88
3.19	Ffynnon Corn / Horn Well, Ynys Enlli	88
3.20	Ffynnon Fair / Mary's Well, Bryncroes	88
3.21	Ffynnon Fair / Mary's Well, Nefyn	88
3.22	Ffynnon Felin Bach / The Well of the Little Mill, Pwllheli	88
3.23	Ffynnon Rhufeinig / Roman Well, nr Criccieth	88
3.24	Ffynnon Sanctaidd / The Sacred Well, Pistyll	89
3.25	Ffynnon Corn / Horn Well, Uwchmynydd	89
3.26	Ffynnon West End / West End Well, Trefor	89
3.27	Ffynnon Lleuddad / Lleuddad Well, Botwnnog	89
3.28	Ffynnon arall Llangybi / Llangybi's other well	89
3.29	Ffynnon Porth Ysgaden / Porth Ysgaden Well, nr Tudweiliog	89
3.30	Ffynnon Aelhaearn / Aelhaearn Well	89
3.31	Ffynnon Dyno Goch / Dyno Goch's Well, Ynys Enlli	90
3.32	Ffynnon Owain Rolant / Owain Rolant's Well / Ffynnon Uchaf / Upper Well, Ynys Enlli	90
3.33	Ffynnon Trwy'r Nant / 'Through the Stream' Well, Llanbedrog	90
3.34	Ffynnon Plas Bach / Plas Bach Well, Ynys Enlli	90
3.35	Ffynnon Cristin / Cristin's Well / Ffynnon Uchaf / Upper Well, Ynys Enlli	90
3.36	Ffynnon Tŷ Pilla / Tŷ Pilla Well, Ynys Enlli	90
3.37	Ffynnon Carreg / Stone Well, Ynys Enlli	90
3.38	Ffynnon Castell Cricieth / Criccieth Castle Well	91
3.39	Ffynnon ganoloesol Penarth Fawr / Penarth Fawr medieval well	91
3.40	Tŷ ffynnon ryngwladol newydd / new international well-house, Felin Uchaf, Llŷn	91

4. CLWYD: the justice of waters — 92

4.1	Ffynhonnau a Sba Trefriw / Trefriw Wells and Spa	94
4.2	Ffynnon Fair / St Mary's Well, nr Trefnant	97
4.3	Ffynnon Elian / St Elian's Well, Llanelian yn Rhos	99
4.4	Ffynnon Sanctaidd Celynin Sant / St Celynin's Well, Llangelynin	102
4.5	Ffynnon Elen / Helen's Well, Dolwyddelan	105
4.6	Ffynnon Drillo / St Trillo's Holy Chapel Well, Rhos on Sea	108
4.7	Ffynnon Beuno / St Beuno's Well, Tremeirchion	110
4.8	Ffynnon Degla / St Tecla's Well, Llandegla	112
4.9	Ffynnon Dyfnog / St Dyfnog's Well, Llanrhaeadr-yng-Nghinmeirch	114
4.10	Ffynnon Sara / Sacran's Well, nr Derwen	117
4.11	Ffynnon Gwenffrewi / St Winefride's Well, Holywell	119
4.12	Ffynnon Ddoged / St Doged's Well, Llanddoged	126
4.13	Ffynnon Beuno / St Beuno's Well	126
4.14	Ffynnon Oswald / St Oswald's Well, nr Holywell	126
4.15	Ffynnon yr Holl Saint / All Saints Well, Gresford	126
4.16	Ffynnon Fach / The Little Well, Crimea Pass	126
4.17	Ffynnon Penrhyn / Lord Penrhyn's Well, Ysbyty Ifan	126

4.18	Ffynnon Sadwrn / Saturday / Saturn Well, Llandudno	127	
4.19	Ffynnon Mair Magdalen / Mary Magdelene's Well, Cerrigydrudion	127	
4.20	Ffynnon Fair / St Mary's Well, Llanrhos	127	
4.21	Pistyll yfed Eglwys Llanrhos / Llanrhos Church drinking fountain	127	
4.22	Ffynnon Gynfran / St Gynfran's Well	127	
4.23	Ffynnon Lletyr Fadoc / Well of Madoc's Lodgings / Ffynnon Rufeinig / The Roman Well, Great Orme, Llandudno	127	
4.24	Ffynnon Tudno / St Tudno's Well, Llandudno	127	
4.25	Ffynnon Fair /Mary's Well, nr Rhuddlan	127	
4.26	Ffynnon Beuno / St Beuno's Well, Holywell	128	
4.27	Ffynnon Goffa Mary Short / Mary Short Memorial Fountain, St Asaph	128	
4.28	Ffynnon Fferm Valle Crucis / Valle Crucis Farm Well, nr Llangollen	128	
4.29	Tŷ Baddon Rhufeinig Prestatyn / Prestatyn Roman Bath-house	128	
4.30	Ffynnon Abaty Valle Crucis / Valle Crucis Abbey Well, nr Llangollen	128	
4.31	Ffynnon Gynhafal / St Cynhafal's Well, Llangynhafal	128	

5. CANOLBARTH CYMRU / MID WALES: towards a scientific explanation 130

5.1	Ffynnon Drewi / The Stinking Well, nr Bronant	132
5.2	*Balineae Silures* (Castell Collen)	135
5.3	Ffynnon Sant Ffraid / St Bridget's Well, nr Swyddffynnon	136
5.4	Ffynnon Llawddog / St Llawddog's (or Ludoc's) Well, Cenarth	138
5.5	Ffynnon Non / St Non's Well, Eglwysfach	139
5.6	Ffynnon Sant Myllin / St Myllin's Well, Llanfyllin	140
5.7	Llanfyllin bridge well	140
5.8	Y Ffynnon ym Mhentre Llandre / The Well at Llandre Village	140
5.9	Ffynnon Cybi / St Gybi's Well, Llangybi	142
5.10	Ffynnon Dyffryn Tawel / The Well of the Silent Grove, Strata Florida	143
5.11	Ffynnon yr Abaty / The Abbey Well, Strata Florida	144
5.12	Ffynnon Hafod Newydd / The Well of the New Summer Pastures, Strata Florida	145
5.13	Ffynnon Tyn-y-Garreg / The Well of the Stone Cottage, Strata Florida	146
5.14	Ffynhonnell Haearnol Rhydd / Free Chalybeate Spring, Llandrindod	147
5.15	Ffynnon Heli Lithia / Lithia Saline Well, Llandrindod Wells	149
5.16	Llandrindod pump room other well	149
5.17	Ffynnon y Llygad / Eye Well, Llandrindod	149
5.18	another Rock Park well, Llandrindod	150
5.19	Llangammarch Wells	152
5.20	Ffynnon Ddrewllyd / Dolycoed Spa, Llanwrtyd Wells	153
5.21	Ffynnon Castell Bronllys / Bronllys Castle Well	157
5.22	Ffynnon Gynidr / St Cynidr's Well, Glasbury	157
5.23	Ffynnon Oer / Cold Well, Swyddffynnon	157
5.24	Pwmp pentref Llanddewi Brefi / Llanddewi Brefi village pump	157
5.25	Ffynnon Creigiau Pen yr Allt / Pen yr Allt Rocks Well, Machynlledd	157
5.26	Ffynnon Fair / St Mary's Well, Pilleth	157
5.27	Ffynnon Fair / St Mary's Well, Llanfair Caereinion	158
5.28	Ffynnon Badarn / St Padarn's Well, Aberystwyth	158
5.29	Ffynnon Gadfan / St Cadfan's Well, Llangadfan	158
5.30	Victoria Wells, nr Llanwrtyd Wells	158
5.31	Garrison Well, Machynlledd	158

5.32 Ffynnon Llywelyn ap Gruffydd /
     Llywelyn's Well, Cilmeri   158
5.33 another Bronant well   158

6. BANNAU BRYCHEINIOG / BRECON BEACONS:
tales as old as time   160

6.1 Ffynnon Angaeron / Aaron's Well,
     nr Goytre   162
6.2 Ffynnon Eluned, Llechfaen   164
6.3 Ffynnon Pen Cefn y Gaer /
     'Penginger' Well, Brecon   164
6.4 Ffynnon y Meddygon Myddfai /
     The Physicians of Myddfai's Well   168
6.5 Ffynnon Isho / St Issui's Well, Partrishow   171
6.6 Ffynnon Gwyddfaen / St Dyfan's Well,
     Llandyfan   174
6.7 Ffynnon y Castell / Castle Well,
     Carreg Cennen   175
6.8 Ffynnon Maendu / Maendu Well, Brecon   177
6.9 Tŷ Ffynnon y Tafarn Newydd /
     The New Inn Well House, nr Cross Ash   179
6.10 Ffynnon Keyna / St Canna's Well
     / The Black Lion Well, Hay-on-Wye   181
6.11 Ffynnon Alarch / The Swan Well, Hay   183
6.12 Ffynnon y Cei / The Wharf Well (or
     Ffynnon y Rhodfa / The Walk Well), Hay   184
6.13 Ffynnon Priordy / Priory Well, Brecon   185
6.14 Ffynnon y Llygad / Eye Well, Brecon   185
6.15 Holy well, Abergavenny   185
6.16 Ffynnon y Castell / Castle Well, nr Cwmyoy   185
6.17 Ffynnon Padrig / Patrick's Spring, Govilon   185
6.18 Ffynnon Eglwys Sant Teilo /
     St Teilo's Church Well, Llandeilo   185
6.19 Ffynnon Ymyl y Ffordd, Llanofer 1 /
     Llanover Roadside Well 1, nr Abergavenny   186
6.20 Cafn y Bwystfil / The Beast Trough,
     nr Abergavenny   186
6.21 Ffynnon Ymyl y Ffordd, Llanofer 2 /
     Llanover Roadside Well 2   186
6.22 Ffynnon Gofer / Nine Wells,
     Llanover Estate   186
6.23 Cafn Anifeiliaid David Watkins /
     David Watkins Animal Trough, Hay   186
6.24 Ffynnon Faelog / St Maelog / Meilig's Well,
     nr Llowes   186
6.25 Ffynnon y Sgirrid / Skirrid Mountain
     Well, nr Abergavenny   187
6.26 Ffynnon Sant Ioan neu Castell /
     St John's or Castle Well, Hay-on-Wye   187
6.27 Ffynnon Anne / St Anne's Well, Trefecca   187
6.28 Ffynnon Logan / Logan's Well, nr Myddfai   187
6.29 Ffynnon Fair / St Mary's Well, Hay   187
6.30 Ffynnon y Dref / Town Well, Hay   187
6.31 Ffynnon y Llygad / Eye Well, Hay   188
6.32 Ffynnon Goeden Bocs /
     Box Tree Well, nr Cwmyoy   188
6.33 Ffynnon yr Esgob Gower /
     Bishop Gower's Well, Llanddew   188
6.34 Ffynnon Syr Charles Morgan /
     Sir Charles Morgan Well, Brecon   188
6.35 Ffynnon Geneu / St Genau's Well,
     Llangenny   188
6.36 Pistyll yfed Gogledd Crughywel /
     North Crickhowell drinking fountain   188

7. GWENT:
borderlands to another world   190

7.1 Baddon Rhufeinig Caerllion /
     Caerleon Roman Baths   193
7.2 Baddon Rhufeinig Caerwent /
     Caerwent Roman Baths   195
7.3 Ffynhonnau Castell Rhaglan /
     Raglan Castle Wells   196
7.4 Castell Cil-y-Coed / Caldicot Castle   199

7.5	Ffynhonnau Castell Casgwent / Chepstow Castle Wells	201
7.6	Ffynnon Sannan / St Sannan's Well, Bedwellty	203
7.7	Ffynnon Gybi / St Cybi's Well, Llangybi	204
7.8	Ffynnon y pentref Llanfair Discoed / Llanfair Discoed village well, nr Chepstow	205
7.9	Ffynnon Rhinweddol / The Virtuous Well / Ffynnon Anne / St Anne's Well, Trellech	206
7.10	Ffynnon Castell Brynbuga / Usk Castle Well	210
7.11	Ffynnon Castell Gwyn / White Castle Well	210
7.12	Ffynnon Gwladys / St Gwladys' Well, Basseleg	210
7.13	Ffynnon y pentref Catbrook / Catbrook village well, nr Chepstow	210
7.14	Ffynnon Chwilgrug / Wilcrick Wishing Well (Y Ffynnon Ofuned), nr Magor	210
7.15	Ffynnon Cynheiddon / St Cenedlon's Well, Rockfield / Llanyronwy	210
7.16	Ffynnon Tewdric / St Tewdric's Well, Mathern, nr Chepstow	211
7.17	Cafn ymyl y ffordd Hendre / Hendre roadside trough, nr Rockfield	211
7.18	Ffynnon ofuned pentref Tredynog / Tredunnock village wishing well	211
7.19	Ffynnon y dref, Trefynwy / Monmouth Victorian town well	211
7.20	Cafn ochr y ffordd, Ynysgynwraidd / Skenfrith roadside trough, nr Raglan	211
7.21	Ffynnon Goffa, Ynysgynwraidd / Skenfrith memorial well, nr Raglan	211

8. Y CWMOEDD / THE VALLEYS: a wounded land 212

8.1	Ffynnon Fair / Mary's Well, Penrhys	214
8.2	Tarren Deusant / The Knoll of Two Saints, nr Llantrisant	219
8.3	Ffynnon Gyffyr / Monks' Bath-house, Margam Park	221
8.4	Ffynnon Mair / Mary's Well, Margam	223
8.5	Ffynnon Gollwyn / St Collwyn's Well, Pyle	224
8.6	Ffynnon Fawr / The Big Well, Nottage	225
8.7	Ffynnon Ddrewllyd / The Stinking Well, Cwm-Twrch Isaf, nr Merthyr Tydfil	227
8.8	Ffynnon Mogwai / Sweetwells, Pont-y-Rhyl, Garw Valley	229
8.9	Ffynnon Dwym / Hot Well or Ffynnon Taf / Taff's Well	231
8.10	Ffynnon Castell Caerffili / Caerphilly Castle Well	233
8.11	Ffynnon Dewi / St David's Well, Nottage	233
8.12	Ffynnon Ciwg / St Ciwg Well, nr Pontardawe	233
8.13	Ffynnon Dôl yr Ogwr / Ogmore Down Well, nr St Bride's Major	233
8.14	Ffynnon a Phwll Bedyddio, Corntown / Corntown Well and Baptismal Pond	233
8.15	Ffynnon Ioan Fedyddiwr neu Ffynnon Sandford / St John the Baptist or Sandford's Well, Newton	233

9. CAERDYDD A BRO MORGANNWG / CARDIFF & THE VALE OF GLAMORGAN: getting and spending 234

9.1	Ffynhonau y Pentre / Salmon's Wells, Penllyn	236
9.2	Ffynnon Santes Anne / St Anne's Well, Llanmihangel, nr Llandow	238
9.3	Ffynnon Yfed Treganna / Canton Drinking Fountain, Cardiff	239
9.4	Ffynnon ymyl y ffordd Dinas Llandaf / Llandaff City roadside well, Cardiff	239
9.5	Ffynnon Sant Teilo / St Teilo's Well, Llandaff Cathedral	240

9.6	Ffynnon y Llaethdy / The Dairy Well, Llandaff Cathedral	240
9.7	Ffynnon Fferm Llwyn-yr-eos / Llwyn-yr-eos Farm well, St Fagans	241
9.8	Ffynnon Sant Fagan / St Fagan's Holy Well	242
9.9	Ffynnon Llyswyrni / Llysworney Well	243
9.10	Pwmp pentref y Bontfaen / Cowbridge village pump	243
9.11	Ffynnon Croes Ham / Ham Cross Well, Llantwit Major	243
9.12	Ffynnon Saint-y-Brid / St Bride's Major village well and pond	243
9.12	Pwmp Eglwys Sain Nicolas / St Nicholas Church pump	243
9.14	Ffynnon Castell Caerdydd / Cardiff Castle Well	243
9.15	Ffynnon Castell Coch / Castell Coch Well	244
9.16	Ffynnon Gattwg / St Cadoc's Well, Pentyrch	244
9.17	Pistyll Yfed Parc Buddug / Victoria Park Drinking Fountain, Cardiff	244
9.18	Pistyll Yfed Caeau Llandaf / Llandaff Fields Drinking Fountain, Cardiff	244
9.19	Pistyll Yfed Gerddi'r Faenor / Grange Gardens Drinking Fountain, Cardiff	244
9.20	Pistyll yfed Canolfan Ddinesig Caerdydd / Cardiff Civic Centre drinking fountain	244
9.21	Ffynnon Llandennis / St Dennis' Well, Cardiff	245

10. ABERTAWE & PHENRHYN GWYR / SWANSEA & THE GOWER PENINSULA: christianity-super-mare — 246

10.1	Ffynnon Castell / The Castle Well, Swansea	248
10.2	Ffynnon Bedr / St Peter's Well, Caswell Bay	249
10.3	Ffynnon pentref Murton Green / Murton Green village well	251
10.4	Ffynnon Cenydd / St Cenydd's Well	251
10.5	Ffynnon Illtud / St Illtyd's Well, Llanrhidian	253
10.6	Ffynnon Sanctaidd / Holy Well, nr Reynoldston	256
10.7	Ffynnon Kithen / Kithen Well, nr Parkmill	256
10.8	Ffynnon y Felin / Mill Well, Parkmill	256
10.9	Ffynnon y Drindod neu Ffynnon Cenydd / Trinity Well or St Cenydd's Well, Ilstone	256

11. SIR GAERFYRDDIN / CARMARTHENSHIRE: rites and wrongs — 258

11.1	Ffynnon Antwn Sant / St Anthony's Well, Llansteffan	260
11.2	Ffynnon Geler / St Celer's Well, Llangeler	261
11.3	Capel Erbach / Erbach Chapel, Porthyrhyd	263
11.4	Ffynnon Capel Begawdin / Begawdin Chapel Well, Porthyrhyd	265
11.5	Dwlch i Dduw, nr Llanon, nr Llanelli	267
11.6	Ffynnon yn Ddragau / The Well of Tears, Bancyfelin, nr Carmarthen	267
11.7	pistyll ymyl y ffordd / roadside fountain, Five Roads, nr Llanelli	267
11.8	cafn ymyl y ffordd / roadside trough, Five Roads, nr Llanelli	267
11.9	Pistyll goffa Rees Goring Thomas memorial fountain, Llanon	267
11.10	'Ogof dy Hygrea' / 'The Grotto of Hygrea', Llanarthne	267

12. SIR BENFRO / PEMBROKESHIRE: pushed to the margins — 268

12.1	Ffynhonnau Sanctaidd Gumfreston / Gumfreston Holy Wells, nr Tenby	271
12.2	Ffynnon Ddeiniol / St Deiniol's Well, Penally	276
12.3	Ffynnon Teilo / St Teilo's Well, Penally	276
12.4	Ffynnon 'Tŷ' / 'House' Well, Penally	276

12.5	Ffynnon Porth Lliw / Port Clew Holy Well, Freshwater East	277
12.6	Ffynhonnau Sain Gofan / St Govan's Wells, nr Bosherston	279
12.7	Ffynnon Drefelen / Bletherstone Church Well, nr Narbeth	283
12.8	Ffynnon Leonard / St Leonard's Well, Crundale Rath, Rudbaxton	284
12.9	Ffynnon Garadoc / St Caradoc's Well Haverfordwest	286
12.10	Ffynnon Tafarn Sain Ffraid / St Bride's Inn Well, Little Haven	287
12.11	Ffynnon Gastell Llawhaden / Llawhaden Castle Well	288
12.12	Pistyll Sanctaidd Castell Henllys / Castell Henllys sacred spring	290
12.13	Ffynnon yr Ychen / St Teilo's Well, nr Llangolman	291
12.14	Ffynnon Gapan / Llanllawer Sainted Well	293
12.15	Ffynnon Wnda / St Wnda's Well, Llanwnda	295
12.16	Ffynnon Nicolas / St Nicholas' Well	297
12.17	Ffynnon Santes Non / St Non's Well, nr St Davids	300
12.18	Ffynnon Ddewi / St David's Well, Porthclais	303
12.19	Pistyll Dewi / St David's Spring St David's Cathedral	305
12.20	Ffynnon Sant Teilo / St Teilo's Well Llandeloy	307
12.21	Ffynnon Faiddog / St Aidan's Well, Whitesands Bay	309
12.22	Naw Ffynnon / Nine Wells, nr Solva	312
12.23	Ffynnon Tregroes / Tregroes Well, Whitchurch	315
12.24	Ffynnon Fair / St Mary's Well, Warren	318
12.25	ffynnon pentref / village well, Pembroke Town	318
12.26	Ffynnon y Stryd Fawr / Main Street well, Pembroke Town	318
12.27	Yr Hen Ddyfrffos / The Old Conduit, Monkton	318
12.28	Ffynnon a chafn ymyl y ffordd / roadside well and trough, nr Stackpole	318
12.29	Ffynnon Sant Ioan / St John's Well, Tenby	319
12.30	Ffynnon bedydd mynwent eglwys Santes Fair Burton / Burton St Mary's churchyard baptismal well	319
12.31	Ffynnon Nicolas / St Nicholas' Well, Monkton	319
12.32	Ffynnon Marged / Margaret's Well, nr Narbeth	319
12.33	Ffynnon Fair / Lady Well, Haverfordwest	319
12.34	Ffynnon Madoc / St Madoc's Well, Rudbaxton	319
12.35	Ffynnon Leonard / St Leonard's Well, Rosemarket	319
12.36	Ffynnon Higgon / Higgon's Well, Haverfordwest	320
12.37	ffynnon pentref / village well, Walton West	320
12.38	Ffynnon Fair / Mary's Well, Maenclochog	320
12.39	Ffynnon pentref ymyl y ffordd / roadside village well, Dinas Cross	320
12.40	Ffynnon Shan Shillan / Shan Shillan Well, Letterston	320
12.41	Ffynnon Buarth Brynach / St Brynach's Well, nr Maenclochog	320
12.42	Ffynnon Llonwen, Llangolman	321
12.43	Ffynnon-y-Cwewll / Quickwell, St Davids	321
12.44	Ffynnon Dogfael / St Dogmael's Well, nr Fishguard	321

12.45   Ffynnon y Cei, Solfach / Solva Quayside
        Well, nr St Davids   321
12.46   Ffynnon Pen-Arthur / King Arthur's Well,
        nr St Davids   321
12.47   Ffynnon Drenewydd / Trenewydd Well,
        nr Llanwnda   322
12.48   Ffynnon Justinian / St Justinian's Well,
        nr St Davids   322
12.49   Ffynnon Wen / Whitewell, St Davids   322
12.50   Ffynnon Llygad / Eye Well, nr St Davids   322
12.51   Ffynnon newydd / new well, nr St Davids   322

Last Words: *Defending The Mountain*   324
bibliography & suggested further reading   332
index of wellspring sites   334

a background to *The Living Wells of Wales*

This is my fifth major volume on the sacred springs, holy wells and spas of Britain, all published by Seren. My first, *Holy Wells: Wales, a photographic journey* (2008) included just 48 sites; in this one, it's more than 300, in twelve topographical sections, travelling throughout Wales, from Anglesey in the north to Pembrokeshire in the south. Of these sites, researched, visited, and recorded photographically, approximately half are explored in depth, and half offered as captioned smaller images at the end of each chapter. And as in all of my wellspring books, I have included Ordnance Survey references to encourage the reader to visit if you haven't already, or to expand your pilgrimages if you have, to these very special places.

and some thank yous

Historically, the main authority on the sacred springs, holy wells and spas of Wales was Francis Jones (*The Holy Wells of Wales*, 1954). His knowledge has been added to by many other individuals and groups since his seminal publication, including Janet & Colin Bord, Paul Davis, Roland Bond, Ian & Frances Thompson, Jane Beckerman, Christina Martin, Jeremy Harte, Gary R Varner, Robin Melrose, Maddy Gray, Elfed Gruffydd, Ian Taylor, Tristan Gray Hulse, TW Pritchard, Terry Breverton, Edna Whelan, James Rattue, Audrey Doughty, Eirlys & Ken Gruffydd, the Wellspring Fellowship and Cymdeithas Ffynhonnau Cymru, and, hopefully, through my own work on wellspring cultures throughout Wales, as well as in England, Cornwall, Scotland and the USA.

I am also indebted to the very many people who have informed and educated me on the wellsprings in their areas, suggesting sites I may have overlooked, offering words of inspiration or of warning, sometimes accompanying me on my many journeys to these often hidden places. They have included Ian Taylor (the Wellhopper) for his insights and friendship during our explorations of North Wales wellsprings; Lee Oliver for his knowledge, contacts and transportation throughout Pen Llŷn; Chris and (the late) Trevor Silverman for their work throughout Pembrokeshire; Rob Owen for his initial suggestions and innovative ideas; Colin Evans, Ynys Enlli historian, ferryman and tour guide; the 'well water artist', Ted Harrison; Dr Peter Ford (and the Hay History Group) for sharing knowledge of the sites throughout Hay-on-Wye; Mike Barrell at the Black Lion Well in Hay; Phil Thomas and Pat Eckley for Ffynnon Fair, Hay; Sid Howells, consultant geologist, for his well at Porth Llew; Roger Hagar and the Treftadaeth Llandre Heritage Group; the inspiring Jacki Sime, Elizabeth Daniels, Doug Malein and Luke Rowlands from Pembrokeshire; Jane Beckerman for her research and renovations at Ffynnon Elian, Llanelian yn Rhos; Keith Gibbs, of The Woodlands Tavern, for escorting me to the Llanfair Discoed well; Diane and Geoff of the wonderful Penrallt Gallery Bookshop, Machynlledd; the congregation at St Michael's Church, Eglwysfach, for their re-imagining of St Non's Well; Monica and Robin of the Myddfai Hall charity who took me on my first visit to the Physicians' Well; Nigel Fletcher, my guide to Ffynnon Drewi, near Bronant; the inspirational Prof David Austin for his seminal work at Strata Florida; Rev Derek Davies at Bletherstone; Caroline Evans, St David's Diocese Faith Tourism Officer, and (the late) Sarah J Geach; Andrew Dugmore, tour guide and story teller; David Morgan Jones and daughter Anwen Davies for their work and welcome at Ffynnon Fraid, Swyddffynnon; Gwyn Jones, Iwan Hughes and the staff at Plas Glyn-y-Weddw Arts Centre in Llanbedrog; Dayfdd Hughes-Davies, designer, storyteller and visionary of Menter Felin Uchaf, Pen Llŷn; Richard Farmer, Elfed Gruffydd and Siân Stacey of the Bardsey Island Trust; Caren and Gwyn Jones at Penarth Fawr, Pen Llŷn; Emlyn Williams on Pen Cilan, Pen Llŷn; Susan E Evans at Ffynnon Engan, Pen Llŷn; Mike Gould (Ucheldre Centre, Holyhead); Ken Murphy and Dyfed Archaeological Trust; Dr Adrian Humpage (RIGS); John Winton; Glenn Davidson; and to Stephen Thomas for his Welsh translations and advice.

Although I have been hugely assisted by and learned so much from all of these generous people, the responsibility for the opinions proffered in *The Living Wells of Wales* and the errors made, obvious to you the reader, are all entirely mine.

WATER THAT PLAYS THE OLDEST MUSIC *
an introduction to the living wells of wales

*Tony Curtis, from his poem 'At Gumfreston Church' [see 12.1]

I've often asked myself what special characteristics wellspring sites possess that have captured our interest so strongly throughout the centuries. There is probably more than one answer.

The earth scientist provides a pretty straightforward explanation: water, evaporating from the oceans, rains onto the land and, where faults appear, falls to lower harder rock where it collects, dissolving its minerals until sufficient pressure pushes it to the surface on its way back to the sea.

Simple, it would seem ... but, in the process of this beautifully balanced perpetual liquid dance, an infinite number of potential journeys are undertaken – physical, mental, creative, spiritual – stimulating a multitude of alternative explanations for and responses to the mystery.

The still water in a natural spring was probably the first mirror within which our ancestors saw themselves ... and it's a vision that is usually accompanied by a view of the sky, constantly moving. Perhaps there's something in that.

Although water is the most yielding of substances, nothing is better at wearing away that which is resistant and hard. Jacques Benveniste was among the first to claim that all water contained a 'memory', the capacity to hold something in its solution of almost all of the bodies through which it had passed, reflecting the thoughts of the sixth century BC Taoist philosopher, Lao-tzu, who wrote that *"the soft overcomes the hard; the gentle overcomes the rigid"* (in *Tao Te Ching*).

opposite:
Trefriw Roman Spa and Well [4.1]
nr Betwys-y-Coed, Conwy

the living wells of wales

Perhaps our interest in these places is because the word 'well' in English points to an absence of illness, a state of 'well-being' (in addition to a water source); or that the word 'spring' also refers to the season of new beginnings; and a 'wellspring' is defined as 'a source of continual or abundant supply'. And in Welsh, 'ffynnon' may have the mid nineteenth century archaic word 'ffwn' as its root, suggesting 'a source' or a 'state of proceeding from', an origination, or even 'breath', the 'fount' of all life. There's also the Welsh word 'ffynnu' which means 'to prosper'.

Or, is it that the eruption of water from the earth was one of the principle determinants of the original geography of human settlement, and that visiting wellsprings which have been in continuous usage for millennia offers the possibility of hearing a faint echo of the stories they once told?

Or perhaps it's the fact that water connects all the shores of the earth, and that human beings, like the planet, are made up predominantly of this essential-to-life liquid; and that the ultimate destination of all waters is a rendezvous with the sea from whence it, and all of us, originally came.

introduction

opposite:
The Holy Well
Holywell Bay,
nr Newquay,
Cornwall
[SW 764 602]

(The images in this Introduction are taken from my previous books on wellsprings throughout Britain to provide a wider perspective for our Welsh sites. This photograph is from my 2010 book *Holy Wells: Cornwall, a photographic journey*)

Or, maybe it's because the water we enjoy today is the self same liquid that existed on Earth millions of years ago, enjoyed by dinosaur and, later, by cave-dweller alike, constantly recycled in a seemingly miraculous, self-sustaining closed system (or mor -prosaically, as Noel Coward reputedly declaimed after flushing his toilet: *"Not goodbye, just au revoir!"*)

Or perhaps, it's all of these things …

Water is one of the most profound of our necessities, both for our physical health as well as – just as importantly, I think – for the stimulation of our imaginations. Sacred springs and holy wells are luminous, liminal places which provide a space at which to consider the connections between rock, sky and water, and an access to wider realities, to other ways of seeing which encourage a dialogue between your god and my god and no god at all.

And here in Wales, it's clear that these ancient liquid tunes (*"held forever as voices in a well"*, according to the poet Gillian Clarke) are still being played … and that their faint notes can still sometimes be heard, if we listen very carefully.

hunting the pluck of water *

Navigate by such stars as are not
  leaves falling from life's
deciduous tree, but spray from the
  fountain
of the imagination, endlessly
replenishing itself out of its own
  waters.

RS Thomas
from 'A Thicket in Lleyn'

The novelist, Ursula K Le Guin was right, I think, when she observed that *"It is good to have an end to journey towards … but it is the journey that matters in the end"*. Pilgrims knew this very well, the struggle and the pain being a significant measure of the experience. For Australian Aborigines, to walk the land was and is to engage in the endless dance of creation, and one of the most constantly attractive aspects of my visits to wellsprings throughout Britain and beyond is also this ability to take us on a series of revelatory journeys.

Some of these are merely geographic, leading us on occassion up dangerous dead ends, or up to our knees in mud; others, though, are travels through time, and through belief – voyages which some might call spiritual.

*Seamus Heaney, from 'The Diviner'

These begin with the pantheistic beliefs of our earliest ancestors; then take us through the coming of the Romans and other invaders to these shores; to the arrival of radical new ideas with Christianity; through the ages of regular attack, abuse and neglect; and further, to the time of the discovery of seemingly more rational and more scientific explanations for these magical springs during the spa era; and, back today – full circle, it would seem – to the tentative beginnings of a more holistic, more open, hopefully more sympathetic relationship with water, with rock and with the earth.

milk, wine, blood

Though diverse, the attributes of wellsprings demonstrate some discernible patterns. Most never freeze or run dry, while some are said to ebb and flow, make strange noises, or are bottomless. The behaviour of fish or eels in wells was often read as omens; the movement of a handkerchief on the water's surface was believed to foretell a partner's faithfulness and likely fertility. Some wells could proffer the name of a thief, provide cures and, on rare occasions, lay curses.

left, top to bottom:
The Well of the Heads
nr Invergarry, Scotland
[NN 304 993]
(from *Holy Wells Scotland*, 2015);

Aquae Sulis
Bath, Somerset
(from *Borderlands*, 2013);

monument to Maggie Wall, burnt as a witch in 1657, Dunning, Scotland
(from *Holy Wells Scotland*)

introduction

right, top to bottom:
'Owl' Nicky
at St Maha's Well
above Loch Lomond, Scotland
[NS 457 918]
(from *Holy Wells Scotland*);
Madron Holy Well
nr Penzance, Cornwall,
[SW 446 328]
(from *Holy Wells: Cornwall*);
The Wishing Well
Alderley Edge, Cheshire, England
[SJ 860 777]
(from *Borderlands*)

Some had the ability to turn objects into stone, others to erupt with milk or wine, or even with blood. Some were said to be haunted by ghosts and guarded by monsters, were home to fairies and doorways into their underground dwellings.

These usually welcoming portals grew into centres for elaborate ceremonies, for storytelling and the presenting of gifts. The rituals associated with receiving well cures, and/or messages, were often complex: some times of the year offered more powerful results than others'; water had to be drunk from a shell, or a special cup, or even a skull; the correct offerings had to be made, words chanted, rhymes recited, rags hung on trees or bushes. And, in return for these (and other) rites, the waters would offer the favours of love, fertility and good health. I've visited wells specialising in cures for warts, for blindness, deafness, scurvy, jaundice, leprosy, rheumatism, epilepsy, paralysis, gout, tuberculosis, skin diseases, indigestion, sciatica, shortness of breath, rickets and piles; for cancer, toothache, drunkenness, melancholy and mental illness; and even for baldness and for broken hearts!

the living wells of wales

above, top to bottom:
St Neot's Well
Poundstock, Cornwall
[SX 204 999]
(from *Holy Wells: Cornwall*);
St Clether's Well Chapel
Bodmin Moor, Cornwall
[SX 203 847]
(from *Holy Wells: Cornwall*);
Duncan Thomson of Strathleven
Artizans at Carman Reservoir Well
nr Dumbarton, Scotland
[NS 376 785]
(from *Holy Wells Scotland*)

how deep it goes, our thirst for their first water *

Explanations of the true meanings of wellsprings have changed ... with time and with belief.

Water appearing naturally, un-aided and unbidden from the hard rock or the dry soil of the earth's belly, would always have had a magical significance for our ancestors, not only as an element essential to life but, just as importantly, as a place where the most powerful of nature spirits resided and where a dialogue with other realities was possible.

When the Romans arrived on these shores, they brought with them a rich new bathhouse culture, and a range of alternative water deities and spirits that were often 'married' with their local equivalents.

And when Christianity eventually spread across the land we now call Wales from the third century onwards, the missionaries – fully recognising the powers of these places to sustain and to inspire – often 're-christened' them with new names, allying them to new legends, while essentially retaining their original meanings and significance for the people. It was at this time that the predominantly female nature of the sites was made masculine, and pagan magical springs became Christian holy wells. But, as Francis Jones in his seminal 1954 book *Holy Wells of Wales* wrote, *"the older deities of well, hill, and megalith survived in a new guise"*.

Churches were built over wells and Christian saints replaced pagan deities as the spiritual benefactor, often at the places where a severed, martyred head had fallen. The red stain of iron found in chalybeate springs provided evidence of a saint's violent and bloody death, at the same time as reminding of the well's original occupant, the female Earth Spirit and her responsibility for procreation and for birth.

The healing properties of the well remained but praise was now due for its services to a new religious master or mistress. The red water in chalybeate wells now became Christ's blood instead of that of the menstruating Goddess.

*from the Scottish writer Valerie Gillies' poem, 'It's the Pits that Make It'

introduction

It was not until the Protestant Reformation of the second half of the sixteenth century that the dominant church decided to undertake the wholesale obliteration of the water cult sites and all other reminders of their 'hydrolatrous' beliefs ... although, thankfully, this was never fully achieved.

Our wellspring sites have lived with this series of sometimes uncomfortable marriages and nearly always troublesome divorces ever since.

but this is true too: stories can save us *

*American novelist, Tim O'Brien

The Living Wells of Wales is not a history book, although it does contain within its pages a great deal of history; and it is not a work of fiction either, although it does retell many unbelievable tales. Most accurately, it is a two-fold celebration of the many, sometimes contradictory levels of meaning that wellspring sites offer, the varying versions of the truth that history, oral accounts, myth, legend, folk tales, poetry and art suggest, alongside my own attempts to observe and capture something of the spirit of these special places through photography.

My approach to these watery places, then, is a 'fluid' one. The Ancient Greek writer Herodotus (484-425 BC) was known in his day as both 'the father of history' as well as 'the father of lies', happy as he was to relate local customs and fabulous stories alongside so-called 'historical' events.

I recently made the difficult trip to the island of St Kilda, 45 miles west of the Outer Hebrides and 110 miles from mainland Scotland, as part of the research for *Sacred North* (March 2018), the book I created with Orthodox priest, Father John Musther.

The origin of the name St Kilda is far from clear. It may be a corruption of Hirta, or Hirtir, the Norse words for 'shepherd', or 'stags', respectively; or it could be based upon the Brythonic word for 'gloom' or 'death'! And although there is no recorded saint named Kilda, the short passage from *Where the World Ends* by Geraldine McCaughrean (2017) that follows is revealing both of the possible origins of the name of this isolated island in the Atlantic, as well as of all other such designations:

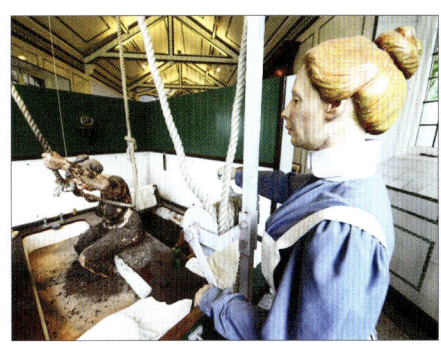

above, top to bottom:

the St Kilda harbour
(from *Sacred North*, 2018);

Chapel Downs Well
Sancreed, Cornwall
[SW 418 293]
(from *Holy Wells: Cornwall*);

Strathpeffer Spa treatments
Ross & Cromarty,
Highlands, Scotland
(from *Holy Wells Scotland*)

So Quill told him the story of St Kilda, who was thrown into the sea by pirates, to drown, but spread his plaid on the water where it turned stiff as any raft and, with his shirt for a sail, he sailed to Hirta and discovered it. 'He built a huge kirk, but it's gone now, alas, because when St Kilda died, the kirk carried him up to Heaven then turned into a cloud.'

'I heard St Kilda was a word writ down wrong in a book,' said Murdo. 'There was no such man.'

'There is now,' said Quill.

The accretion of levels of memory through the telling and telling of old tales means that even if something probably didn't actually happen, in one very important sense the telling makes it 'true'.

It's the same, I believe, with the folk tales and customs that grapple with the multiple meanings of the real and imagined worlds surrounding our sacred spring and holy well sites. As the stories are told and the rites conducted, they become part of us in the telling and in the performance.

This is Martha H Noyes writing about the culture, history and struggles for independence of the people of the Hawaiian Islands in *Then There Were None* (2003):

History, like statistics, can be bent, argued, and interpreted to fit any point of view. But the language of the heart, the sounds of the spirit, are beyond argument.

Sir Arthur Quiller-Couch, writing in the second half of the nineteenth century about the limits of our knowledge of these often mysterious places, describes holy wells as being *"buried in the remotest past, in an age before record"*, and that *"our speculations ... are of necessity vague and unsatisfying"*. He concluded that *"Each individual observer offers in his turn his theory drawn from the buried past."*

We all write, and comment, and photograph, and act, after all, from where we are. We dig where we stand. (And, incidentally – given that well-guardians were nearly always women, and that it was almost exclusively female deities that were originally worshipped here – I think, that it can be both 'his' and 'hers'!)

introduction

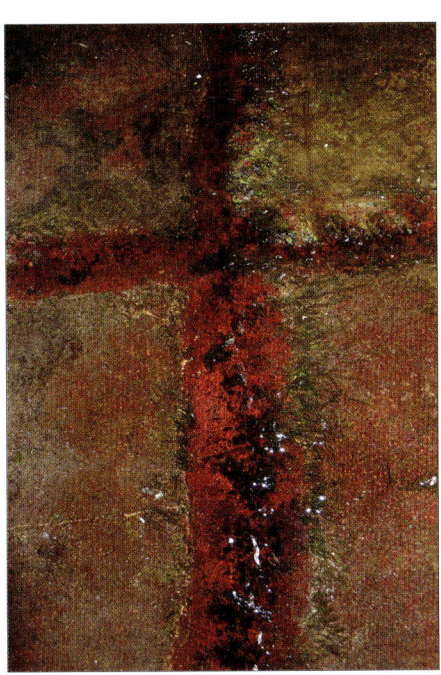

It's impossible to fully know and understand the past, and the beliefs that motivated people to do what they did. This *Living Wells of Wales* text reflects my own explorations of the histories of these ancient springs – as far as they are known – alongside the legends and the tales handed down, most often through oral accounts, as well as the equally important contributions of our poets and writers, moved by these places and their often incredible claims.

This creativity of re-interpretation has always, in my view, been at the very heart of the diverse and contradictory odysseys around belief and around faith with which any study of holy wells forces us to engage. But, in a world where 'kinetic activity' really means being shot; 'extraordinary rendition' sending prisoners of war to another less savoury country to be tortured; and 'collatoral debt obligations' the USA's bad mortgages which played such a leading role in the world's latest economic crash, we should not confuse these imaginative explorations with the muddying of the waters through obfuscation or 'fake news'. The latter are strategies to confuse and ultimately control; the former one of the principal means by which we have always explored and tried to better understand the more mysterious aspects of our world.

This is Scottish author and academic Ali Smith (in an interview with Scotland's First Minister, Nicola Sturgeon, at the 2018 Edinburgh Book Fair):

We are living in a culture that insists on lying ... It insists on telling us information about which we are left wondering whether it is true or not ...

Fiction and lies are opposites of each other. Lies go out of the way to distort and turn you away from the truth. But fiction is one of our main ways of telling the truth.

opposite, top to bottom:

Tetbury Wells
Malvern Hills, Worcestershire, England
[SO 595 679] (from *Borderlands*);

St Boniface's Well
Munlochy, Ross & Cromarty, Scotland
[NH 641 537] (from *Holy Wells Scotland*);

St Bernard's Well
Edinburgh, Scotland
[NT 245 742] (from *Holy Wells Scotland*)

left, top to bottom:

The Queen's Well
Glen Mark, Angus, Scotland
[NO 421 828] (from *Holy Wells Scotland*);

St Drostan's Well
New Aberdour, Aberdeenshire, Scotland
[NJ 887 646] (from *Holy Wells Scotland*);

St Winefride's Well
Woolston, Shropshire, England
[SJ 322 244] (from *Borderlands*)

the living wells of wales

showing our true colours

Like the ultimately unanswerable questions concerning the 'real' meanings of our wellspring sites, I am often asked by people who see my photographic images, *"Are these the real colours?"* My answer is usually to show them my hand and ask them what colour it is ... then to hide it under a table or in my pocket and ask the same question again. (It's a little perhaps like the old Buddhist query regarding whether a sound is made by a tree falling in a forest if no-one is there to hear it.)

Colour is just the reflection of light onto a surface. It changes by the second and by the season, by the weather and the time of day and, in a photographic representation of a scene, colours and perspectives are also determined by what sensor and what lens is in use, by the nature of the screen on which it is viewed, and, if printed, by the inks, the press, the papers, etc.

And beyond all of these variables, we all see the same image differently anyway, through our different eyes ... and with the different perceptions of the world we have developed.

left:

Holy Well
Holy Well Bay,
nr Newquay,
Cornwall
(from *Holy Wells: Cornwall*)

the living wells of wales

What is offered in my photographs of wellspring sites and in the retelling of their histories and tales is *a* view, not *the* view; *a* truth, not *the* truth.

But perhaps the syncretism of all of these images and all of these different accounts may offer a faint reflection of what is potentially most important and most significant in our lives, *"selling"*, in the words of appropriately-named African American abolitionist Sojourner Truth (1797-1883), *"the shadow to support the substance"*.

above, left to right:

The Marquis Well
Cairn Gorm, Banffshire, Scotland:
the highest well in Britain
(from *Holy Wells: Scotland*);

Hospital Fountain
Great Malvern, Worcestershire, England
[SO 781 474] (from *Borderlands*);

Helier Brune Well
Unst, Shetland, Scotland:
the most northern well in Britain
[HP 594 047] (from *Sacred North*)

the path to
St Nicholas' Well
Monkton, nr Pembroke
[12.31]

1 A MEETING OF OPPOSITES:
ynys môn / anglesey

*In the bare midst of Anglesey they show
Two springs which close by one another play;
And, 'Thirteen hundred years agone', they say,
'Two saints met often where those waters flow'.*

from 'East and West'
by Matthew Arnold (1822-1888)

The Christian history of Ynys Môn is dominated by two great male and two great female figures: the saints Seiriol and Cybi, and Dwynwen and Gwenfaen. Seiriol and Cybi built their monasteries at opposite ends of Anglesey, St Cybi at Caergybi (now known as Holyhead) and St Seiriol at Penmon at the south-east corner of the island. It was said that such was their friendship that they would meet weekly for prayers at Clorach Fawr near Llanerch-y-medd in the centre of the island, where each had a holy well. Sadly today, Cybi's well [1.11] is a crudely-capped ruin lying over a low wall, while Seiriol's, on the opposite side of the road, has been lost entirely.

As a result of their weekly peregrinations, St Cybi – walking south – was given the nickname Cybi Felyn ('Cybi the Dark', or 'Tanned'), while St Seiriol – walking with his back to the sun – was known as Seiriol Wyn ('Seiriol the Fair').

opposite:

Ffynnon Sant Seiriol / St Seiriol's Well [1.1], Penmon, Anglesey

the living wells of wales

1.1 a site for sore eyes

**Ffynnon Sant Seiriol /
St Seiriol's Well**
Penmon, nr Rhosybol
SH 6305 0797

It's not difficult to see these namings and this simple tale harking back to a much earlier time, reflecting the ancient importance of sun, moon and stars; and there is ample evidence at the wellspring sites on Ynys Môn (as elsewhere throughout Wales) of these and other early beliefs connecting the heavens, the earth and its waters with the lives of our earliest ancestors.

Originally known as Ffynnon Fair, St Seiriol's Well is set into a rock wall at Penmon in the south-east corner of Anglesey, beside an impressive complex of religious and secular buildings. It seems to have acquired the name more familiar to us today to mark the arrival in the sixth century of Welsh-born prince Seiriol (said to have been one of the three sons of King Owain Danwyn of Rhos) as the first abbot of the priory here. The saint's well and circular cell, plus the adjacent church, dovecote, fishpond and priory all still survive in various states of reconstruction and decline.

Its isolated monastic setting and the inspiration of its spiritual leader attracted a regular band of dedicated hermits and monks to Penmon.

In later life, however, the saint sought an even greater degree of peace and solitude, moving across the short stretch of water to Ynys Lannog, where he eventually died in 550 AD. He is thought to have been buried there, although some claim that his remains are in Penmon Church.

The island was re-christened Ynys Seiriol in his memory until the Vikings re-named it Priestholm. Since the nineteenth century, it has been known as Puffin Island, and today is a Special Protection Area, no longer for hermits like Seiriol but now for wildlife, including its great colony of cormorants, plus its guillemots, razorbills, shags and kittiwakes ... as well as its eponymous puffins.

Seiriol's image cured disorders of the eye, a claim reflected to this day in the name for the periwinkle (or sea snail) on Anglesey: Llygad Seiriol or 'Seiriol's Eye'!

left:

Seiriol and Cybi murals
in Holyhead
showing their light and
dark complexions

opposite,
clockwise from top left:

the entrance to
St Seiriol's well-house;
St Seiriol stained glass
window, Penmon Church;
pilgrims' grafitti at Ffynnon Seiriol;
inside Seiriol's well-chamber

Ynys Môn / Anglesey

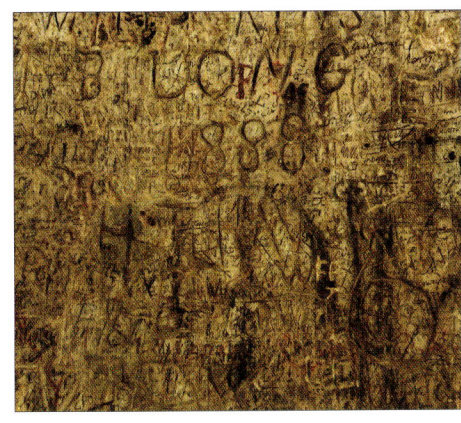

1.2 the dreams of lovers

**Ffynnon Dwynwen /
St Dwynwen's Well**
Llanddwyn Island,
nr Newborough
SH 3867 2885

As well as Seiriol and Gybi, we should not be surprised to find two important female saints on Ynys Môn, Anglesey being known as Môn Mam Cymru or 'The Mother of Wales'. Their experiences, however, were much less agreeable than those of their male counterparts.

Legend tells that Dwyn – more commonly known today as Dwynwen, or 'the blessed Dwyn' – was one of the twenty-four children of King Brychan Brycheiniog ... and the most beautiful! But this is the only element of her story that attracts consensus.

In one tale, Dwynwen is pursued by the tyrant Maelgwyn Gwynedd and flees from Ireland to Wales. In another, her desperate journey is made in reverse. Some say that she crossed the water on foot, an action that established the belief in her ability to protect seafarers. Another tale tells of her falling in love with the prince Maelon Dafodrill at a feast arranged by her father ... but again there are variations concerning the outcome.

In one, Dwynwen's father forbids her union with Maelon as he has already offered her hand to a rich prince from a nearby town; in another, Maelon is unfaithful; and in yet another, the young prince tries to seduce the blessed Dwyn.

Either way, Dwynwen is distraught and asks her god to erase her and Maelon's love for each other. Dwynwen is then offered three wishes: her first is that Maelon, who had been turned into a block of ice for his indiscretions, be released; her second, that she might never fall in love again; and her third that henceforth every lover's dream should come true.

Dwynwen established her church on the isolated rocky island which now bares her name on the south-westerly point of Anglesey, and lived the rest of her life here as a nun. Once a permanent island connected to the mainland by a stone causeway, it is now only fully-isolated at high water (so, if you are visiting, check the tide timetables).

Her well was a favourite destination for the crippled in body (specialising in cures for aches, stitches and pleurisy), as well as in the heart. Some said that a fish or a number of eels lived in her well that could provide the name of a future lover or tell of the likely faithfulness or otherwise of a partner.

Pilgrims would spend the night on Gwely Esyth, a high spot above the well, and would carve their names in the turf when a cure had been successfully achieved.

Notwithstanding her earlier claims to calm the seas, Dwynwen's church and rectory were eventually engulfed by sandstorms and largely destroyed, though the site retains to this day much of its ancient spiritual allure.

Dwynwen has become Wales' patron saint of lovers, and 25 January is celebrated as St Dwynwen's Day, the Welsh equivalent of the feast day of the obscure Roman martyr, Valentine.

left:

the ruins of
St Dwynwen's Chapel
on Llanddwyn Island

opposite near:

the most likely location
of St Dwynwen's Well

opposite far:

the lighthouse on
Ynys Llanddwyn

The exact location of Ffynnon Dwynwen is disputed.

In my first book on the wellsprings of Wales (*Holy Wells Wales*, 2008), I stated that it was the large stone-lined chamber (known as Merddin Cil) across the main path from what remains of the church that was the location, as this was (and still is) the place sited on the island's interpretive panels.

Ian Taylor (*www.wellhopper.wales*), an expert on the wells of North Wales, however, believes hers is the spring on a cliff above the sea on the north side of the island, less than fifty yards from her church.

There is also a spring on the mainland known as Crochan Llanddwyn where many of the Dwynwen-connected divination practices may have once taken place.

Like all places of dreams and of legends, it is difficult, and perhaps ultimately unnecessary, to be perfectly certain.

the living wells of wales

left:

Dwynwen's cross
on Ynys Llanddwyn

1.3 for want of sense

**Ffynnon Wenfaen /
St Gwenfaen's Well**
nr Rhoscolyn,
Ynys Gybi / Holy Island
SH 2594 5436

*Full oft have I repaired to drink that spring,
Waters which cures diseases of the soul
As well the body! And which always prove
The only remedy for want of sense.*

Lewis Morris (1701-65)
on St Gwenfaen's Well

Gwenfaen was probably the daughter of Paul Hen (or 'Old Paulinus') of Manaw, and sister of Peulan and Gwyngeneu, both also 'saints' who lived on Holy Island. Her exposed well, sunk into the ground on a remote headland on the southernmost tip of Ynys Gybi, was once famous for its cures for mental illnesses and depression. Wenfaen in Welsh means 'white stone', and after drinking here, two pieces of quartz were asked as payment to the well and its saint.

At a time when the battle for souls was raging between the local Druids and the new Christian faith, it is said that, while being pursued by the former, Gwenfaen, fearing for her life, climbed a rock and was spirited away by angels.

Ynys Môn / Anglesey

right:
St Gwenfaen's Well
on Ynys Gybi
(and a view of
nearby Rhoscolyn)

1.4 kill or cure

**Ffynnon Eilian /
St Eilian's Well**
Llaneilian,
nr Amlwch
SH 4657 9330

Water from the well of Ffynnon Eilian issues from a fissure in a north-facing crag in the cliffs above Porthyrychen, before meandering to the sea. A dozen years ago, there was little to see here except for the cleft in the rock and the trickle of its once-sacred waters, but in 2014 work began to restore the well chapel walls, complete today with a saint figure and a slate plaque to encourage passers-by on the Anglesey / All-Wales Coastal Path to pause, as many did in the past when this site was a major place of pilgrimage.

Legend claims that Eilian had been sent from Rome as an emissary of the Pope in the mid fifth century, landing with his family, supporters, personal effects and cattle at Porthyrychen. Some say that, if you look very carefully, you may still be able to see the freshwater-filled hoof prints of Eilian's oxen in the rocks.

The chief lord of Anglesey at that time was Caswallon Lawhir ('Caswallon of the Long Hand') who, annoyed by this unexpected and potentially threatening arrival, seized the party and its belongings.

In response, Eilian struck the monarch blind, only restoring his sight after being granted the area the saint's pet doe could cover before being caught. One version of this tale claimed that the animal was chased and killed by one of Caswallon's greyhounds, and that an enraged Eilian cursed the land in response.

Caswallon's 'long hand' is thought to have referred both to his physical appearance (the late medieval poet, Iolo Goch claimed that he could *"reach a stone from the ground to kill a raven, without bending his back"*) as well as his firm control over his lands and people. Either way, it seems that he had met his match in this visitor and the new faith he brought with him.

Eilian's Well was said to have initially sprung forth to quench the thirst of Eilian and his human and animal party after their arduous sea journey. Like Gwenfaen's Well [1.3], it came to be highly prized for the relief of mental health problems, although – like its namesake in Llanelian yn Rhos in Conwy [4.3], which also faced north, a prerequisite, it seems, for success – it also gained a reputation as a curse well sometime in the early eighteenth century. Locally, it was known as the Witching Well.

The most common rituals associated with curse wells included scratching the name or initials of the intended victim on a piece of slate with a pin, then bending the pin and throwing it into the water; writing the culprit's name on a piece of paper and hiding it in one of the cracks in the rock face; stabbing a dummy (or 'poppet') of the person to be cursed; or, on rarer occasions (and possibly for maximum effect), piercing a live frog with a skewer to which was attached a cork at either end, and floating it in the well waters, the curse being active it was claimed for as long as the poor creature remained alive.

opposite:

the restored Ffynnon Eilian well site complete with saint's statue

above:

images of St Eilian's Well, 2007 and 2018

the living wells of wales

1.5 losing the battle

**Ffynnon Llanfihangel Dinsylwy /
Llanfihangel Dinsylwy Well**
nr Llanddona,
Anglesey
SH 5880 8146

On all three of my visits to this site, I have experienced what seemed to me to be a powerful, sometimes disturbing ambiance.

The well and church here – nominally dedicated to St Michael – is situated between an Iron Age Hill fort (Din Sylwy) with its flat top known as Bwrdd Arthur (or 'Arthur's Table') and the raging sea. A possible explanation is offered by a tale told of witches landing at nearby Llandona beach, though Baring Gould in his 1903 *A Book of North Wales* suggested that they were probably Irish criminals set adrift in a coracle with no paddles who, being refused food or drink by the fearful locals, struck a staff into the earth and created a new and magical spring.

If the fine, unadorned chapel with its probable fifth century origins here is contending against what it may once have been seen as the powers of darkness, I think it is clearly losing the battle.

left:
Llanfihangel Dinsylwy well
and St Michael's chapel,
Llanddona

opposite:
St Patrick's Well
and Cave,
Llanbadrig

1.6 the most peaceful spot on earth

**Ffynnon Badrig /
St Patrick's Well**
Llanbadrig,
nr Cemaes Bay,
Anglesey
OS 3754 9468

Like St Eilian's Well [1.4], this site is another made spiritually important by an arrival by sea, this time, however, from a significantly shorter though equally eventful journey.

The most popular account tells of the shipwrecking of St Patrick, the patron saint of Ireland, on the small rocky island known as Ynys Badrig (or 'Middle Mous'), a hundred yards or so from the mainland. Managing to swim ashore, Patrick found refuge from the stormy seas in a welcoming cave (Ogof Padrig) and refreshment from its fresh spring waters (Ffynnon Badrig). In thanks for his survival, he founded a church on the land directly above this cave and its well.

An alternative and less dramatic origin tale suggests that this was the bay from which St Patrick set sail to evangelise the Irish; although others claim that its founding was by a different Patrick, Padrig ab Alfryd of Gwaredog in Arfon.

the living wells of wales

Ffynnon Badrig is reached by a 'goat path' that descends steeply down the cliff where, once again, the saint's footprints (Òl Traed Sant Padrig) are said to be visible. It was much celebrated for its cures, especially of children's ailments, rheumatism and toothache.

It is difficult to be certain of the actual source of the well, numerous pools of fresh water flowing through channels in the rocks and falling to the sea. I think that *Wellhopper* Ian Taylor once again has the right response: *"... in its modern interpretation it is the body of fresh water in its entirety that forms Ffynnon Badrig, whether the source of this is a single spring or two or more springs drawing from the same subterranean foundation."*

This holistic approach would, no doubt, please His Holiness the Dalai Lama who, when on a visit to Patrick's Church at Llanbadrig, pronounced it *"the most peaceful spot on earth"*.

above:

Ian Taylor,
below Ffynnon
Badrig

1.7 looking both ways

**Ffynnon Goch / The Red Spring
(or Lord Boston's Sulphur Well)**
Penrhoslligwy,
nr Llanallgo,
Anglesey
SH 4859 8602

The impressive, castellated 'gothic' turret in which Lord Boston's so-called 'Sulphur Well' is housed dates from 1864. There is none of the distinctive pungent aroma of sulphur emanating from the well today, though this may have been the case in previous times. Indeed, the site is known locally as Ffynnon Goch (the 'Red Spring') and its offerings as 'copper water' from the colour of its now clearly chalybeate (or iron-rich) waters.

Chalybeate wells became popular in the seventeenth century, reaching peak interest in the nineteenth century spa movement, and continuing here into the 1940s, with its waters bottled and sold at fairs across Anglesey and beyond.

Although an article on Ffynnon Goch (from the *Proceedings of the Anglesey Antiquarian Society*, by E Neil Baynes, 1928) suggested that it had a reputation for cursing – with the usual involvement of pins, dolls and frogs – Ian Taylor believes that this has little support and may even be a confusion with another site.

right:

Lord Boston's
Sulphur Well,
Penrhoslligwy

How many of these places were used for health, how many for hate? Perhaps they had both facilities depending on your needs, offering the dual powers of persecution and of praise, of revelation and revenge, of curse and of cure.

Ynys Môn / Anglesey

and ...

1.8: Ffynnon Allgo /
St Gallgo's Well
Llanallgo,
nr Moelfre,
Anglesey
GR 499 848

1.10: Ffynnon Gwrachod /
The Witches Well
Holyhead,
Anglesey
GR 224 823

1.11: Ffynnon Gybi /
St Cybi's Well
Clorach Fawr
nr Llanerchymedd,
Anglesey
SH 4490 8414

1.9: Ffynnon Sant Cyngar /
St Cyngar's Well
Llangefni,
Anglesey
SH 4574 7588

1.12: Ffynnon Santes
Ceinwen /
St Ceinwen's Well
nr Cerrigceinwen,
Anglesey
SH 423 737

2 WALLS AND BRIDGES: gwynedd

Two of Wales' greatest castles stand in Gwynedd (Harlech and Caernarfon), as well as the evocative remains of a Roman settlement (*Segontium*), though their building was far from supportive of the native people of Wales.

Forts and castles needed a ready supply of liquid sustenance like everywhere else, particularly at times of siege, so they were often constructed at a location where the twin necessities of elevation and a reliable source of clean drinking water were to be found, as well as a place (as at *Segontium*) where a reminder of the water deities and customs left behind could be observed and practised.

(I am aware that both the Llŷn Peninsula and Anglesey are currently part of the county of Gwynedd but, based upon their distinctive roles within Welsh wellspring history, I have decided to give them sections of their own.)

opposite:

Ffynnon Enddwyn /
St Enddwyn's Well [2.8]
above Duffryn Ardudwy,
Gwynedd

the living wells of wales

2.1 dreams and nightmares

Caer Rufeinig *Segontium* / *Segontium* Roman Fort
Caernarfon,
Gwynedd
SH 485 624

where a spring rises or a river flows, there should we build altars and offer sacrifices

Seneca, Roman first century AD Stoic philosopher

The Roman army first invaded the area we now know of as Wales around the mid-first century AD. Then, in 60 AD, they stormed Anglesey with the aim of exterminating its Druidic cult, central to the faith systems of the local people.

As Rome's armies pushed west and north across Britain, a long chain of military outposts and towns was created to both wage war upon the local tribes and, when this was successfully achieved, to consolidate their conquests. The auxiliary fort of *Segontium* was established c.77 AD to control the Menai Straits and sever the link between Anglesey and Snowdonia, and in the process, to further subdue the local populations.

It remained occupied until at least 365 AD, when a smaller replacement fort (Hen Waliau) was built a little way to its west, this time to also defend against Irish pirates.

Segontium was mentioned in the *Mabinogion*, the collection of stories of battle, love and magic which is our

earliest surviving British prose, written in Middle Welsh in the twelfth and thirteenth centuries from oral sources. In *The Dream of Macsen Wledig*, we are told of one Magnus Maximus (or Macsen Wledig), a Roman emperor who has a dream of making a journey over the highest mountain in the world through forests and over seas that ends in a great hall in a fine castle in a far away land. Here he sees a beautiful maiden and, upon waking from his dream, vows to search the whole Empire to find her, which he eventually does ... in *Segontium*. Her name was Elen and she was the daughter of a Caernarfon chieftain. This part of the story ends with their marriage, a suggestion perhaps of the good sense of uniting Roman and local interests.

At *Segontium*, there are the remains of a well in a once-colonnaded court, here, as well as three bath-houses. These would have introduced both the sophisticated Roman discipline of cleanliness, at the same time as offering a panoply of new water spirits to add to those already revered by the locals.

The most significant of the Roman water sect sites in Britain was that established in 43 AD around the mineral springs of *Aquae Sulis* at Bath in Somerset. The cult of the goddess Sulis Minerva there seems to have been based upon an amalgam of the multi-talented *Minerva* – the Roman goddess of medicine, poetry, wisdom, commerce, weaving, crafts and magic – and *Sulis*, the local Celtic deity of the thermal springs.

A similar cultural syncretism is evident at Caerwent. *Mars-Ocelus* reflecting the 'marriage' of a native Celtic nature god with a leading Roman divinity.

Most deities found in Roman bath-houses had, not surprisingly, a strong association with health: statues of *Asclepius*, the ancient Greek god of medicine and healing, and his daughters *Iaso* (Medicine), *Aglaea* (Healthy Glow), *Hygieia* (Hygiene), *Aceso* (Healing), and *Panacea* (Universal Remedy) were commonplace, to ensure the full benefits of the healing waters.

Military bath-houses – usually built outside the main fortifications – often called upon the favours of another Roman deity, *Fortuna Balnearis* ('Fortuna of the Baths') for protection, especially when campaigning in remote and dangerous outposts like those in Wales.

The architectural conventions of the great public Roman thermae usually stipulated the provision of a number of rooms of varying temperature: a cold room (or *frigidarium*) in which to disrobe, as well as to cool down and to take a cold bath at the end of the treatment; a warm room (or *tepidarium*) in which to acclimatise the body in readiness for the hot room (or *calidarium*) with its heated floor.

Some establishments included an even hotter room, the sweat chamber (or *laconicum*, named after *Laconia*, the homeland of the uncompromising Spartans). At Caerleon near Newport in South Wales, the magnificence of the first century legionary fortress spa facilities [7.1] is clear to see.

Taking a bath in the Roman era was much more than an opportunity to wash off the dirt from the day: it was a religious experience, a reconnecting with one of the elemental forces which played such a dominant part within their systems of belief.

opposite:
the main well at *Segontium* fort

left:
the bath-house complex at *Segontium*

Washing the body and purifying the spirit were closely linked, separating the civilised man from the barbarian.

the living wells of wales

2.2 imagination and reality

Ffynhonnau Castell Caernarfon / Caernarfon Castle wells
Gwynedd
SH 477 626

Nature so fitted and seated, that it stands impregnable, and if it be well manned, victualed, ammunitioned, it is invincible ...

John Taylor, from *A Short Relation of a Long Journey made Round or Ovall by encompassing the Principalitie of Wales, Etc.*, 1652

The castle at Caernarfon was built by Edward I as a physical embodiment of the legendary fortress – *"the fairest that man ever saw"* (in Lady Charlotte Guest's translation) – imagined by Macsen Wledig in his *Mabinogion* dream. Like the much earlier fort of *Segontium*, it was constructed to repress Welsh hopes of nationhood, this time following the defeat and death of Llywelyn ap Gruffudd, the last Welsh Prince of Wales, at Cilmeri in December 1282. [see **5.32**]

Water at Caernarfon Castle was certainly *"well ... victualed"*, with two huge 50 foot deep wells (in the Well and Granary Towers), plus a very large cistern (on top of the Cistern Tower) which collected rainwater from the roofs.

2.3 victory and defeat

Ffynhonnau Castell Harlech / Harlech Castle wells
Gwynedd
SH 582 313

Stunningly situated Harlech Castle is another of the group of fortresses built by Edward I in the last quarter of the thirteenth century to defend his interests against the rebellious Welsh.

A subsequent native uprising in the early years of the fifteenth century saw Owain Glyndŵr recapture Harlech (as well as Aberystwyth) Castle in the spring of 1404, cementing his authority in Mid Wales, until it was retaken by Harry of Monmouth, the future Henry V, in 1409.

opposite:
one of the two near-identical wells at Caernarfon Castle

above:
the well at Harlech Castle;
the inner court, Harlech Castle

the living wells of wales

2.4 crushed

**Ffynnon Fair /
St Mary's Well**
Bron Fair,
Maentwrog,
Gwynedd
SH 6655 4047

Legend suggests that the strange rounded stone set beside the entrance to the church at Maentwrog was thrown by the sixth century giant / saint Twrog, from the top of Moelwyn, a hill to the north of the village, crushing a pagan altar in the valley below where the church now stands. It is said that, if you look very closely, you can see the saint's handprints in the indentations on the top of the missile. It was this story and this stone – probably an ancient ceremonial menhir – which gave the village its name (Maen Twrog / 'Twrog's Stone').

The well (and church) here are now both dedicated to St Mary. The slate-boxed Ffynnon Fair once supplied water for the neighbouring houses but is today in an overgrown, damaged and neglected state, following a fall of the earth bank and the 'need' to extend the car park for the adjacent row of houses.

left:

images of Ffynnon Fair, Maentwrog, 2007 and 2018

opposite left:
stained glass window of St Twrog at St Mary's Church, Maentwrog

opposite right:
view of St Mary's Church through its porch;
Can you see the saint's handprints in 'Twrog's Stone'?

gwynedd

2.5 rubbish

Ffynnon Gwyfil / Gwyfil's Well
Plas Brondanw Estate,
nr Porthmadog
SH 618 424

The roadside entrance to the Grade 2 Listed Gwyfil Well is conveniently shaped to accept rubbish bins.

Ironically, the fine wrought-iron and stone gateway, topped with its acorn finial, and designed by Sir Clough Williams-Ellis (the architect and owner of the Brondanw Estate), were built as an anti-pollution measure to safeguard the purity of the spring waters.

2.6 gone

Ffynnon Faglan / St Baglan's Well
Llanfaglan, nr Caernarfon
SH 460 609

Once an important spiritual site for both pagan and Christian worshippers, Ffynnon Baglan is one of the saddest examples of wellspring destruction in Wales. Formerly a grand walled structure with seats and a masonry chamber, when I first visited it in 2007 it was an unimpressive pile of broken stones set into the corner of a ploughed field. Now, all trace of even these has gone.

The recent attacks on the well are not, it seems, new. These words from a Mrs Roberts of Cefn-y-coed near Carnarfon, (reported in *Sacred Wells in Wales* by John Rhŷs and TE Morris in *Folk-Lore*, Volume 4 [1893]), detail both the many medicinal uses of the site, as well as its neglect:

The old people who would be likely to know anything about Ffynnon Faglan have all died. The two oldest inhabitants, who have always lived in this parish, remember the well being used for healing purposes. One told me his mother used to take him to it, when he was a child, for sore eyes, bathe them with the water, and then drop in a pin. The other man, when he was young, bathed in it for rheumatism; and until quite lately people used to fetch away the water for medicinal purposes. The latter, who lives near the well, at Tan-y-graig, said that he remembered it being cleaned out about fifty years ago, when two basins-full of pins were taken out, but no coin of any kind. The pins were all bent, and I conclude the intention was to exorcise the evil spirit supposed to afflict the person who dropped them in, or, as the Welsh say, dadwitsio. No doubt some ominous words were also used. The well is at present nearly dry, the field where it lies having been drained some years ago, and the water in consequence withdrawn from it.

What does still remain, however, rising above where Ffynnon Baglan once offered its cures and exorcisms, is an ancient forested tumulus and, at its top, a perfectly-preserved baptismal font, scooped out of a large boulder by a combination of nature and man.

left:
Ffynnon Gwyfil
Plas Brondanw Estate

above:
the remains of
Ffynnon Faglan in 2007

opposite:
the 'eye' of the stone font
on the tumulus above
Ffynnon Faglan

the living wells of wales

left, top to bottom:
St Baglan's Church exterior;
the font at the top of the Iron Age mound above Ffynnon Faglan;
interior of St Baglan's church with its mid-eighteenth century pews

opposite:
Ffynnon Beris, Nant Peris, Snowdonia

At church and castle sites, you can often feel a human presence as well as the survival of ideas and of beliefs, the walls seemingly charged with the accumulation of acts of faith and tradition. Prayers offered up leave traces, faint residues, memories even, like smoke from candles darkening rafters.

The towers of our cathedral, chapel and castle sites are built in the direction of the sky, sometimes for protection, to defend and exclude; sometimes to demonstrate power, prestige and wealth; and sometimes looking heavenwards for inspiration and to praise god. Wellsprings, by contrast, always look down, to the earth's liquid belly.

While church and castle buildings are solid, most wellsprings flow to fill the spaces nature or humankind provides. Even when we try to contain them in rock and stone, they often move position, erupting elsewhere. Wells participate in our world without possessing it. Instead (in most cases) of building high walls, the main view at wellspring sites is always downwards, connecting us with what lies beneath. And while all of our fine buildings inevitably crumble and decay, no one molecule of water ever ceases to exist.

These special places offer the possibilities of access to other realities, encouraging us to move gently from the everyday a little way towards the extraordinary, and on a good day even, from the earthly to the potentially divine.

As well as two of our finest examples of castles (and three of our saddest accounts of wellspring neglect and destruction), a pair of our most interesting wellspring sites are also to be found in Gwynedd, both with stories to tell:

2.7 fishy tales

Ffynnon Beris / St Peris' Well
Nant Peris,
nr Llanberis,
Snowdonia
SH 6084 5836

Symbolically, the fish that lives in the well swims in the channel between the seen, the unconscious and the conscious.

Nigel Pennick, from
Celtic Sacred Landscapes, 1996

The symbol of the fish represented wisdom, knowledge and fecundity in the ancient mythologies of most cultures, including the Welsh. The sacred trout, seen by the lucky few in Ffynnon Beris, was believed to be an omen of good luck for pagan and Christian bathers alike, as well as an indication of a successful cure for scrofula, warts, tumours and rheumatism, the well being particularly efficacious for children suffering from rickets.

In November 1896, the *Liverpool Mercury* newspaper reported on the installation of two new fish into the pool following the death of its fifty-year-old occupant, and included the following words: *"Invalids in large numbers came, during the last century and the first half of the present century, to this well to drink of its 'miraculous waters'."*

Little is known of the possibly early Christian saint, Peris. He may have been one of the many children of the sixth-century legendary prince Helig ap Glannog of Tyno Helig, whose offspring were responsible for the establishment of at least seven churches throughout the North Wales area, including that at Llangelynin [4.4]. Peris is thought to have retired to the solitude of this area in later life, and passed his final days here. Although the curing properties of the well were attributed to his daily drinking from its waters, it is far more likely that its magical qualities were recognised many centuries before his arrival, and that he adopted this site for Christianity.

In the last few years, the well's owners have encouraged the use of Ffynnon Beris for christenings and baptisms – the parents and godparents sitting on the slate steps – for wedding blessings, choir performances, and other religious and community celebrations, and are even planning to re-introduce a fish to the well.

opposite and right:
Ffynnon Beris, Llanberis

the living wells of wales

2.8 gender fluid

Ffynnon Enddwyn / Enddwyn's Well
nr Dyffryn Ardudwy, Gwynedd
SH 6052 2655

Little is known of the possibly female St Enddwyn. Even her gender, it seems, is open to question. Afflicted with a sore throat, Enddwyn is said to have bathed in this well while on her/his way to Trawsfynydd ... and was immediately cured, a custom repeated by many pilgrims in the years that followed. Its speciality was the relief, not surprisingly, of glandular diseases, though it was thought to also cure skin disorders, sore eyes and arthritis. The tradition here included drinking a cup of the water, then applying some of the moss that grew beside the well as a plaster onto the ailing part of the body. It has been reported that crutches and walking sticks were left at the site as proof by those restored to full health. Some also believed that throwing pins into the well would protect from evil spirits.

The evocative remains of St Enddwyn's Well are an impressive lichen-walled structure, remotely situated in hills overlooking Tremadoc Bay, some 700m above sea level. Often shrouded in mist – giving the site a magical and dramatic appearance and feel – it is well worth the considerable effort of getting to this place where heaven meets earth, and where the certainties of land fade into the mutability of water.

below: Ffynnon Enddwyn, nr Duffryn Ardudwy, with (on a good day) views over Tremadoc Bay

and ...

2.9: Ffynnon Cegin Arthur /
The Well of Arthur's Kitchen
Llanddeiniolen,
Gwynedd
SH 554 649

2.10: Ffynnon Eidda /
Eidda's Well
nr Blaenau Ffestiniog,
Gwynedd
SH 762 437

2.11: Ffynnon-y-Capel /
Chapel Well
nr Dolgellau,
Gwynedd
SH 751 225

2.12: Ffynnon Bedydd
Sgotaidd /
Scotch Baptism Well
Harlech,
Gwynedd
SH 583 311
a nineteenth century
large baptismal tank,
near Capel Rehoboth
(formerly Capel Uchaf)
built in 1820 by the
Scotch Baptists

2.13: cafn ceffylau /
horse trough
Harlech
SH 586 311

3 TO BE A PILGRIM:
pen llŷn / the llŷn peninsula

*a land that hoards its past
and merges all of time
in the present ...*

from *Tide-race*
by Brenda Chamberlain

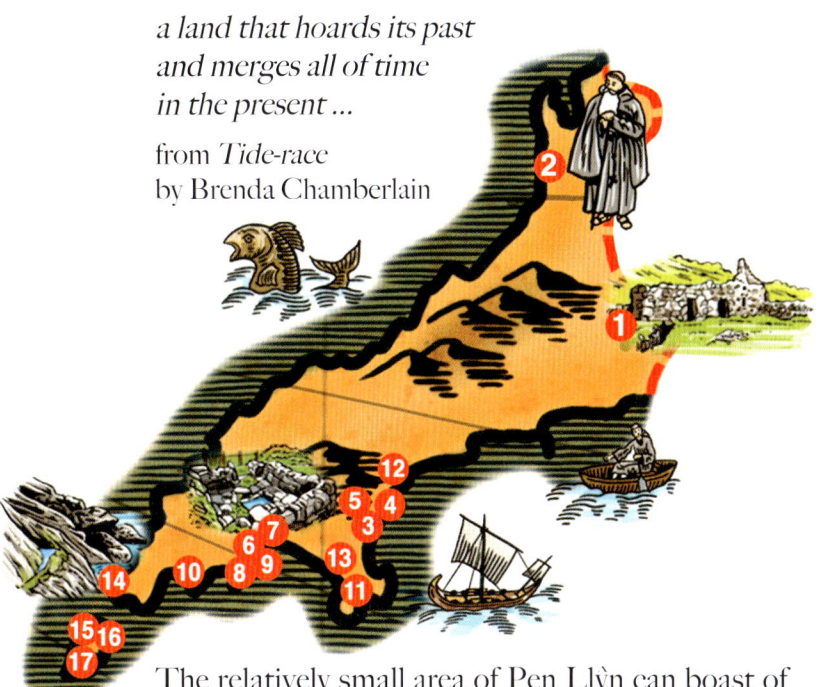

The relatively small area of Pen Llŷn can boast of more than its fair share of holy wells, mainly because of the pilgrim routes that traversed its lands heading towards a crossing to Ynys Enlli, the sacred isle of Bardsey. Most of the wellspring sites on the mainland here would have served as spiritual service stations for the pilgrims who walked, rode or were carried on well-worn trails both north and south of the peninsula which grew closer to the sea as they moved closer to their destination. And, once there, in the words of the poet Christine Evans, you found yourself *"where what mattered / happened."*

opposite:

Ffynnon Gybi /
St Cybi's Well [3.1]
Llangybi,
Pen Llŷn

The wellsprings on the Llŷn peninsula would have developed in importance through this constant trade, as, in afterlife collateral, three trips to Enlli were deemed to equal one to Rome. From the fifth century onwards, saints like Cadfan, Deiniol, Dyfrig, Einion, Lleuddad, Tudwal, Cybi and numerous others retreated to the island to die, a practice which attracted many other holy folk to follow in their footsteps on what became known as *"the road to Heaven"* and *"the gate to Paradise"*. (It is worth noting that the idea of a saint used by the early Celtic church was markedly different from that of their Latin counterparts, the former using the term much more freely to refer to any especially good Christian member of the church community, rather than a personage canonised by Rome.)

Enlli was famous as 'the island of 20,000 saints', where today, in the words of the poet, Gillian Clarke, *"Any pebble or shell / might be the knuckle-bone / or vertebra of a saint"* (from her 'Fires on Llŷn'). And, as well as the human remains, as many as twenty wellspring sites still survive to this day on Enlli.

Although most visitors and locals alike are unaware of the riches through which they pass on the way to seaside towns and castles, or which sit near their doorsteps, there are still regularly visited wellspring sites throughout Pen Llŷn.

Ffynnon Gybi, near Pwllheli is the jewel in the Llŷn wellspring crown as probably the principal stopping-off point on the pilgrimage routes to Enlli. And people still descend the slippery rocks to the much less accessible Ffynnon Fair or Mary's Well, on the very tip of the land overlooking Bardsey Island, at Uwchymynydd.

These special places still attract pilgrims of various denominations and none, as well as poets and writers inspired by their locations and by their stories. RS Thomas was Pen Llŷn's most famous contemporary bard, with his church, St Hywyn's, perched high above the waves at Aberdaron: *"From here, only sea-roads / run on"*, Ruth Bidgood.

In his often troubled relationship with his god, Thomas remembers (in his poem 'The Moon in Lleyn') that the *"parish / has a saint's name time cannot / unfrock"*, and smells of the *"scents / Of dead heroes and dead saints"* (from 'Border Blues').

And this is RS Thomas' poem, 'Ffynnon Fair', about Llŷn's St Mary's Well:

They did not divine it, but
they bequeathed it to us:
clear water, brackish at times,
complicated by the white frosts
of the sea, but thawing quickly.

Ignoring my image, I peer down
to the quiet roots of it, where
the coins lie, the tarnished offerings
of the people to the pure spirit
that lives there, that has lived there
always, giving itself up
to the thirsty, withholding
itself from the superstition
of others, who ask for more.

Pen Llŷn and Ynys Enlli are richly represented in poetry, as a book like *A Llŷn Anthology* (edited by the late Dewi Roberts, 2007) illustrates. I'd particularly recommend the tragic poem 'Ffynnon Fair' by Michael Ponsford; Harri Webb's 'Enlli'; 'Vespers' by Christine Evans; and 'The Moons of Llŷn [for RS Thomas]' by Alun Llwyd.

3.1 for the relief of pilgrims

**Ffynnon Gybi /
St Cybi's Well**
Llangybi,
nr Pwllheli,
Pen Llŷn
SH 427 413

St Cybi is reputed to have been born in Cornwall and died on Ynys Cybi (the island of Holyhead, off Anglesey) in 555 AD. He must have been a great traveller because he is said to have also visited Ireland, the Holy Land and Rome, as well as most parts of Wales, the latter fact attested to by the number of wells and chapels which bear his name, found in places as far apart as Gwent, Pembrokeshire, Mid and North Wales, and here on Pen Llŷn.

Legend has it that his Llŷn well was created when the saint struck his staff on the ground. What remains today is an ancient, stone-walled spring and adjacent larger well chamber for bathing, plus a later caretaker's cottage built around 1750 where the well guardian lived ... as well as a convenient privy for the relief of pilgrims.

opposite:
the path to Ffynnon Gybi

right:
St Cybi's Well

Cybi's Well cured warts, lameness, blindness, scrofula, scurvy and rheumatism. One of the treatments here demanded the drinking of well and sea water in equal measures, then bathing in the well and sleeping the night in the cottage. This act of 'incubation' was thought to attract the saint back to his well to activate the healing process.

In addition to St Cybi's alleged curative properties, the well was believed to have had the power to foretell the romantic intentions, or otherwise, of men. On the eve of the pagan festival of Beltane, women dropped handkerchiefs or feathers (or sometimes even pieces of bread) into the larger of the two pools and closely studied the direction in which they moved: southwards indicating their lover's future constancy, northwards his potential for infidelity.

left and opposite:
Ffynnon Gybi /
St Cybi's Well,
Llangybi

pen llŷn / the llŷn peninsula

This is Ruth Bidgood's response to
Llŷn's famous Ffynnon Gybi:

Holy saint Gybi,
by your sacred well,
by your mercy to lovers, I ask
with the ancient ritual of divination,
spreading my handkerchief on the waters,
to float towards blest south or cursed north –
is my man honest, or will I weep?

I pray my offering
drifts to the south.
Oh God! it floats north!
No, no, there are leaves in the well –
I free them, nudging it south.
Wind in the gorse all around
sounds prickly and dry,
like an old man's laugh.

3.2-3.5 north and south

Approaching Ynys Enlli along Llŷn's northern coastal paths, you would be sure to visit **Ffynnon Beuno / St Beuno's Well**, at Clynnog Fawr [3.2 / SH 412 493]. A dip in the freezing waters here, followed by a night on the cold stones of the saint's tomb in his church nearby was believed to cure the 'falling sickness' (or epilepsy) in children, as well as impotence in men. If you managed to get any sleep on the tomb, the cure would be successful. Pennant, writing in 1788 (*Tours in Wales*), reported of the tomb and the custom:

"I myself once saw on it a feather bed on which a poor paralytic from Merioneddshire had lain the whole night after undergoing the same ceremony."

And in an unlikely borrowing from the Roman Mithraic cult, bullocks were said to have been slaughtered and offered to Beuno in the church here, to ensure the 'well-being' of local cattle.

In addition to the seventh century saint's holy well and the tomb where his remains are believed to have been interred, another major attraction here was (and still is) Maen Beuno

('St Beuno's Stone'), incised with a Latin cross plus markings reputed to have been made by Beuno's own fingers. It is now situated within his church, the last of the many Celtic monasteries he founded (c. 616) after criss-crossing the country throughout his life.

(We will hear more of Beuno and his abilities to cure, especially with regard to his niece, later [4.11 / Ffynnon Gwenffrewi / St Winefride's Well].)

above:
Ffynnon Beuno,
Clynnog Fawr

opposite:
Ffynnon Gybi,
Llangybi

the living wells of wales

pen llŷn / the llŷn peninsula

opposite:

Ffynnon Beuno,
Clynnog Fawr

above left to right:

entrance to St Beuno's Church,
Clynnog Fawr;
one of the finely-carved wooden
pew ends at St Beuno's Church;
St Beuno's Stone

the living wells of wales

On the southern pilgrimage routes through Pen Llŷn, travellers would have visited the many wells around Mynytho, including Ffynnon Fyw, Ffynnon Arian, and Ffynnon Sarff (although most of these seem to have avoided a christening away from paganism towards the new faith); the four fine wells at Plas yn Rhiw; and then, finally, when nearing Uwchmynydd's precious view of the holy isle, Ffynnon y Saint at Aberdaron.

Once dedicated to St Curig, the two large, finely re-constructed pools of Ffynnon Fyw (or Dduw) / The Living (or God's) Well [3.3 / SH 3091 3088] in Mynytho are visibly polluted, currently suffering, most likely, from seepage from a domestic septic tank.

Thought to have once effected cures for blindness, Ffynnon Fyw was in its heyday an important site for community celebrations.

opposite left, top to bottom:

Ffynnon Fyw, showing signs of pollution; two images of Ffynnon Fyw, pre-reconstruction, 2007

above:

Ffynnon Fyw, Mynytho

pen llŷn / the llŷn peninsula

Francis Jones (*The Holy Wells of Wales*, 1952) identifies **Ffynnon Arian / The Money** (or **Silver**) **Well** [3.4 / SH 3039 3113] as a wishing well, although we know precious little else about it.

right:
Ffynnon Arian,
Mynytho

pen llŷn / the llŷn peninsula

opposite and left:

Ffynnon Sarff /
The Serpent Well,
Mynytho
with Lee Oliver
from Keep Wales Tidy

A magical snake with the powers of divination was said to have once lived in the waters of **Ffynnon Sarff** (or **'The Serpent Well'**) at Mynytho [3.5 / SH 2950 3190].

And **Ffynnon Fair / Mary's Well** [SH 311 329], at Foel Fawr, also in Mynytho, could reveal the name of a thief: *"One had to throw bread into the well, whispering the name of the suspect at the same time. If the bread sank, then the person was guilty!"* (Elfed Gruffydd, *Llŷn*, 1998)

the living wells of wales

3.6-3.9 a spectacular spot

There are also many interesting well sites in the National Trust-owned area of Plas yn Rhiw on Llŷn:

Ffynnon Aelrhiw / Aelrhiw Well [3.6 / SH 233 285] – with its association with the early seventeenth century Plas yn Rhiw manor house, its ornamental gardens into which Aelrhiw's waters still flow, and the spectacular views across Cardigan Bay – was famous for its ability to treat skin disorders.

Baring-Gould fails to identify a saint named Aelrhiw in any of the Welsh genealogies, instead suggesting that the name might be a corruption of Y Ddelw Fyw or 'the Living Image', which occurs on some Welsh calendars with the feast day of 9 September, which coincides with that of the St Aelrhiw once celebrated at Rhiw. The well was noted for curing afflictions of the skin, and in particular for an ailment known as Man Aeliw ('Aeliw's spot'), named, I assume, after its record of successful cures here.

Virtually inaccessible some five years ago, it has recently been restored by AHNE Pen Llŷn AONB, Keep Wales Tidy and volunteers. It is good to see that local people are once again both using the waters from this well for medicinal purposes, as well as assisting with its upkeep.

above and opposite:
Ffynnon Aelrhiw, falling to the gardens of Plas yn Rhiw

the living wells of wales

pen llŷn / the llŷn peninsula

opposite:
Ffynnon Aelrhiw,
Plas yn Rhiw

below left:
snowdrops
at Plas yn Rhiw

below:
near Ffynnon Saint,
Plas yn Rhiw

Ffynnon Saint / Saint's Well [3.7 / SH 242 295] – which specialised in curing complaints of the eyes – is an evocative site, set below the Neolithic axe factory on Mynydd Rhiw from which blades were exported far and wide.

the living wells of wales

pen llŷn / the llŷn peninsula

Ffynnon Pant / Pant Well [3.8 / SH 231 278] is stunningly situated in a wall between two fields overlooking Porth Neigwl, opposite the suggestively-named Awelon, with its Arthurian possibilities.

opposite:

Ffynnon Saint,
Plas yn Rhiw

left and above:

Ffynnon Pant,
Plas yn Rhiw

the living wells of wales

And a fourth nameless wellspring which I have called Ffynnon Plas yn Rhiw / Plas yn Rhiw Well [3.9 / SH 238 285] is set within the park's beautiful woodlands, not far from the house.

(Sadly, the once-important Bryn y Ffynnon / Hill Well [SH 242 303] in Rhiw – with its historic cottages and pigsty – has recently become inaccessible due to insensitive tree felling.)

above and right:
Ffynnon Plas yn Rhiw

opposite left:
Ffynnon y Saint, nr Aberdaron
opposite right, top to bottom:
Porth Neigwl from Pen Cilan;
landowner Emlyn Williams at
Ôl Troed March Engan;
Lee Oliver unearthing
Ffynnon Pen-y-Groes;
Ôl Troed March Engan

3.10-3.11 water, metal, stone

As we have already seen, there are a number of wellsprings on Llŷn which currently have hinged, metal lids, some of which are in a poor state of repair.

Ffynnon y Saint / Saint's Well [3.10 / SH 1654 2671], near Aberdaron, offered a final opportunity for Enlli pilgrims to drink its medicinal waters, and to pray at the altar of Allor Hywyn (a large flat stone destroyed when the nearby bridge was built) before proceeding to cross to Bardsey Island.

The isolated **Ffynnon Pen-y-Groes** [3.11 / SH 293 248] on Pen Cilan, south of Llanengan, has the added attraction of its ancient stone, known as Ôl Troed March Engan [SH 294 249] and the Neolithic burial chamber [SH 312 235] at Cilan Uchaf at its south-eastern tip, as well as very fine views.

In the recent past, Ffynnon Pen-y-Groes serviced nine local houses until piped tap water was introduced in the 1950s, but it is intriguing to ponder how long people who lived here have used this source. Mynydd Cilan, on Pen Cilan, is a part of Llŷn thought to have been occupied for more than 15,000 years. The ancient stone near to the well is named after and said to show the hoof print of Einion (or Engan)'s horse which leapt from the nearby Castell Cilan to save his master's life sometime during the fifth or sixth century. Einion was the Prince of Llŷn, and brother to the saints Seiriol and Meirion; and he was also to claim that religious title. It was Einion who gifted Ynys Enlli to Cadfan, the island's first abbot, *"to become a monastic refuge for Saints weary of the world"* (Baring-Gould & Fisher). Water was collected from this stone, as well as from Ffynnon Pen-y-Groes, for medicinal purposes, to heal warts and other skin diseases. Engan became the patron saint of Llanengan (see also his well behind Llanengan Church / [3.13]).

the living wells of wales

3.12-3.13: beyond retention

The designs and fabric of holy well and sacred spring sites have changed over time, as beliefs and faiths have discovered new ways to explain the unexplainable, building layer upon layer of masonry and of meaning. It is strange, then, that the current prevailing attitude towards the care – when they are cared for – of our wellsprings seems most often to be to stop history at the latest modification This is a strategy in danger of signing the death certificates for these sites as places of consequence and vitality in our lives.

There are exceptions to the rule, of course, where people are continuing and extending the dialogue with our wellspring cultures: Ffynnon Gwenffrewi / St Winefride's Well [4.11] in Holywell, Flintshire, still welcomes its thousands of pilgrims annually to bathe in and drink its waters; queues still regularly form at Hay Slad Spout [SO 766 448] in the Malvern Hills, in Worcestershire, to fill their buckets with pure and free spring water; and 'cloutie' wells, like St Boniface's [NH 641 537] at Munlochy, in Scotland, and Ffynnon Rhinweddol or The Virtuous Well [7.9] in Trelleck, Monmouthshire still attract the soiled offerings of the sick and the unhappy in a tradition that goes back way before the start of Christianity.

opposite: Ffynnon Pen-y-Groes, Pen Cilan

But despite these few good examples, most people are unaware of the significance of the sites on their doorsteps, often resulting in their neglect.

Today, many are used as rubbish bins for discarded cans and crisp packets; some are polluted by the seepage of farm chemicals; destroyed by forestry, or road and housing 'developments'.

While I fully recognise the archaeological imperative to retain and secure historic remains for future generations (and the importance of the development of transport infrastructure, the building of houses, and the growing and harvesting of trees), I want to question why we aren't continuing today to make our own physical, spiritual and community responses to these once-important sites.

The good news is that, on Llŷn there are some inspiring examples of just this kind of wellspring future thinking. During the building of the amphitheatre at the Plas Glyn-y-Weddw Arts Centre [3.12 / SH 329 315] in Llanbedrog, a well was discovered. Many would have seen this as an inconvenience and found a way of diverting its waters away from the new structures. In contrast, however – and recognising the historical and ecological importance of the well – it was incorporated into the modern build, the spring being capped at the centre of the seating area (though still visible with a little digging), while the waters flow out into a drinking fountain within the wall leading to the theatre. Currently, there is a 'Do Not Drink' sign on the fountain, though this I am told they intend to reverse, releasing the spring once again to serve its originally intended life-giving purpose.

left: The Amphitheatre Well, Plas Glyn-y-Weddw, Llanbedrog, with Lee Oliver (KWT), Iwan Hughes (manager) and Gwyn Jones (director)

the living wells of wales

Another quite different response which left the original ancient well intact but used its waters to create a new and impressive feature, is that constructed within the garden of (and by) Mrs Susan E Evans of Tan y Fynwent, Llanengan. Ffynnon Engan / St Engan's Well [3.13] / SH 2931 2707], near Abersoch, is associated with the saints Peris and his servant Cian, and has a history of miracles.

It probably had its latest build phase sometime in the late sixteenth century, and, while maintaining that structure with great care, Mrs Evans has created a lower pool into which the original well's waters flow, a structure which looks back in its design to a much earlier period in the sacred spring's history.

pen llŷn / the llŷn peninsula

3.14: the final steps

Ffynnon Fair / Mary's Well
Uwchymynydd
nr Aberdaron,
Pen Llŷn
SH 1395 2519

One of the most dramatically-situated of all of Wales' holy wells, Ffynnon Fair's natural basin is perched precariously amongst cliffs above the sea on the very tip of Pen Llŷn, accessed only via a steep and slippery rock climb down Grisiau Mair ('Mary's steps' or 'ladder'). The well is regularly covered by the tide but returns to its pure water state after each salty ingression. It is said that pilgrims would try to find the marks of the hooves of Ceffyl Mair ('Mary's horse') and the scratchings of Mary's fingers on the rocks before drinking its holy waters here. The ruins of Capel Mair ('the chapel of St Mary') sit in the field above, overlooking Ynys Enlli, the final destination of pilgrims who rested here.

Neither cures nor wishes at Ffynnon Fair were easy to gain, however. The ritual involved taking a mouthful of liquid from the spring below, climbing up the rocks and then walking around the chapel without spilling or swallowing any of the water, a feat that seemingly could not have been achieved by any but the already fit and healthy.

opposite:
Ffynnon Engan 'extension'
(with owner, Mrs Susan Evans)

left, top to bottom:
Llanengan Church; church window;
ancient pews

above:
Ffynnon Engan, Llanengan

the living wells of wales

above, top:

Ynys Enlli / Bardsey Island

above centre, left to right:

Ynys Enlli from Uwchymynydd;
Grisiau Mair / 'Mary's steps'
leading to Ffynnon Fair;
Lee Oliver and Rhedyn
on the path to Ffynnon Fair

left:

waves over Ffynnon Fair

opposite:

Ffynnon Fair, Uwchymynydd

This is the poet Susan Richardson's evocative response to Ffynnon Fair:

Grief has led her here
in its hooded goatskin cloak,
with its crooked staff,
its cussed devotion.

She stutters
down Grisiau Mair, each step
a slippery syllable on the stuck-out tongue
of cliff. The sea is a whip
that means to increase her suffering,

while Bardsey belongs to a bestiary,
hump-backed hulk, jaws frothing.

She supposes she should pray
but doesn't know the language –
and anyway, her voice is taut
as oxhide stretched
over a timber frame, unsteadied
by eddies of pain.

She turns, instead, to the well's whisper
of water, tinged
with a wish-glint of silver coins.

It will take more than one sip
to dispel her accidie
but already she can sense the squint
of a fresh beginning, the twitch
of a shearwater's wings.

the living wells of wales

3.15-3.17: the island of twenty thousand saints

It is a strange Enlli fact that – despite the sacred nature of the island and the number of saints buried here – none of the wells on Bardsey are named after any of them. The nearest ecclesiastical connection is a collection of possibly seven small round pools on Mynydd

Enlli, known as **Ffynnon Barfau** / (perhaps) **The 'Well of the Beards'** [3.15 / SH 123 223], to which the island's monks were believed by some to have climbed each morning to shave their heads, using the waters as natural mirrors.

Their creation was the work, it is said, of a giant who jumped from Maen Bugel, sinking his feet deep into the mountainside rock.

It is claimed that Lleuddad turned the water into milk by stirring it with his staff at **Ffynnon Baglau** (**Ffynnon Bryn Baglau** or **Ffynnon Dalar**) [3.16 / SH 119 218]. On another occasion, the saint instructed his followers to plant their staffs into the ground around the well, which soon sprouted into fully-grown trees. The lame would leave their crutches here after being cured, and there is yet another story of Lleuddad's quarrel with Cadfan somehow being settled here with the use of these discarded items.

Ffynnon Baglau is one of the few major wells on Ynys Enlli not currently utilised as a domestic water supply. It is also one of the most impressive in terms of both construction and location (set as it is beside the single road running across the island from the landing stage at Y Cafn to the Abbey), although it is today unattractively fenced and topped with barbed wire, its former glories hidden and (nearly) inaccessible to all.

pen llŷn / the llŷn peninsula

Miracles were said to have been performed at the impressively situated **Ffynnon Dolysgwydd / Dolysgwydd Well** [3.17 / SH 118 211], although – as with much else in wellspring culture – these claims have their doubters.

opposite left:
Ffynnon Barfau /
The Well of the Beards,
Ynys Enlli

opposite centre
and far left:
Ffynnon Baglau,
Ynys Enlli

left:
Ffynnon Dolysgwydd,
Ynys Enlli

It's often difficult to distinguish between what has been recorded in historical accounts and the works of invention inspired by these sites, though maybe both of these are just different products of our imagination, means to explain the things we cannot fully comprehend.

the living wells of wales

and ...

3.18: Ffynnon Gwynhoedl /
Gwynhoedl Well
Llangwnnadl,
Pen Llŷn
SH 209 332
Hidden within bushes across Yr Afon Fawr from its historic church, this is the possible site of the grave of Gwynhoedl, its patron saint.

3.21: Ffynnon Fair /
Mary's Well
Nefyn,
Pen Llŷn
SH 307 406

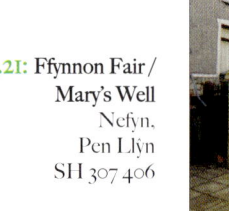

3.19: Ffynnon Corn /
Horn Well
Ynys Enlli
SH 122 222
The island's main well is said to have been excavated by the monks. Today, with its plastic lid and wooden-gated protection, it is still used by residents, in a continuous 1500 year thirst-quenching history.

3.22: Ffynnon Felin Bach /
The Well of the Little Mill
Pwllheli,
Pen Llŷn
SH 365 354
A site associated with the poet Cynan (Albert Evans Jones): writing from the horrors of his WWI trenches, in *Ffynnon Felin Bach*, his National Eisteddfod-winning poem, he remembered with fondness his mother filling her pitcher at this well:

> O! let me again the joy
> This spring could give me as a boy.
> When water from some Heavenly Hill
> With cleansing grace my heart would fill.
>
> And here some virtue still must lie
> To cool your fever, passer-by.

3.20: Ffynnon Fair /
Mary's Well
Bryncroes,
Pen Llŷn
SH 227 314
Lee Oliver takes a drink ...

3.23: Ffynnon Rhufeinig /
The Roman Well
Betws-Fawr,
above Criccieth,
Pen Llŷn
SH 466 398

pen llŷn / the llŷn peninsula

3.24: Ffynnon
Sanctaidd /
The Sacred Well
Pistyll,
Pen Llŷn
SH 330 423

3.27: Ffynnon
Lleuddad /
Lleuddad Well
nr Llangwnnadl,
Botwnnog
SH 219 327

3.25: Ffynnon
Corn / Horn Well
Uwchmynydd,
Pen Llŷn
SH 141 254
with Bardsey Island
in the distance

3.28: Ffynnon arall
Llangybi /
Llangybi's other well
on the path to
Ffynnon Gybi [3.1]
SH 426 412

3.29: Ffynnon Porth Ysgaden
/ Porth Ysgaden Well
nr Tudweiliog
SH 219 374
On the Cefnamlwch Estate,
in a beautiful situation overlooking the sea, set below
the remains of a coal-fired
lime kiln that once supplied
farmers for use on their land

3.26: Ffynnon
West End /
West End Well
Trefor,
Pen Llŷn
SH 363 467

3.30: Ffynnon Aelhaearn
/ Aelhaearn Well
Llanaelhaearn,
Pen Llŷn
SH 384 446
This once-impressive
curative site now lies
locked and concrete-
and bramble-covered
by the side of a busy road
below the Iron Age Tre'r
Ceiri Hillfort, associated
as it is with the Vortigern
legends.

the living wells of wales

3.31: Ffynnon Dyno Goch / Dyno Goch's Well
Ynys Enlli
SH 117 211
An eel was said to have once lived in the well here.

3.34: Ffynnon Plas Bach / Plas Bach Well
Ynys Enlli
SH 119 217

3.32: Ffynnon Owain Rolant / Owain Rolant's Well
(or Ffynnon Uchaf / Upper Well)
Ynys Enlli
SH 122 221
Enlli's most naturally-attractive well, emerging from two scrapes against the mountain's rock wall to the north of Ty Capel

3.35: Ffynnon Cristin / Cristin's Well
(or Ffynnon Uchaf / Upper Well)
Ynys Enlli
SH 120 21

3.36: Ffynnon Tŷ Pilla / Tŷ Pilla Well
Ynys Enlli
SH 119 213

3.33: Ffynnon Trwy'r Nant / 'Through the Stream' Well
Llanbedrog, Pen Llŷn
SH 326 319

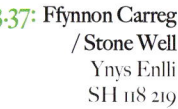

3.37: Ffynnon Carreg / Stone Well
Ynys Enlli
SH 118 219

90

pen llŷn / the llŷn peninsula

3.38: Ffynnon Castell Cricieth / Criccieth Castle Well
Pen Llŷn
SH 500 377
The water cistern here, situated in the floor of the castle's entrance passage, was fed by a natural spring.

3.39: Ffynnon ganoloesol Penarth Fawr / Penarth Fawr medieval well
nr Abererch, Pwllheli
SH 419 376
Caren and Gwyn Jones' large circular medieval well at Penarth Fawr has been kept alive by an impressive new glass covering.

3.40: ty ffynnon ryngwladol newydd / new international well-house
Felin Uchaf, Pen Llŷn
SH 203 289
Dafydd Hughes-Davies at his visionary *Felin Uchaf* cultural and eco complex, where he has created a new wellspring building which looks both backwards as well as forwards, for people of all faiths and none (plus resident frog)

4 THE JUSTICE OF WATERS: clwyd

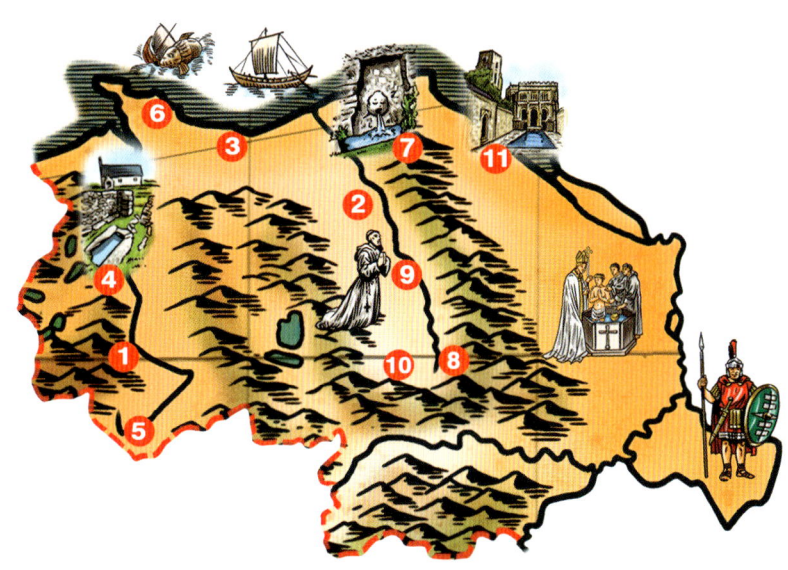

opposite:

Ffynnon Dyfnog /
St Dyfnog's Well [4.9]
Llanrhaeadr-yng-Nghinmeirch,
Denbighshire

The borders of both the nation of Wales and of its regions have changed regularly over time, under the pressures of invasion and of politics. In this Clwyd section, I have included the traditional (1535) counties and the contemporary (1996) unitary authorities of Conwy, Denbighshire and Flintshire, as well as Wrexham, historically a part of Denbighshire but granted separate County Borough status in 1996. Clwyd – named after the river that runs through it – was abolished as a county in the same year.

Sacred springs and holy wells draw other borders for us, feint lines between the real and the imagined. They have been described as 'thin places' where the skin between the corporeal and the spiritual is stretched to almost nothing, and where, as a consequence, invitations to enter may be answered with greater ease. It is at these points that wellsprings were thought to have had the power to offer a measure of relief, a sign, a message perhaps, sometimes a cure, sometimes even a degree of justice in an unjust world.

But other lines being drawn, with gates, fences, barbed wire and 'keep out' signs which exclude instead of welcome. Some once important well-spring sites are closed to our visits and to our gaze today. I have a big problem with this. These places hold our history. They are part of our heritage, part of where we have been, what we have fought over, what we have and in some cases still do believe in.

A sad recent development was the closure and deterioration of Ffynhonnau a Sba Trefriw / Trefriw Wells and Spa [4.1 / SH 780 652], situated on the western slopes of the Conwy valley, near Betwys-y-Coed. Once described as *"the healthiest place in Wales"* (Morris Jones writing in *Hanes Trefriw*, 1879), its chalybeate waters have been in use for millennia.

Trefriw is just a few miles south of the Roman fort of *Canovium*, and beside Sarn Helen, the major Roman road that ran from this military settlement to another at Tomen-y-mur, and on to *Moridunum* at present day Carmarthen. Not surprisingly, then, the copious spring at Trefriw was recognised and used by the XXth Roman Legion many centuries before its chalybeate and sulphur-rich waters were developed into one of the country's most important spa destinations in the early eighteen hundreds.

left:
Trefriw Wells Spa today

opposite:
Trefriw Wells Spa in 2007
Note the weighing scales with the notice that reads:
*"To WEIGH oneself OFTEN
Is to KNOW oneself WELL.
To know oneself WELL
Is to BE WELL."*

Trefriw's popularity grew throughout the nineteenth and into the first half of the twentieth century with its health-seeking, well-healed visitors arriving by steamer from Conwy, and by train. It is interesting to note that Trefriw's first passenger boat, introduced in 1847, was called the *St Winifred*. At its height in the early years of the twentieth century, six steamers a day were carrying more than one thousand visitors on the ninety-minute journey to its pump rooms, bath houses, tea shops, restaurants and hotels.

One explanation for the origin of the name of the village is tref ('farmstead', or alternatively 'town') and briw ('a wound'), referring to the ability of the waters here to heal, a claim supported by many, and not least, local Trefriw Spa regular, Mary Owen 'the oldest subject in Great Britain', who died in 1911 at the age of 108!

Those seeking cures were further enticed by Trefriw Spa's five-star reviews: *"inconceivably nasty and correspondingly efficacious"* (in Baddeley's *Thorough Guide to North Wales*, 1895), and *"As sulphate chalybeates are the best of all chalybeates, the Trefriw is the finest chalybeate water in Great Britain"* (from the eminent Dr Hayward of Liverpool).

the living wells of wales

4.2: the fount of the virgin's ruined shrine *

Ffynnon Fair / St Mary's Well
nr Trefnant, nr St Asaph,
Denbighshire
SJ 0290 7107

Today, the steamers and the visitors have gone, but the medicinal waters still flow and are still in demand. Spatone is now based here, packaging and distributing their *Iron+* products internationally, continuing the practice of the Victorian period when a two-month supply shipped anywhere in the world cost the very considerable sum of forty-two shillings.

In the recent past, there was a path open to visit the original spring and to view the Roman and later remains, and a small impressive museum displaying an old slate bath, an elbow and a hip bath within the treatment rooms, as well as a tea shop.

All of this is now gone (or, at least, no longer accessible), with the original well site fenced and padlocked.

Another of my great angers in the world of Welsh wellsprings is the site of Ffynnon Fair in Denbighshire:

St Winefride's Well at Holywell [4.11] and Ffynnon Fair near Trefnant were linked by a popular pilgrimage route, as, intriguingly, are the fine designs of their basins. The earliest part of the now-roofless chapel building is thought to date from the thirteenth century, with the chancel being added and the fine polygonal well pool of hewn stone rebuilt in the fifteenth.

Following the Reformation, the well began to fall into disrepair and, by the eighteenth century, the chapel was in ruins and pilgrimages had ceased, although it did continue to build upon its reputation – like that of Bodrhyddan [4.25] – for secret weddings, becoming known by some as 'the Gretna Green of North Wales'.

Today, only the ivy-clad stones returning to nature, and the constant chatter of the spring waters are left to testify to its long history of worship and of love. But even worse, the site now, on private land, is doubly-inaccessible, first at the entrance to the field at the end of which it stands, then chained at the gate to its iron-fenced enclosure.

Fount of the vale! thou art sought no more
By the pilgrim's foot, as in time of yore,
When he came from afar, his beads to tell,
And to chant his hymn at Our Lady's Well.
There is heard no Ave through thy bowers.
Thou art gleaming lone midst thy water
   flowers!

Felicia Hemans

opposite:
the ferrous stalactites at Trefriw Wells' Roman spring

right:
Ffynnon Fair, 2018

* Felicia Hemans (1793-1835) from her poem, *Ffynnon Fair / Our Lady's Well*

In truth, my 'pilgrim's foot' still wants to visit Ffynnon Fair, as well as the many other closed wellspring sites throughout Wales.

What clearly is needed here is what already exists in Scotland. *The Land Reform (Scotland) Act 2003* gives everyone rights of access over land and inland waterways throughout Scotland, as long as they act responsibly and care for the environment. This 'freedom to roam' embodies within law the belief that the land belongs to all of us (although, of course, it currently doesn't) and that we should have the right to access it, walking our own paths and – like at places like Trefriw Spa and Ffynnon Fair – being allowed to create our own definitions of what these and the other important once-and-future places can still mean for us.

opposite:
Ffynnon Fair,
nr Trefnant,
Denbighshire
in 2009

4.3: the most dreadful well in wales *

Ffynnon Elian / St Elian's Well
Llanelian yn Rhos,
nr Colwyn Bay, Conwy
SH 8607 7692

Not in the mystic Aelian's grove,
Did feather'd songsters sing of love;
But birds of omen harbour'd there,
And fill'd with boding shrieks the air

Charlotte Wardle, from *St Aelian's, or the Cursing Well*, 1814

So-called curse wells have been present within the annals of sacred waters since our earliest records.

The Romans certainly used their springs as places where they could seek restitution or revenge. Their practice was to inscribe a tablet with a 'message' to a deity, naming the malefactor and sometimes asking for a very specific punishment. A tablet found in *Aquae Sulis* in Bath addressed to the god *Sulis Minerva* reads, *"Dodimedis has lost two gloves. He asks that the person who has stolen them should lose his mind and eyes in the temple where she appoint"*. And, on another occasion, following the theft of a favourite silver ring, the victim asked that the thief be *"accursed in his blood and eyes and every limb, or even have all of his intestines quite eaten away"*!

This method of requesting natural justice, restitution or help for any of life's difficulties was also on offer at at least one well in North Wales. At Ffynnon Elian in Llanelian yn Rhos, initials were scratched onto slates or stones before being placed in the well, and a request asked of the saint via the medium of the well guardian.

Initially considered to be a site with strong healing and wish-granting properties, Ffynnon Elian was said to have sprung forth to quench the thirst of the obscure St Elian sometime in the sixth century, although it is almost certain that the benefits of its waters would have been recognised well before the christianising of the site.

At the end of the seventeenth century, the Welsh polymath Edward Lhuyd (1660-1709) observed that petitioners were required to pay a groat (a silver coin worth four English pennies) or its equivalent value in bread in order to obtain a cure for a sick child here. He also reported that the well was used by 'Paphistiaid' (Catholics), an indication that although Catholicism had been outlawed since the time of Henry VIII, there were people who continued to ask for help and healing at the old and trusted sources.

* Wirt Sykes, writing in *British Goblins*, 1881

the living wells of wales

Some time in the last quarter of the eighteenth century, however, the reputation of the well was to change from that of a healing pilgrimage destination to a place where people could wish ill upon their neighbours. The Welsh naturalist and antiquarian, Thomas Pennant (1726-1798) was the first to publish a description of Ffynnon Elian in which the word 'curse' was recorded:

... the well at Saint Aelian... has been in great repute for the cure of all diseases, by means of the intercession of the saint who was first invoked by earnest prayers in the neighbouring church. He was also applied to on less worthy occasions and made the instrument of discovering thieves, and of recovering stolen goods. Some repair to him to imprecate their neighbours and to request the saint to afflict with sudden death, or with some great misfortune, any persons who may have offended them.
(from *A Tour in Wales*, 1778)

Although Pennant clearly acknowledged the dual nature of Ffynnon Elian, he went on to offer a personal anecdote that probably did more than anything else to cement the negative reputation of the site:

... three years have not elapsed since I was threatened by a fellow (who imagined I had injured him) with the vengeance of St Aelian and a journey to the well to curse me with effect.

above and opposite:
the restored Ffynnon Elian,
Llanelian yn Rhos,
Conwy

From that time onwards, English travel writers in particular were happy to perpetuate the myth and to reduce the site's options to that of a *"wickedly malicious well"* which *"holds still a strong influence over the ignorant mind"* (Wirt Sykes, *British Goblins*, 1881). Some wrote about *"the cursing hag"*, *"the baneful fountain"*, the grove of trees surrounding the well as *"dripping with evil"*, and that *"implacable Welshmen would walk 40 miles to curse their neighbours"*. The following story of one Pedws Ffowk appeared in *The Welsh Fairy Book* (1908) written by W Jenkyn Thomas, and is worth quoting in its entirety:

Pedws Ffowk was for three years afflicted with a complaint which nobody could understand. She was well and yet she was not well: she was sick and yet she was not sick. That is to say, she had no ache or pain, and her appetite was good. But all the time she became thinner and thinner, until at last she was nothing but skin and bone. She went to doctor after doctor, but they could not find out what was the matter with her. She consulted quacks also, but even they did her no good.

Finally, she went to a wise man. He, after hearing her story, said, "Someone has put you into St. Elian's Well."
"What do you mean by that?" asked Pedws.
"Someone has gone to the woman who keeps the well," answered the wise man, "and put your name on the register, and thrown a pin into the well, together with a pebble with your initials on it."
"Well, what is the harm of that?" inquired Pedws, who had not heard of the power of the cursing well.
"You are cursed," was the reply, "and unless the curse is removed, you will pine away and die."
"But what am I to do?" said Pedws, now thoroughly frightened.
"You must go to the woman who keeps the well, and pay her to take you out of the well," was the wise man's advice.

Pedws lost no time in going to the guardian of the well, who, for a small fee, agreed to examine her register. Sure enough, the name of Pedws Ffowk was there inscribed, and the date of the entry corresponded with the time when she had begun to waste away. On the payment of another and a larger sum of money the priestess of the fountain agreed to take out of the water the stone on which the initials of Pedws Ffowk were scratched.

From that moment flesh began to grow on her bones, and before long her clothes, which had hung upon her like rags upon a scarecrow, were filled out as well as they had ever been.

Pedws lived to a good old age, and her greatest trouble was that she never found out which of her best friends had put her into the well.

the living wells of wales

The poets and travel writers who provided the fragments of sensationalist evidence of this *"backward and primitive"* people, were, however, not the only enemies of Ffynnon Elian. Methodism arrived here in the latter years of the eighteenth century and, in 1829, outraged members of the congregation destroyed the site, taking every stone away, and very possibly using some of the original well structure to build their own chapel nearby.

Jane Beckerman – on whose land St Elian's Well now sits and who is sensitively restoring the site – has explored in detail the context and attraction of the well's dual characteristics to curse and to cure:

Life was hard in Wales from the end of the eighteenth century. The Napoleonic Wars took Welsh men away from their farms and their other occupations; Enclosure Acts took away common land, making life harder for the landless to graze a few animals; and the weather was particularly bad from the end of the eighteenth century until the third decade of the nineteenth ... People must have felt 'cursed' by life, when illness and poverty were so near at hand; and the promise that the 'curse' could be removed, by simply 'taking out' a pebble or slate with an individual's initials on it would have seemed very inviting. There was a cost involved, at a time when money was very scarce, but the ancient power of this well must have been deeply ingrained in the local community and those further afield. It would not have continued to be used if this had not been the case.

Beckerman – in her 'reading against the grain' as contemporary historians call it – offers an intriguing re-interpretation of St Elian's Well as a place for adjusting the balance of life, for finding a small measure of justice in an unjust age, in stark contrast to the more commonly propagated view of the site as a centre for all things evil.

(I am indebted to Jane Beckerman for much of the above information, gleaned from her 2009 Masters thesis *'Ffynnon Elian: Reputation and Reality, 1700-1850'* for the University of Wales Bangor – now published as *Unholy Water? Ffynnon Elian 'The Cursing Well'* – which inspired in me new insights into the usages of our sacred springs.)

4.4 sink or swim

Ffynnon Sanctaidd Celynin Sant / St Celynin's Well
Llangelynin,
nr Hendre, Conwy
SH 7512 7369

The chapel and well of St Celynin, another six-century holy man, is hidden high up in the mountains above the Conwy Valley in one of the most isolated and peaceful positions of any chapel in Wales.

Celynin himself dates from the sixth century and was one of twelve sons of Helig ab Glannog, whose territories were thought to have been flooded, and now lie under Beaumaris Bay and Lavan Sands, their remains becoming visible at very low tides a mile or so off the coast at Penmaenmawr. It was as a result of losing their family lands in this way that the sons became monks at Bangor on Dee and on Bardsey.

Celynin's Well – set into the southwest corner of the churchyard wall – specialised in treating sick children who were immersed in its waters, then wrapped in a blanket and allowed to sleep at a house at Cae Iol, nearby. The success or otherwise of the cure could be judged by placing an item of the child's clothing on the water: if it floated the child would recover; if it sank then the cure had failed and the child would most probably die.

clwyd

opposite:

Jane Beckerman,
the landowner
and well guardian
of Ffynnon Elian,
Llanelian yn Rhos,
nr Colwyn Bay

above:

the path to
St Celynin's Well and Church,
Llangelynin

4.5 alive again

Ffynnon Elen / St Helen's Well
Dolwyddelan,
nr Blaenau Ffestiniog,
Conwy
SH 7366 5251

We have already encountered an Elen or Helen at *Segontium* [2.1] as the heroine of *The Dream of Macsen Wledig*, one of the *Mabinogion* tales. She has often been equated / confused with Helena of Constantinople, discoverer of Christ's cross, and the mother of Constantine the first Christian ruler, a belief to which weight was perhaps added by tales of Roman soldiers using 'her' well as a picnic site, and the discovery of Roman coins nearby.

There was also a belief that the village name, Dolwyddelan, was derived from Dolydd Elen ('Elen's Meadow'), though it is more likely that it comes from the Irish saint, Gwyddelan, who preached in this area sometime between the fourth and sixth centuries, and to whom the church here is dedicated. Said to steam during cold winter months, the site – now known locally as Ffynnon Elen (though also almost certainly originally dedicated to Gwyddelan) – was particularly efficacious for sickly children and for paralysed limbs.

More than a decade ago, Ffynnon Elen was almost completely hidden, overgrown with ferns and brambles, the path to it difficult to travel.

I am glad to report, however, that work on the site began in June 2014 (led by archaeologist Bill Jones with members of the Dolwyddelan Historical Society, and supported by the site owners Elen's Castle Hotel, and the National Park Authority), and that today the well has been restored to something near its former glory.

above:

Ffynnon Elen /
St Helen's Well,
Dolwyddelan,
hidden in 2007

opposite,
clockwise from left:

Ffynnon Elian,
Llangelynin;
the Men's Chapel
to keep the unwashed drovers away from the main congregation;
the inscription of the Lord's Prayer and Ten Commandments in Welsh on the wall beside the altar,
to which a skull and crossbones have been appended;
St Elian's Well

clwyd

opposite:

Ffynnon Elen,
Dolwyddelan,
2018

left, top to bottom:

St Gwyddelan's Church,
Dolwyddelan,
exterior and interior;
Gwyddelan's hand bell
(found in 1850, buried
in the ground),
hanging from the beams
above the nave

4.6 small is beautiful

**Ffynnon Drillo /
St Trillo's Holy Chapel Well**
Marine Drive,
Llandrillo yn Rhos /
Rhos on Sea,
nr Llandudno,
Conwy
SH 8413 8113

With seats for just six worshippers, St Trillo's Chapel is considered to be the smallest in Britain. It is said to have been built at the place, sat next to the sea, where St Trillo established his first church in the sixth century, on the site of a pre-Christian sacred spring.

Trillo is thought to have been the son of King Ithel Hael of Llydew (Snowdonia). He came to Wales as a missionary with some members of his family, including his brothers, saints Tegai and Twrog, and his sister Llechid. He was a monk on the holy island of Bardsey before establishing his church at Llandrillo, where he lived as a hermit from 570 AD. When he died in 590, his body was returned to Bardsey for burial.

The well, which sits under a grate directly below the chapel altar, is dedicated to both St Trillo and St Elian.

clwyd

opposite:

St Trillo's Chapel,
Rhos on Sea

above, left to right:

the tiny interior of St Trillo's Chapel
with his holy well under the altar;
the stained glass windows of
St Elian and St Trillo in his chapel

the living wells of wales

4.7 face time

**Ffynnon Beuno /
St Beuno's Well**
Tremeirchion, nr St Asaph,
Denbighshire
SJ 0835 7235

St Beuno is considered by some to be the sixth century patron saint of North Wales. He is reputed to have restored the life (as well as the head) of his niece, Winefride at Holywell [4.11]; and it may be through the gaping mouth of her head here at Tremeirchion that water spouted from its large walled reservoir, in a clear reference back to the ancient Celtic Cult of the Head. The spring's pagan connections are further suggested by the presence of the Stone Age Cae Gwyn caves in the valley beyond the old well-house.

The water from Ffynnon Beuno was believed to have had strong restorative properties, healing rheumatism, sore eyes, warts, eczema, epilepsy and paralysis, if drunk or immersed within. The large one metre-deep bathing pool, the metal hand-pump and the substantial house adjacent – which would probably have been originally built as the well guardian's cottage, and has in later times been both a shop and a pub – all attest to the importance of the site for pilgrims and those in need of a cure.

clwyd

opposite:

the gaping mouth of the
severed head of St Winefride(?),
at Ffynnon Beuno,
Tremeirchion

above, left to right:

the handpump outside Ffynnon Beuno;

the ancient pilgrims' cross in the grounds of
St Beuno's Church in Tremeirchion
(Like the well, its history reflects the ebbs and flows of Christianity in Wales.
It is thought to have been carved and erected in the fourteenth century or earlier,
but was toppled in the mid-seventeenth century as part of the Puritan purge of
"Monuments of Superstition and Idolatry". In 1862, J Youde Hinde of Rhyl
found the crosshead beneath a yew tree in the churchyard.
It has now been restored, and was re-dedicated in September 2004.
It was also celebrated for its miracles.)

4.8 st tegla's disease

Ffynnon Degla / St Tegla's Well
Llandegla, nr Ruthin,
Denbighshire
SJ 1948 5228

In Welsh, epilepsy is sometimes referred to as Clwyf Tegla or 'St Tegla's Disease', so it is no surprise that the sacred waters of Ffynnon Degla are famous for curing this disease (as well as scrofula). The site (*"Only second in fame to Winifred's"*, according to Wirt Sykes writing in his *British Goblins*) is to be found on the north bank of the River Alyn in Llandegla in Denbighshire, its waters emerging into a small chamber from beneath two shading trees.

Tegla's Well was consecrated in the Christian age to the fourth century Welsh hermit princess Degla, although it almost certainly had much deeper roots. Tristan Gray Hulse has argued that *"The identity of the Welsh saint Tegla was so far forgotten at Llandegla by the high middle ages that she was apparently identified ... with the possibly apocryphal but certainly far more famous first-century saint Thecla of Iconium"*.

Whatever its origins, an elaborate ritual which mixed pagan and Christian practices was required here in order to ensure an effective cure.

The well had to be visited on a Friday night after sunset when the patient's feet and hands were washed, before reciting the Lord's Prayer while walking around the well three (in some versions, nine) times carrying in a basket a cockerel (if male) or a hen (if female).

The unfortunate bird would then be pricked with a sharp pin which was thrown into the waters, after which a groat would be paid to the parish clerk.

This was followed by three (or nine) circuits around the church, carrying the bird and again repeating the Lord's Prayer, after which the patient entered the building and placed another groat in the poor box. The next stage of the 'treatment' involved lying under the altar using only a bible as a pillow and the communion cloth as a coverlet until daybreak, when the patient placed the bird's beak in his / her mouth and blew, before eventually letting the poor creature go.

After putting a final piece of silver in the poor box, the patient returned home to await the anticipated death of the cock or the hen that would signify the successful transference of the disease into the bird.

"The parish clerk of Llandegla in 1855 said that an old man of his acquaintance 'remembered quite well seeing the birds staggering about from the effects of the fits' which had been transferred to them", according to Wirt Sykes.

This act clearly reflected the ancient pagan practice of 'scapegoating' in which an animal or a person (originally, the king) took on the suffering of the people, the most significant example of which, in Christian times, was Jesus' sacrifice to take on the burden of the sins of the world.

opposite:

detail from the fine interpretive panel at Ffynnon Degla, Llandegla

left:

Ffynnon Degla

the living wells of wales

4.9 who cares ?

Ffynnon Dyfnog / St Dyfnog's Well
Llanrhaeadr-yng-Nghinmeirch,
Denbighshire
SJ 0798 3347

there is nothing we suffer to get so near us as the tokens of the remote

Henry James (1843-1916),
from *Cathedrals and Castles*, 1905

The large oblong eighteen-inch-deep pool of St Dyfnog's Well is filled by a number of springs that flow from the hillside at the head of its beautiful tree-lined valley.

St Dyfnog was the confessor of the Caradog family, and venerated throughout Clwyd from the sixth century onwards. The story is told that the well only received its healing powers after the saint stood in its cold waters as a penance, in just a shirt, belted with an iron chain, for some undisclosed misdemeanour. It thereafter specialised in relieving 'scabs and itch', which may possibly give us a clue to his 'crime'.

In the eighteenth century, the site was blessed with changing rooms for the many visiting bathers, and the spring was *"enclosed in an angular wall, decorated with small human figures"*, according to Thomas Pennant.

The Llanrhaeadr Preservation Society has recently been supported by the Heritage Lottery Fund in Wales (as well as Cadwyn Clwyd, the rural enterprise agency) to run an ambitious "£300,000 community scheme to establish a religious tourist attraction, environmental centre and education facility" at Llanrhaeadr, based upon the history and remains of Ffynnon Dyfnog. This is great news for wellspring supporters, particularly as of late the site was beginning to show some dangerous signs of degeneration.

I have regularly bemoaned the neglect that most of our Welsh wellspring sites suffer, but there are places throughout Wales where the opposite problem is apparent, places that have been cleaned to within an inch of their spiritual lives – stones scraped to the bone – in acts almost as destructive as those where wellsprings have been abandoned and destroyed.

So care here, as elsewhere, needs to be taken. I have heard some disturbing local comments about the degree to which the Llanrhaeadr plans for a 'religious tourist attraction' could potentially detract from the natural setting of the site through its laudable objectives to make access easier. I want as many people as possible to experience these wonderful places, but there clearly needs to be a balance struck between restoration, ease of access, and the retention of the character and spirit of the site.

What follows are, I think, wise and challenging words, taken from the *Wellhopper*'s blog of 3 January 2014:

Ffynnon Fair at Bryncroes and Ffynnon Fyllin at Llanfyllin show what the impact being cared for by some municipal groundsman can be.

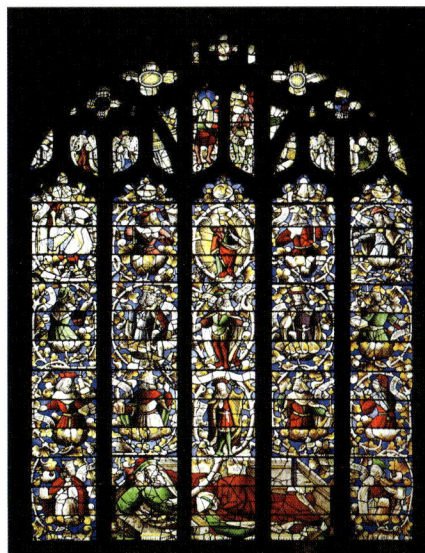

Concrete and closely cropped grass, litter bins and safety railings preserve the structure of a well whilst at the same time seem to drain the life and character out of the site, just as the neatly clipped lawns in a CADW castle cannot reproduce the reality of the mud and grime, the feasting and slaughter, and the hustle and the bustle of the everyday life of the people who once lived and died in the castle in centuries past.

And this is part of what I wrote in my 2013 book, *Borderlands*:

... perhaps, as Henry James suggested, our search is now for the "tokens of the remote" rather than for the "remote" itself. St Winifred's in Holywell when packed with bathers on a hot weekend, or even the banks of the Ganges at Varanasi at the height of its festivities both felt to me more like Barry Island on a Bank Holiday Monday than the sanctified sites I had conjured. What remains of our once-elaborate well sites, and what we seem to value most, are mere glimpses of a distant and silenced past, in which we may not have felt as comfortable in their heydays as we now do alongside their remnants.

Like both our real and our imagined journeys to ancient places – their columns once upright and brightly-painted, their temples thronged with worshipers – I, for one, seem happiest to sit alone amongst the stark and tumbled ruins, now washed clean of too much artifice by the rain and bleached white by the sun.

opposite:

Ffynnon Dyfnog, Llanrhaeadr

left:
The 1533 Jesse window at the Llanrhaeadr Church depicts Jesus' family tree, from Jesse, the father of King David, and is amongst the most impressive late medieval stained glass windows in Wales.

the living wells of wales

above:
the late anthologist, Dewi Roberts
at Ffynnon Dyfnog

above:
Allan Hughes works with Krithia Roberts
at the Anvil Pottery at Llanrhaeadr-
yng-Nghinmeirch.

4.10 her hand in marriage

**Ffynnon Sara /
Saeran's Well**
nr Derwen,
Denbighshire
SJ 0643 5154

A well promising relief from rheumatism, skin diseases and cancer, Ffynnon Sara lies peacefully within a grove of holly bushes and conifer trees beside the Mynian Brook whose trickling music provides the pleasant soundtrack to every visit. Believers would fully immerse themselves in the waters here and offer pins to the well or money to the well-keeper to increase their chances of a successful outcome.

Some have claimed that this well is dedicated to the Irish saint Saeran, Saeron or Saran, whose name may have been corrupted locally to that of Sarah or Sara (although an alternative explanation suggests a naming after a woman called Sara, who lived in the cottage nearby and tended the well). And in the 1690s, the well was reported as being called Ffynnon Pyllau Peri, after a nearby farm.

below, left to right:
the gate to St Mary's Church, Derwen;
the Gothic-style pre-Reformation cross in Derwen churchyard

Saeran was a missionary bishop who travelled in this area in the sixth century. His (her?) well was on the old Pilgrim's Way from St David's in the south-west to Holyhead in the north-east.

One famous Ffynnon Sara tale told of a young woman who was about to get married but suffered from eczema. Worried that she would not be able to fit her wedding ring onto her painful fingers, she resorted to the well and was, it is said, completely cured.

left and above:

Ffynnon Sara, Derwen
where 'Health and Safety' meets
the living wells of Wales!

opposite:

stained glass window of
Winefride and her uncle
at St Winefride's Well:
Beuno wasn't the greatest
plastic surgeon, it seems!

4.11 the spring in eternity

**Ffynnon Gwenffrewi /
St Winefride's Well**
Holywell,
Flintshire
SJ 1851 7627

One of the most compelling stories of an ancient sacred spring's Christian incorporation is that of St Winefride's in Holywell. Hers is a tale of purity, lust, murder, justice, resurrection ... and plastic surgery.

Winefride (or Gwenffrewi) was a North Wales saint of the seventh century, the daughter of Welsh nobleman Tyfid ap Eiludd and his wife Gwenlo. There are a variety of versions of the innocent Winefride's tale but all agree that she planned to become a nun, probably alongside her aunt Tenhoi who was the abbess of Gwytherin, near Llanwrst in Denbighshire.

One day, so one account goes, Caradoc a local chieftain's son, stopping on his journey, tired and thirsty, asked Winefride for a drink, and looking into her eyes fell immediately in love. Some say he asked her to marry him on the spot; others that he was already married and that his intentions were much less honourable. Whatever the case, she refused him and he tried to take her by force.

Enraged by her rejection, Caradoc took out his sword and cut off her head. As a result, it is said, of her purity and goodness, a great spring immediately erupted out of the ground at the spot where her head fell. This was to become the elaborate shrine of St Winefride at Holywell, often referred to as 'The Lourdes of Wales':

... the ground stained with her blood cracked, and a rapid spring gushed out in that place full of water, the stones of which to this day are seen bloody as on the first day.

translation from the Latin,
from anon., *First Life*, c.1130

Luckily for Winefride, however, her maternal uncle, St Beuno was celebrating mass in his small wooden chapel nearby and was able to re-attach the head and restore her to life. Caradog, in contrast, cursed by Beuno – something at which he seems to have been very skilled – was taken by the devil, melting slowly and painfully into the earth, never to be seen again.

After the ordeal, the chroniclers reported that Winefride returned to her religious vocation, first founding a convent near Holywell, before joining her aunt at Gwytherin, and eventually becoming the abbess there herself, where she eventually died and was buried in 650 or 660.

After her death and following many reports of miraculous cures at her well, a major Winefride cult developed and, by 1138, such was her popularity that her remains were transferred to Shrewsbury Abbey and thousands visited both Shrewsbury and Holywell annually to pay their respects and to seek guidance and healing.

Legend tells of one miraculous cure during the relics' journey to Shrewsbury when a man took a pinch of dust from St Winefride's skull, mixed it with water and gave it to a sick man to drink ... with astonishing results.

... many times this most benign virgin relieves dropsical persons, restores the paralytic, heals the gouty, cures the melancholy. No less does she remove sciatica, eradicate cancer, cure shortness of breath, extirpate piles...

The Life of St Wenefred, in AW Wade-Evans' *Vitae Sanctorum Britanniae et Genealogiae*, 1944

the living wells of wales

above, left to right:

Ffynnon Gwenffrewi, Holywell
(The current statue of St Winefride here
dates from the 1880s,
replacing the original which was
destroyed during the Reformation.);

pilgrim grafitti, recording a cure
at St Winefride's Well;

a fine drawing of Winefride
at the well museum, Holywell

opposite:

the main well
at St Winefride's

clwyd

During the Reformation, Wales, in particular, was seen as being *"in an evil condition as to religion, the inhabitants remaining still greatly ignorant and superstitious"* (Archbishop Parker of Canterbury, 1564), and so was set in motion the attack on *"all nefarious conventicles of the wicked and the superstitious dogmas of the papists"* (Bishop, 1576).

Nearly all of Winefride's many relics were destroyed during this time, including in 1540, her magnificent shrine at Shrewsbury Abbey. The sole surviving remnant is part of her skeleton, too small to be properly identified but believed to be a piece of one of the saint's finger bones, which is now housed, appropriately, at Holywell where her story began.

the living wells of wales

in water in deep devotion up to their chins for hours, sending up their prayers

Thomas Pennant, 1781

With more than 1,300 years of continuously recorded Christian use, St Winefride's Well in Holywell is the grandest well building in the British Isles.

Its elaborate two-storey, late fifteenth and early sixteenth century Late Perpendicular Gothic construction with its star-shaped well, large bathing pool and first-floor chapel have all survived almost intact since their completion in 1512 under the leadership of Abbot Pennant of Basingwek.

St Winefride's shrine escaped the terminal attacks inflicted upon many other Catholic holy centres during the Reformation (including that at Shrewsbury), such was its perceived importance, its money generating potential, and the regularity of its delivery of seemingly verifiable cures:

On the banks are hundred of sick folk who have arrived on crutches, but who can run back home.

anon, *The Miracles of Wales*, 1820

clwyd

In 1189, Richard I visited this calcium and iron-rich spring as, on later occasions, did his successors Henry V (who, in 1416, arrived on foot to give thanks for his victory at Agincourt), as well as Edward IV and James II, the latter in the company of his queen to ask for a son, a wish that was granted soon afterwards in 1688.

And the young Princess, later to become Queen Victoria visited the holy well while on holiday in the area in the 1820s.

opposite:

the bathing pool
at St Winefride's,
with 'Beuno's Stone'
in the foreground

left top:

discarded crutches in the
museum at St Winefride's

left other:

contemporary pilgrims
at Ffynnon Gwenffrewi

Perhaps the most famous 'cure' recorded at Holywell was that of Winefrid White. Here is the 1806 testimony of the surgeon Samuel Stubbs, reported in J Milner's *Authentic Documents relative to the Miraculous Cure of Winefrid White, of Wolverhampton, at St. Winefrid's Well... On the 28th of June 1805*:

I first visited the aforesaid Winefrid White ... Sept. 1, 1802; at which time, ... I found her in a very debilitated and languishing state, owing to an internal disorder, accompanied with the most fatal symptoms. These brought on an enlargement of the vertebrae, with a relaxation of the ligaments, and a paralytic affection, particularly of the left side; so that, at length, the patient could not hold herself upright, nor move herself from place to place, except in the most feeble manner, and by the help of a crutch ... I have frequently seen her and conversed with her since, without discovering any change in her for the better, down to the 22d or 23d of last June; being two or three days before she is reported to have made a journey to Holywell ... All the above mentioned fatal symptoms ... have disappeared. The ligaments of the vertebrae are contracted and firm, as I ascertained yesterday ... These changes so extraordinary, compleat, and performed in so short a time, I am unable to account for, by any principle of medicine I am acquainted with, or by any experience I have had in it."

And, more than a decade later, this from Fr Metcalf, writing in *The Life and Miracles of Saint Wenefride*, 1817:

The aforesaid Wenefride White is living at the present day, in a state of perfect health, and now superintends a Catholic charity school in Wolverhampton ... The witnesses to the above cure are numerous and consist of persons of different stations, religions, countries, and places of residence, with Protestants, Catholics, English, Welsh, residents in Wolverhampton, Liverpool, and Holywell, who could not possibly be combined for the purpose of attesting a series of falsehoods.

Others visited St Winefride's for spiritual uplift alone or to seek confirmation of their faiths. This is the journal entry for 8 October 1874 of the poet and priest Gerard Manley Hopkins:

Barraud and I walked over to Holywell and bathed at the well and returned very joyously. The sight of the water in the well as clear as glass, greenish like beryl or aquamarine at the surface with the force of the springs, and shaping out the five foils of the well quite drew and held my eyes to it.

The strong unfailing flow of the water and the chain of cures from year to year all these centuries took hold of my mind with wonder at the bounty of God in one of His saints, the sensible thing so naturally and gracefully uttering the spiritual reason of its being ... and the spring in place leading back the thoughts by its spring in time to its spring in eternity ...

This is a site of international importance that is still visited by more than 36,000 people annually, a figure that is increasing year on year.

Today, a diverse range of pilgrims make their way to Holywell, including those growing in number who have, according to David Birchall of the St Beuno's Ignatian Spirituality Centre in Tremeirchion "*a spiritual need but do not want to join churches*".

opposite:
contemporary pilgrims at Ffynnon Gwenffrewi

clwyd

the living wells of wales

and ...

4.12: Ffynnon Ddoged /
St Doged's Well
Llanddoged,
Conwy
SH 8059 6378
This and the following three wells are all examples of neglect: the once sacred spring here has been crudely capped, its legend only surviving in the name of a cul-de-sac, in the new estate, the very building of which spelt its demise.

4.15: Ffynnon yr Holl Saint /
All Saints Well
Gresford,
Wrexham
SJ 3459 5520

4.13: Ffynnon Beuno /
St Beuno's Well
Gwyddelwern,
nr Corwen,
Denbighshire
SJ 075 469

4.16: Ffynnon Fach /
The Little Well
(+ Carreg Mihangel /
Mihangel Stone)
Crimea Pass,
nr Dolwyddelen,
Conwy
SH 7035 4959

4.14: Ffynnon Oswald /
St Oswald's Well
nr Holywell,
Flintshire
SJ 1684 7760

4.17: Ffynnon Penrhyn /
Lord Penrhyn's Well
Ysbyty Ifan,
Conwy
SH 8517 5003

clwyd

4.18: Ffynnon Sadwrn /
Saturday (or Saturn) Well
Llandudno,
Conwy
SH 8075 8210

4.22: Ffynnon Gynfran /
St Gynfran's Well
Llysfaen,
nr Colwyn Bay,
Conwy
SH 8931 7759

4.19: Ffynnon Mair
Magdalen / Mary
Magdelene's Well
Cerrigydrudion,
Conwy
SH 9538 4894

4.23: Ffynnon Lletyr
Fadoc / The Well of
Madoc's Lodgings
(or Ffynnon Rufeinig
/ The Roman Well)
Gt Orme,
Llandudno,
Conwy
SH 7652 8379

4.20: Ffynnon Fair /
St Mary's Well
Llanrhos,
nr Llandudno,
Conwy
SH 7917 8020

4.24: Ffynnon Tudno /
St Tudno's Well
Llandudno,
Conwy
SH 7706 8378

4.21: Pistyll yfed Eglwys
Llanrhos / Llanrhos
Church drinking fountain
Llanrhos,
nr Llandudno,
Conwy
SH 7694 803

4.25: Ffynnon Fair /
Mary's Well
Bodrhyddan Hall,
nr Rhuddlan,
Denbighshire
SJ 0451 8757

127

the living wells of wales

4.26: Ffynnon Beuno /
St Beuno's Well
Holywell,
Flintshire
SJ 1841 7619

4.27: Ffynnon Goffa
Mary Short / Mary Short
Memorial Fountain
Elwy River bridge,
St Asaph,
Denbighshire
SJ 0362 4263

4.28: Ffynnon Fferm
Valle Crucis / Valle
Crucis Farm Well
nr Llangollen,
Denbighshire
SJ 203 443

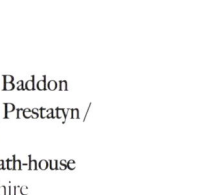

4.29: Tŷ Baddon
Rhufeinig Prestatyn /
Prestatyn
Roman Bath-house
Denbighshire
SJ 0621 1755

4.30: Ffynnon Abaty
Valle Crucis /
Valle Crucis
Abbey Well
nr Llangollen,
Denbighshire
SJ 2044 4161

4.31: Ffynnon Gynhafal /
St Cynhafal's Well
Llangynhafal,
Denbighshire
SJ 1331 3830

128

embroidered kneeling cushion of
Ffynnon Beuno and its well guardian's cottage,
from St Beuno's Church, Tremeirchion

5 TOWARDS A SCIENTIFIC EXPLANATION:
canolbarth cymru / mid wales

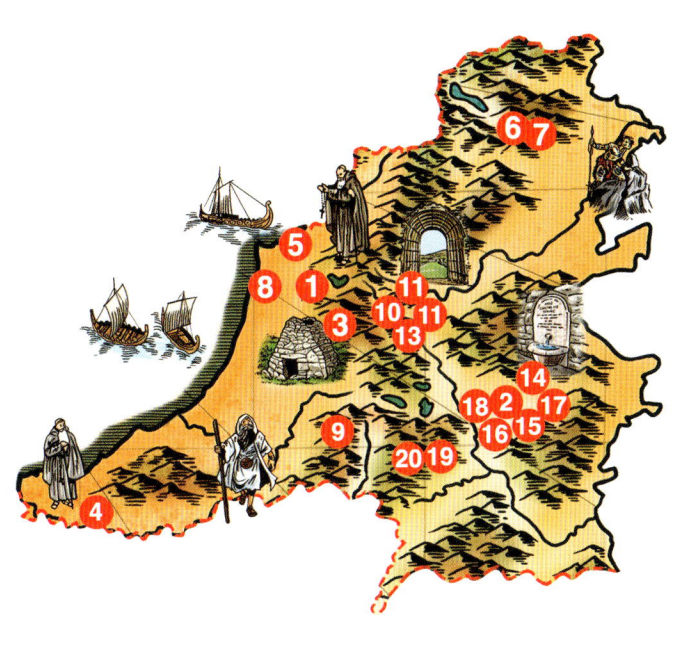

The Mid Wales council areas of Ceredigion and Powys offer the perfect palimpsest of wellspring history, leaving layer resting upon layer of masonry and meaning for us to fathom as new explanations were developed and discarded over time. From pre-Christian pagan sites to those introduced by Roman invaders; from those adopted and adapted by the new Christian faith to those that they tried to destroy; from the age of new scientific explanations during the spa era to the evidence of their demise, all of these are available for exploration here.

And it is within the complexities of this history that any research and intervention into wellspring culture must begin: with an open-hearted recognition of the often-contradictory levels of meaning and usage exposed, based ultimately upon a respect for the abiding divinity of water.

(Although the Brecon Beacons straddles Powys – as well as the north-western part of Monmouthshire and parts of eastern Carmarthenshire, and some of the Valleys' unitary authorities – I have not included it in any of these other sections, as it merits a chapter of its own.)

opposite:
Ffynnon Drewi /
The Stinking Well [5.1]
nr Bronant,
Ceredigion

the living wells of wales

5.1 the breath of the devil

**Ffynnon Drewi /
The Stinking Well**
nr Bronant, Ceredigion
SN 675 622

I was glad to have been accompanied on my most recent visit to Ffynnon Drewi (or The Stinking Well) by local resident, Nigel Fletcher.

Ffynnon Drewi seems so-called not as a corruption of our patron saint's name but rather in reference to the site's smell, drewi in Welsh meaning 'a stench' or 'stink'.

The journey over the exposed and treeless moorland was very wet, and the area directly below the three wells themselves treacherous with deep and clinging mud. While there, I thought that perhaps the site should be renamed the 'Sinking Well'.

The smell rises through the wells' waters, in some people's view from the breath of the devil, who presumably on my visit was trying to pull us down towards him. The place, with its three evocative springs sitting side by side, certainly has a strongly pre-Christian feel.

above:
Nigel Fletcher
at Ffynnon Drewi /
The Stinking Well,
nr Bronant

opposite:
one of the three wells
at Ffynnon Drewi

cruelty and culture

Although Julius Caesar led the first Roman expedition to Britain in 55 BC, it was not until 43 AD – when Claudius landed with 50,000 well-trained fighting men – that our real engagement with this most organised of empires began. Within five years, Rome had subjugated much of the southern part of the country. Many who survived the early onslaught of this brutal military superpower fled west to the heavily forested hills of Wales where they continued for many decades to offer stubborn resistance to the notion of a Roman province of *Britannia*.

The first attacks on the area we now know of as Wales were around 47 AD. At this time, the territory was occupied by five tribal groupings: the Deceangli in the north-east; the Ordovices in the north-west and central areas; the Cornovii in the central borderlands; the Demetae in the south-west; and the Silures in the south-east.

Caradoc (or Caractacus), the great resistance leader, had been driven west into Wales by the Roman forces, from where he led a successful guerrilla campaign with the local Ordivice and Silure tribes until his defeat and capture at the battle of Caer Caradoc on the Welsh border in 50 AD.

By 90 AD, most of the native Welsh population had been suppressed and almost all of what was to become England and Wales had fallen under various degrees of Roman rule, with the possible exception of the lands of the Ordovices (significantly omitted on a mosaic map in the Forum in Rome said to show the full extent of the Roman Empire).

The strategy of the Roman invaders was a combination of cruelty and culture, their aim to both conquer and co-opt. The bath-house at these sites of occupation was an ever-present component of this imperial architectural and ideological blueprint, introducing both the sophisticated Roman discipline of cleanliness, at the same time as offering a new panoply of water spirits to add to those already revered by the local people.

right and opposite:
Next to nothing remains above ground of the Romano-British Castell Collen and its *Balneae Silures* military bath-house.

5.2 love and war

Balineae Silures
Castell Collen,
nr Llandrindod Wells, Powys
SO 628 055

The little known Roman fort at Castell Collen, a mile or so north-west of Llandrindod Wells, sits on the crest of a knoll overlooking a horseshoe bend in the river Ithon. It was once the site of eighteen training camps founded in the Flavian period by Julius Frontinus in his campaign to subdue the Silures, and is the most significant example of Roman defences in central Wales.

Given the scale of the site and the number of soldiers it catered for, it is not surprising to find that Castell Collen had an extensive bath-house complex – known as *Balneae Silures*, in recognition of the local Celtic tribe.

As the power of the Roman empire faded, Castell Collen was abandoned (in around 400 AD) and, over the years that followed, the site, like so many others, was raided for its stone for local buildings, leaving little above ground level today to suggest the scale and importance of this once formidable military base. Excavated in 1911, then again more extensively between 1954 and 1956, one of the most intriguing items found here was a silver ring with its crudely inscribed message '*AMOR DVLCIS*' meaning 'sweet love'.

adopted and adapted

Building on the foundations left by these and other predecessors, Christianity was quick to co-opt these powerful watery places from our deepest past:

5.3 from goddess to saint

Ffynnon Sant Ffraid / St Bridget's Well
Cynhawdre Farm, Gwenhafdre Isaf, nr Swyddffynnon, Ceredigion
SN 675 671

The gestation of the Bridget or Bride (Ffraid in Welsh) myth is a long and interesting one. Beginning life as a Celtic goddess, Bridget was adopted and adapted by Christianity as the saint Bridget, such was her power within the popular imagination. Baring-Gould and Fisher report that she *"procured honey from a stone for the poor"* and *"converted butter that had been turned to ashes to butter again"*. Also, *"whenever it rained heavily she would throw her white winnowing sheet on the sunbeams"*. It is claimed that *"when her father desired her to marry someone she did not like, one of her eyes fell out of its socket"*; that *"she sailed on a piece of turf from Ireland"*; and, at a time of famine, she made a beautiful fish without a single bone out of rushes. These brwyniaid (or 'smelts') were known as pysgod Sant Ffraid (or 'St Bride's fishes'), and it is said that fishermen in Pembrokeshire used to pray at the Chapel of St Bride before setting sail, though these fantastical tales may well be the conflation of two or more interesting and saintly women.

Bridget's origins are reflected in the design of her well-housing here, a typically Irish beehive structure (a little like that at Maendu in Brecon [6.8]. In its tree sheltered spot, heavily-garlanded with mosses, lichen and ferns, it reverberates with the timelessness of her legendary layers of existence in fact and in fiction.

St Bridgit's Well was in medieval times part of the Strata Florida estate and visited by its travelling monks. Anwen Davies, her father David Morgan Jones and late mother Jasmine, the owners of the farm on whose land Ffynnon Sant Ffraid sits, are to be praised both for the welcome they also give to passing pilgrims keen on visiting the well and the great care they have shown for the site over very many years (often against all bureaucratic odds, and entirely at their own expense).

right and opposite:
Ffynnon Sant Ffraid / St Bride's Well, Cynhawdre Farm, nr Swyddffynnon, Ceredigion (with landowner and well guardian, David Morgan Jones)

the living wells of wales

5.4 a tyranny of neatness *

**Ffynnon Llawddog /
St Llawddog's (or Ludoc's) Well**
Cenarth, Ceredigion
SN 268 416

The spring here, falling to the river Teifi and its historic bridge and cascades, is said never to fail, whatever the weather.

For me, though, Ffynnon Llawddog is somewhat over engineered, though an important addition to the Mid Wales well scene.

5.5 where god hides

**Ffynnon Non /
St Non's Well**
St Michael's Church,
Eglwysfach,
Ceredigion
SN 685 956

Ffynnon Non is a holy well site which has been sensitively re-imagined (with the aid of a legacy from Celia Groves, a grant from the Welsh Historic Gardens Trust, and the generosity of the Jones family of Dolen Fâr, Eglwysfach). It was re-dedicated to St Non, the mother of our patron saint, in a moving service in September 2017, appropriately by Bishop of St Davids Joanna Penberthy (the first female bishop in the Church in Wales), although there is little evidence that Non strayed this far north.

In 1993, Hugh Rees of Eglwysfach remembered as a boy seeing *"hundreds of people visiting the well from far and near to wash in her water"*. He confirms that people had *"great benefit from the water, especially those suffering from 'Rheumatism'"*, though RS Thomas who was the vicar of this parish between 1954 and 1967 wrote of being *"within listening distance of the silence we call God"* here, and asked (in his poem, 'In Church'), *"Is this where God hides / From my searching?"*.

opposite:

Ffynnon Llawddog /
St Llawddog's (or Ludoc's) Well,
Cenarth

above:

Joanna Penberthy,
the Bishop of St Davids
at the September 2017
Dedication Service of
Ffynnon Non / St Non's Well,
Eglwysfach

A site fully restored and cared for by its community of which I am less keen, however, is Ffynnon Sant Myllin / St Myllin's Well [5.6 / SJ 138 195], in Llanfyllin, near Welshpool, Powys, though the Town Council's work here won a Prince of Wales Award in 1987.

'What a nice well would that be,' said a labouring man to me one day, 'if all that rubbish was cleared off.' The 'rubbish' was some of the most beautiful mosses and lichens and ferns and other wild growths that could possibly be seen. Defend us from the tyranny of trimness and neatness showing itself in this way!

William Wordsworth (1770-1850) *

For me – as it seems it would have been for Wordsworth, too – it's a little too manicured and its aluminum rails compare badly with those at (for example) St Non's ... although it's a lovely place to sit and survey the town.

The (intrusive) interpretative board at the site states that the sixth century St Myllin (or Moling) was the first in Britain to baptise by immersion.

And to add insult to injury, the village well [5.7 / SJ 143 196] at Llanfyllin, next to the old bridge over the river Cain, has been in use for more than a decade as a receptacle for rubbish bins and boxes.

5.8 looking forward

Y Ffynnon ym Mhentre Llandre / The Well at Llandre Village
nr Aberystwyth, Ceredigion
SN 6233 8690

More positive ideas are being developed around Llanfihangel Genau'r Glyn ('St Michael's Church in the Mouth of the Valley') at Llandre, including the renovation and celebration of the village's ancient healing well. An article in the *Aberystwyth Observer* of 1867 claimed that: *"All those who are suffering from rheumatism should bathe in Llanfihangel Well, which is known to have cured a large number of persons afflicted with this painful disorder"* (quoted in Randall Evans Enoch's 2010 book, *Llanfihangel Genau'r Glyn: the history of a community*).

The Treftadaeth Llandre Heritage Group led by their innovative treasurer, Roger Hagar, has already opened up the well site (filled in just before the onset of World War II) and landscaped the area; created an inspirational Poetry Path in the woodland above the church (recently damaged by Hurricane Emma); designed some attractive interpretive panels on the area's history, topography and wildlife; and laid out the impressive Llandre Heritage Trails in the old, steeply-wooded churchyard.

I greatly look forward to seeing what they will do next with their historic holy well.

 canolbarth cymru / mid wales

opposite, left to right:

Ffynnon Sant Myllin /
St Myllin's Well,
Llanfyllin, Powys;
the old bridge well, Llanfyllin;
Roger Hagar at Y Ffynnon ym
Mhentre Llandre /
The Well at Llandre Village

left:

Llandre Well

the living wells of wales

There are at least three villages in Wales with a holy well now named after St Gybi. He occurs at Clorach Fawr in Anglesey [1.11], and in Monmouthshire [7.7].

His well at Llangybi in Ceredigion (5.9 / SN 578 478) is a simple unspoilt place, remarkably peaceful despite its location next to the busy A485 road racing between Tregaron and Lampeter.

right:
Ffynnon Cybi / St Gybi's Well,
Llangybi,
Ceredigion

canolbarth cymru / mid wales

the primacy of the waters

The monks knew well the value of this spot, here were – nay, still are, their wells of healing waters, – iron, sulphur, chalybeate – used with benefit by the natives today.

George Eyre Evans, 1903, local antiquarian (quoted in *Poetry from Strata Florida*, 2013)

5.10-13 the living wells of Ystrad Fflur

The groundbreaking *Strata Florida Research Project* is being led by the always inspiring David Austin, Professor Emeritus of Archaeology at the University of Wales Trinity St David. Of most significance within the pages of this book is his confirmation that the structure in the Abbey is indeed a holy well (something I had always believed, despite the guidebook saying differently). These are his words:

The Cistercian Abbey of Strata Florida (Ystrad Fflur) was re-founded in 1184 on what we now believe was the site of an earlier ('Celtic') monastery. At the heart of that sacred place was a holy well, perhaps already within a stone building. In creating the new Abbey, the ancient Holy Well was designed to be at the crossing of the new cruciform-plan church and in front of the High Altar. It retained its old east-west alignment while the church itself was aligned on sunrise and sunset on St David's Day. The water for this holy well was channelled into the Abbey through the Afon Glasffrwd (or the 'blue or green force').

Along the course of this stream are four other holy wells which feed into it, while the source – formerly a small

but now in-filled lake two miles to the south-east – has twenty-six mainly early Bronze Age monuments gathered around it, linked by narrow sunken footpaths to the water's edge.

What Professor Austin has revealed here is the historical primacy of the springs in what he calls "*an ancient sacred landscape, based on the life-giving waters into which the Abbey was carefully inserted*".

right:
Professor David Austin
at **Ffynnon Dyffryn Tawel /
The Well of the Silent Grove**,
Strata Florida,
nr Ystrad-Meurig,
Ceredigion
[5.10 / SN 7505 6522]

left:

Ffynnon yr Abaty / The Abbey Well, Strata Florida, [5.11 / SN 7455 6576]

canolbarth cymru / mid wales

What more truly romantic spot can be imagined or desired than that round 'Ffynnon dyffryn tawel', the 'well of the silent grove'? ... its cool waters still bubble forth, much as they did when pilgrims to the Abbey slacked their thirst at its welcome brink.

George Eyre Evans, 1903

above, left to right:

Ffynnon Dyffryn Tawel /
The Well of the Silent Grove,
Strata Florida;

**Ffynnon Hafod Newydd /
The Well of the New Summer
Pastures**
Strata Florida
[5.12 / SN 7604 6394]

the living wells of wales

above:

**Ffynnon Tyn-y-Garreg /
The Well of the Stone Cottage**
Strata Florida
[5.13 / SN 7608 6402]

5.14-18
taking the waters

The fortunes of the wells of Wales and elsewhere improved dramatically in the late eighteenth century when a new 'scientific' recognition of the beneficial properties of natural springs exploded into the fashion for medicinal spas, giving a huge new lease of life to the fortunate towns where they occurred.

Signifying the presence of a mineral spring, the word 'spa' comes from the town of Spa in Belgium where locals claimed that drinking its iron-bearing waters had from medieval times cured a variety of illnesses.

The popularity of this new/old practice of 'taking the waters' saw those rich enough flocking in their thousands to Llandrindod, Trefriw [4.1], Llanwrtyd, Llangammarch and elsewhere to drink from and immerse themselves in their saline, sulphur, iodine, alum, magnesium, barium chloride and chalybeate basins and pools. Visiting a spa during the 'season' now became the height of good taste and sophistication, as much a place to be seen as to be cured.

But hydropathy treatments were often extreme and full of discomforts, as terrifying in some cases as the custom known as 'bowsening', inflicted upon the mentally-disturbed in much earlier days when the unfortunate was pushed backwards into a sacred pool, a practice repeated until the demons fled the demented!

Included in the later spa towns' 'punishments' were 'wet sheeting', where a patient was wrapped like a mummy in soaking linen sheets; and the 'douche', when stinging ice-cold water was showered over the naked cure-seeker from above, below or, in some cases, from all sides, which one eighteenth-century patient aptly termed *"a good rehearsal for Purgatory"*.

And of the 'lamp bath', another who experienced that torture wrote:

"There is nothing so likely to draw the gravy out of a man ... it is for all the world like being a fat goose before a slow fire"!

right:
entrance to
Rock Park & Spa,
Llandrindod Wells

the living wells of wales

The three kinds of springs – iron, sulphur and saline – found at what we now call Llandrindod Wells, are said by some to have had their origins in Celtic mythology. The story is told of an ancient hero who saves a maiden's life by literally 'liquidising' the three devils that were pursuing her, with the aid of iron, brimstone and salt.

Although Llandrindod was to become the premier spa town in Wales in the mid-nineteenth century – even considered by some to offer serious competition to the grand English resort of Bath – it seems likely that the curative properties of the mineral waters here were known and appreciated much earlier by the Romans who occupied the Castell Collen military site [5.2], one mile north-west of the present town.

The first reliable record of 'taking the waters' at the chalybeate spring in Llandrindod was as early as 1696, when the Vaughans of Herefordshire were said to have stayed for three weeks. The springs were rediscovered in 1732 by a Mrs Jenkins, the tenant of Lower Bach-y-Graig farm. She sold the water to travellers and the fame of its healing properties soon spread. The farm became known as the Pump House, and later was developed as the celebrated Pump House Hotel.

canolbarth cymru / mid wales

opposite:
new spa visitors at **Ffynhonnell Haearnol Rhydd / the Free Chalybeate Spring**, Rock Park, Llandrindod Wells [5.14 / SO 055 608] (The word chalybeate derives from the Chalybes, mythical creatures which inhabited Mount Ida in northern Asia Minor and were said to have invented iron-working.)

right, top to bottom:
Ffynnon Heli Lithia / Lithia Saline Well in Rock Park [5.15 / SO 054 608];

a recently-renovated well below the Pump Room in Rock Park [5.16 / SO 058 608];

In 1983, water from **Ffynnon y Llygad / The Eye Well** [5.17 / SO 055 608] in Rock Park was sent to the then Prime Minister Margaret Thatcher. There is no evidence that it improved her vision.

In 1754, a German physician and spa expert who suffered from a variety of diseases visited Llandrindod, drank from its salty and sulphuric springs and was cured. His encouraging comments on the medicinal qualities of the waters set in train international recognition of Llandrindod as a major spa town:

Their good effects are so conspicuous that they give place to none in Europe ... as yet I have not met with any of the same kind that surpass these at Llandrindod.

Dr D W Linden, from his 1756 *Treatise on the Medicinal Waters of Llandrindod*

Accounts of the medical successes of these places – often graphic, like this one which appeared in a 1774 journal – were common:

A man who lives near the spring... told me he was ill for several years and so windy and costive that his life was a burden to him. He appealed to several apothecaries and physicians who gave him no relief. He at last took to the waters of which he drunk 23 pints which brought from him an excrement so hard as could make little or no impression on when stamped with the heel of a shoe! This man is upwards of 70 years old and has drank the water frequently after and hath never had a sick day since that time and looks though grey the healthiest man I have seen of his age.

the living wells of wales

canolbarth cymru / mid wales

The popularity of the Llandrindod waters during the eighteenth century was short-lived, however, as the town's remoteness and its attraction to gamblers and drinkers led to an early decline, not to be halted until the mid-nineteenth century with the advent of the Central Wales Railway. Arriving from Knighton in 1865, and eventually connecting with Shrewsbury in one direction and Swansea in the other in 1868, the town was now within easy reach of the urban centres of the North West, the Midlands and South Wales.

At its height, more than thirty mineral springs, two assembly rooms, a pump room, an ornamental lake, hotels, public houses, tea rooms, churches, shops and everything else needed by the traveller in search of a watery cure sprang up to cater for as many as 90,000 mostly wealthy visitors each year at Llandrindod, as the town was transformed into a prosperous and fashionable spa resort:

... there were six attendants in white coats, three each side, serving the various waters. Some days the queue would be nearly up to the park entrance. On one Bank Holiday morning, over 1,000 glasses of water were sold before 9.00am. Some people bought weekly tickets and waters were also delivered daily to the hotels and boarding houses in one or two-gallon jars.

Consumption of between sixteen and eighteen pints a day was normal, and such were the purging qualities of the waters here that one man was reported to have discharged a worm seven feet long and two inches wide after imbibing.

And as well as ingesting the waters, a wide range of alternative procedures were on offer, including hydro-electric sulphur baths, carbonic acid baths, cold showers and douches, and scary-sounding pseudo-scientific treatments involving 'Leucodescent Rays', 'Galvanic and Faradic Current Cataphoresis', 'D'Arsonval High Frequency' installations, and the use of the 'Nagelschmidt Sinusoidal Current' apparatus!

opposite:

another of the restored springs in Rock Park, Llandrindod Wells
[5.18 / SO 056 609]

above, left to right:
The Old Pump Rooms;

the still-impressive Gwalia Hotel, situated at the entrance to Rock Park (now the Radnorshire offices of Powys County Council);

The Old Pump Rooms are now the Rock Park Complementary Health Centre.

the living wells of wales

5.19 bringing home the bacon

Llangammarch Wells
nr Builth Wells,
Powys
SN 945 476

The sulphur and bromide spring situated on the banks of the river Irfon at Llangammarch was believed to have been 'discovered' in 1837 by a local farmer searching for a lost pig. The animal was found wallowing in a muddy, unpleasant-tasting pool, the medicinal value of which was later recognised and publicised widely. The water was unique in containing large quantities of barium chloride, particularly beneficial it was thought for the heart, the circulation and the complexion. The 'discovery' transformed this ordinary Mid Wales village into a destination of choice for the rich, including European royalty.

Today, the roofless ruins of the red brick bath-house and pump room are all that remains of Llangammarch Spa's years of splendour, although the nearby Lake Hotel still has its water pumped to its rooms.

5.20 the miracle of health

**Ffynnon Ddrewllyd /
Dolycoed Spa**
Llanwrtyd Wells
nr Builth Wells, Powys
SN 872 470

Although the medicinal properties of Ffynnon Ddrewllyd – another 'stinking well' due to the very strong presence of sulphur in its waters – were most fully exploited during the mid-nineteenth century spa era, knowledge of the spring's ability to provide cures, particularly for ailments of the muscles and joints, was recognised many centuries earlier.

The rather unlikely story is told of a local vicar, the Rev Theophilus Evans, who suffered amongst other things from scurvy. One day, in 1732, he witnessed a toad bathing in a roadside puddle and, noting the animal's extreme good health, implausible as it might seem, decided to drink some of the same water there and then … and received an immediate cure! This, it is said, was the spur for the major investments that followed, with the building of pump rooms, bath-houses, luxury hotels and guest-houses, transforming this rural hamlet into a prosperous centre for the medical pilgrim. In the past, it had been awe-inspiring saint's tales that attracted the masses to these wellspring sites; now it was the miracle of health.

The elaborate spa buildings were reached via a splendid avenue of trees, wide enough for horse-drawn coaches to carry their ailing patients to the treatment rooms.

The well water is white in appearance, created by the precipitation of certain minerals. The impression of what looks like milk issuing from a natural spring was not uncommon: it is said to have occurred at St Winefride's Well in Holywell [4.11] for three days after the saint's death, as well as at St Illtyd's Well on Gower and Ffynnon Cegin Arthur [2.9] in Gwynedd. In pagan times, the outpouring was thought to be a gift from the breasts of Mother Earth.

The spa age was a unique episode in social history, fascinating for its contrasts between artificial languishings and cultivated fragility and those imposed mortifications of the flesh, in health's name, that today would try an athlete in perfect physical condition.

Muriel Searle
from *Spa and Watering Places*, 1977

opposite:
the now nearly inaccessible site of Llangammarch Wells, and a broken and discarded bath tub

left:
the tree-lined avenue leading to the spa buildings at Llanwrtyd Wells

the living wells of wales

above:

images from before (2008), during (2012, with members of the Victorian Society at Ffynnon Drewllyd, on a wells tour led by the author), and after (2018) the 'renovation' of the well-house at Dolycoed Spa, Llanwrtyd Wells

opposite:
The Dol-y-Coed Hotel started life as a humble farmhouse. It was modernised and extended in 1735 to satisfy the every need of the wealthy spa visitor, and is currently the home of Charcroft Electronics.

canolbarth cymru / mid wales

In time, however, the treatments on offer at spa towns like Llanwrtyd Wells were replaced by a new kind of hydropathy, available at seaside resorts, with the added benefits of sunlight, aromatic pines and bracing sea air. In addition, local authorities were beginning to provide more easily accessible and cheaper alternatives to the spas in municipal baths and swimming pools. And the advances in medical knowledge that culminated in the creation of the Nation Health Service in 1948 offered effective treatments for all the ailments that the spas claimed to relieve, resulting in the decline and closure of most of these once-thriving establishments.

Llanwrtyd – claimed to be the smallest town in Britain – had to find new reasons to survive once the spa tourists had departed for good. This it did with the invention of mountain bike trails, beer festivals and, most imaginatively, the annual Man versus Horse marathon and the World Bog Snorkling Championships!

The same cannot be said, it seems, of the renovations taking place at its spa site. For years the buildings sat derelict. Now they have been converted into homes and the domed well housing has been demolished, and a new conservatory-style PVC extension erected in its place surrounding the mosaic-decorated well basin which at its height could deliver up to 4,500 gallons of sulphur-rich water a day.

the living wells of wales

In the late twentieth century, a growing recognition of the damage we are doing to our planet, alongside an uneasiness with our increased reliance upon prescription drugs, has sparked a renewed curiosity in and search for alternative remedies, distanced from the reach of the global pharmaceutical industry.

Throughout the world, including here in Wales, a new interest in sacred springs, holy wells and curative waters is being witnessed, and new spa centres are being developed, often along the lines of those with which the Romans would have been familiar ... but without, perhaps, the fellowship or good offices today of an all-powerful deity.

above:

the milky-white waters that issue from Ffynnon Ddrewllyd, Llanwrtyd Wells

canolbarth cymru / mid wales

and ...

5.21: Ffynnon
Castell Bronllys /
Bronllys Castle Well
nr Talgarth,
Powys
SO 149 347

5.22: Ffynnon Gynidr /
St Cynidr's Well
Glasbury,
nr Hay-on-Wye
SO 164 413
Originally dedicated to the
sixth century saint, today the
elaborately-constructed,
timber-framed canopy,
erected in 1900, is in memory
of Walter Fenwick de Winton
of nearby Maesllwch Castle,
who was killed in action
in Africa in 1892.

5.23: Ffynnon Oer /
Cold Well
Swyddffynnon,
Ceredigion
SN 692 663

5.24: Pwmp pentref
Llanddewi Brefi /
Llanddewi Brefi
village pump
nr Narberth,
Ceredigion
SN 662 553
one of the very few
working water pumps
in Wales

5.25: Ffynnon Creigiau
Pen yr Allt / Pen yr
Allt Rocks Well
Machynlledd
SH 747 011

5.26: Ffynnon Fair / St Mary's Well
Pilleth, nr Knighton, Powys
SO 256 683
Owain Glyndŵr recorded one of his most important
successes in his struggle against the English near here,
on St Alban's Day (22 June 1402). He defeated an army
led by Sir Edmund Mortimer, through the employment
of superior tactics and the skills of the Welsh longbow-
men, despite having a much smaller force.
Glyndŵr's soldiers quenched their thirst, here,
both before and after their victory.

the living wells of wales

5.27: Ffynnon Fair /
St Mary's Well
Llanfair Caereinion,
nr Welshpool,
Powys
SJ 1036 06480
in an image from
its church window

5.31: Ffynnon yr Arflu /
Garrison Well
Machynlledd
SN 746 009
another well with a possible
Roman connection in
Machynlleth, thought to have
supplied the soldiers while
stationed here

5.28: Ffynnon Badarn /
St Padarn's Well
Aberystwyth
SN 697 812

5.32: Ffynnon Llywelyn ap
Gruffydd / **Llywelyn's Well**
Cilmeri, nr Builth Wells
SO 001 514
the place where it is said the
Prince of Wales' head was
washed after he was killed in
battle on 11 December 1282
(Victoria Society visit, 2012)

5.29: Ffynnon Gadfan /
St Cadfan's Well
Llangadfan,
nr Welshpool
SJ 010 104
Efforts have been made
here to interpret this once
important site, but it is
today a sad and gloomy
spectacle.

5.30: the equally
unimpressive remains of
**Ffynhonfa Buddug /
Victoria Wells Spa**
nr Llanwrtyd Wells,
Powys
SN 867 469

5.33: another well
at Bronant
SN 625 674
in the grounds
of *Talfryn*,
Nigel Fletcher's house,
near to Ffynnon Drewi
[5.1]

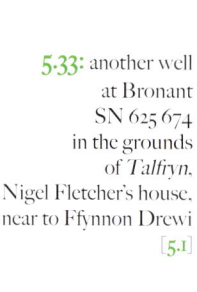

canolbarth cymru / mid wales

Free Chalybeate Spring,
Rock Park, Llandrindod Wells
[5.14]

6 TALES AS OLD AS TIME:
bannau brycheiniog / brecon beacons

Wales' varied landscapes are often the best witness to its history, and to the many stories invented to explain our lives, struggles and beliefs. Knowledge of the tales the land tells – in this case of the waters that spring from its surface throughout the Brecon Beacons – offers one of the best means by which to understand this small though significant part of our country.

Currently – despite a history of neglect and sometimes even the willful destruction of sacred spring and holy well sites, and the amnesia regarding our wellspring cultures – there is still much to be celebrated, especially within the Beacons area.

Some special places that have been in continuous use for millennia continue to offer the possibility of hearing faint echoes of the voices of the people who drank and bathed, gave their offerings, made their pleas, and told their stories here.

opposite:
Ffynnon Maendu [6.8]
Brecon

6.1 what's in a name?

**Ffynnon Angaeron /
Aaron's Well**
nr Goytre,
Monmouthshire
SO 2976 0519

This stunningly situated pin well – now named after Angaeron, Aeron or Aaron, a mythical figure lost in time – is one of the county's crown jewels, sitting peacefully beside a stream on the Goytre Wharf to Myndd Garn Wen Brecon Beacons Park Circular Walk path.

right, clockwise from left:
path to Ffynnon Angaeron / Aaron's Well;
fence in carpark of Horseshoe Inn at Pen Croes-hir at start of the walk;
Ffynnon Angaeron

opposite:
Ffynnon Angaeron

In the fourteenth century, it was called Ffynnon Rhufeinig ('the Roman Well') and Ffynnon Ofuned ('the Wishing Well'), adding more intrigue to its origins and offerings. In 1890, when it was cleaned out, many pins and an expensive brooch were discovered.

6.2-6.3 st eluned and the celtic cult of the head

A parallel tale to St Winefride's [4.11] is that of Eluned. At least two holy wells are dedicated to Eluned (or Eilwedd, Lludd, Alud, Tayled, Elevetha or Almedha) in the Brecon area: one at Llechfaen [6.2 / SO 080 285]; the other below the Slwch Tump, also known as the Ffynnon Pen Cefn y Gaer / 'Penginger' Well [6.3/ SO 0579 2861]. And some believe that the elaborate two-sided Bishop Gower's Well [6.33] at Llanddew, a little to the north-east of Brecon, was also once dedicated to her.

Eluned, one of the many daughters of King Brychan of Brycheiniog, was thought to have been a fifth century Christian convert who sought refuge in the area after previously being persecuted for her religious beliefs at Llanddew, Llanfilo and Lechfaen, where, it is said, she was ousted by the locals (some say for her beliefs, others for her disheveled appearance, some even for her thievery!). She finally found protection – albeit temporarily – through the kindness of a local lord, at Slwch Tump, a hilltop enclosure of Iron Age origins.

Like Winefride, Eluned was pursued by a lustful prince ... with similar consequences, resulting in the creation of yet another significant curing well.

This is part of an account – written in the late seventeenth century by Hugh Thomas – which concludes the story:

... her importunate lover went to her retirement where, finding her alone at prayers, a violent fear surprised her soul, so that she sought to flee down to the Lord's house at the bottom [of the hill], which the young Prince perceiving, mad with rage and despair,

pursues her, cuts off her head which, rolling a little down the hill, a clear spring of water issued out of the rock where it rested.

The Celts valued the head above all other parts of the body, believing it to be the seat of the soul and the power-centre of human action, and – with the tree and the well – an essential medium for communication with the 'OtherWorld'.

There are many examples of places that combined well worship with a belief in the Celtic Cult of the Head. And, as we can see with the tales of Eluned and Winefride (amongst many others), these convictions did not end with the introduction of Christianity. In very many christianised sites, there are tales told of saints' heads being struck off (and sometimes, like in the case of St Winefride, being stuck back on again) or, as in Ffynnon Beuno at Tremeirchion [4.7] of water gushing from the mouth of a saint's head.

Despite being a major pilgrimage destination in the past, today Eluned's 'Penginger Well' is a rarely visited, deep, dark hole, unattractively covered by railway sleepers and wire or, alternatively (there is some disagreement as to the exact location) hidden in a clump of overgrown bushes.

left:
a rock near
St Eluned's Well,
below Slwch Twmp

bannau brycheiniog / brecon beacons

above, left to right:
Jan Shivel at Ffynnon Eluned
below Slwch Tump

the alternative site for
Eluned's 'Penginger' Well,
with, left to right,
Mike Williams (Brecon Cathedral),
Dr Adrian Humpage (South-east Wales Regionally
Important Geodiversity Sites Group),
Dr Peter Ford (Hay History Group), and
Alex Makovics (Keep Wales Tidy)

the living wells of wales

In contrast, the site of Eluned's Lechfaen Well and trough was reconstructed and renovated by the village in 1998, led with care and passion then and since by Helen and Brian Sheppard.

They organised the digging out of the well which was completely covered with earth, renewing the banks and the seating, planting flowers in boxes, and today maintain the site as a focus for community activity. Barbecues are held here, as well as carol services at Christmas, school picnics, and other events; and they have innovative ideas for the fabric and further use of the site into the future.

An Eluned Festival was organised by Brecon Cathedral in 2017 to celebrate the saint's day on 1 August, harking back to the feasts held annually in her chapel near Slwch Twmp, significantly perhaps, on the same date as the pagan harvest festival of *Lughnasadh* or *Lammas*.

This is Gerald of Wales (Giraldus Cambrensis) describing such a feast and its miraculous occurrences in his *Journey Through Wales* of 1188:

... attended by a large concourse of people from a considerable distance, when those persons who labour under various diseases, through the merits of this blessed virgin, receive their wished-for health.

The circumstances which occur at every anniversary appear to me remarkable. You may see men or girls, now in the church, now in the churchyard, now in a dance, which is led round the churchyard with a song, on a sudden falling on the ground as in a trance, then jumping up as in a frenzy, and representing with their hands and feet, before the people, whatever work they have unlawfully done on feast days; you may see one man put his hand to the plough, and another, as it were, goad on the oxen, mitigating their sense of labour by the usual rude song; one man imitating the profession of a shoemaker; another that of a tanner.

You may see a girl with a distaff, drawing out the thread, and winding it again on the spindle; another walking and arranging the threads for the web; another, as it were, throwing the shuttle and seeming to weave.

On being brought into the church, and led up to the altar with their oblations, you will be astonished to see them suddenly awakened and coming to themselves.

Thus, by the divine mercy, which rejoices in the conversion – not in the death – of sinners, many persons, from the conviction of their senses, are at these feast days corrected and amended.

The 2017 St Eluned event was good ... but not quite as good as that!

opposite:
Helen and Brian Sheppard, the Llechfaen Eluned Well guardians

right:
the handpump at Ffynnon Eluned, Llechfaen

6.4 the best of health

**Ffynnon y Meddygon Myddfai /
The Physicians of Myddfai's Well**
Glasfynydd Forest,
nr Myddfai, nr Llandovery,
Carmarhenshire
SN 806 287

Another great wellspring-related tale concerns the Physicians of Myddfai. Though not easy to find, and with a location once again contested between a number of sites, the Physicians of Myddfai's Well offers us a complex and inspiring story of ancient Celtic magic, alternative medicine, and violence (once again) against a woman ... as well as a very good walk.

The legend tells of an impoverished, young Carmarthenshire farmer, at the end of the twelfth century, grazing his flock of sheep in the shadow of the wild Black Mountain escarpment. He spies a magical woman emerging from the inky black waters of Llyn y Fan Fach ... and resolves to have her as his wife.

His unusual wooing relied upon the offering of baked goods. (Mary Berry would have been pleased!) Rejected on two occasions, he finally gets the recipe right (with the help of his mum), and the Lady agrees to be his bride ... but on two conditions, the most important of which was that he must treat her with respect, and never strike her, the consequence of this happening three times being her immediate return to the lake, along with her very large animal dowry.

They lived happily at a farm called Esgair Llaethdy, about a mile from Myddfai, and, after nine months, the Lady gave birth to the first of their three sons, who they named Rhiwallon.

At the boy's christening, however, the Lady sobbed, knowing her new family's fate, and, her husband – annoyed by her behaviour on this most special of days – struck her.

She reminded him of his promise and the condition of their marriage, and he swiftly begged her forgiveness, which she readily gave. Later still though, she cried again, this time at a wedding (because she knew that the bridegroom would soon die), and the farmer struck her once more.

Finally, she laughed at the bridegroom's funeral (because she knew that his suffering was now over), and the farmer hit her for the third, and fateful, time.

above:
Llyn y Fan Fach, Carmarthenshire

The Lady turned immediately and began to walk towards Llyn y Fan Fach, taking with her all of the animals her father had granted the couple. As she crossed their land, every sheep, lamb, cow, calf, hen, duck, goose, pig and horse followed her. And her husband was never to see her again, destined now to raise their three boys, alone.

As the sons grew, they missed their mother terribly, and often went to the lake to try to catch a glimpse of her. She eventually appeared to Rhiwallon and told him that he should study medicine. On each occasion thereafter, she offered parts of her knowledge to her sons, instructing the boys where to find the most powerful of herbs, and the medicines and poultices to create with them.

Using the natural products they gathered from the surrounding area – mixed with the spring water from their now famous well – the Physicians of Myddfai created cures and remedies for all ailments, arguably making this small Carmarthenshire village the birthplace of modern medicine, and laying the foundations for the best health care available, far in advance of much on offer in Europe at the time.

opposite:
The Physicians of Myddfai's Well
Sadly, after recent insensitive tree-felling, the site around the well resembles the Somme, post-battle.

the living wells of wales

There is some disagreement – as so often is the case in the re-telling of ancient tales – concerning the severity of the husband's blows. In some accounts, they were mere touches, taps on the shoulder to remind the Lady that her behavior was unacceptable; some commentators have even seen her actions as fully warranting her husband's responses; others that the touches were perhaps accidental.

And the poet, Gillian Clarke – who translated T Llew Jones' *One Moonlit Night* in which this tale is retold – adds a further level of explanation ... that the forbidden touches were with metal:

My father told me this proved the story was very old, marking a time when the Celts, or Iron age people, first came to Britain, and the people of the Stone Age were afraid of their metal swords, shields and jewelry.

And this is from Gillian Clarke's own poem, 'Healers', from her *Physicians of Myddfai* trilogy (published in *Making the Beds for the Dead*):

Somewhere down the line
myth became history,
and slow repeating time
passed down the story
in the mother tongue
to the young.

From them we might have learned
the healing power of plants.

The Physicians used over 200 plants, many of which can still be found in the area. And, luckily for future generations, Rhiwallon – who had become the personal doctor to Rhys Gryg, Lord of Dinefwr and Llandovery castles – wrote down more than 500 of their remedies (later copied, along with the legend of the Lady of the Lake – itself also recorded in the *Mabinogion* – in the fourteenth century *Red Book of Hergest*, from which most of our knowledge comes).

Many of these healing recipes reveal a very contemporary, holistic approach to medicine. Rhiwallon, his brothers, his three sons, Cadwgan, Gruffydd and Einon, and their many descendants, believed it seems in treating the whole person rather than just the symptoms of sickness. For good health, they advised moderation in food, work and sleep; keeping well wrapped up in winter; not consuming too much meat or alcohol; and drinking plenty of water. Here are a few of their specific recommendations:

Whosoever shall have lost his reason or speech, let him drink the juice of the primrose.

If you would at all times be merry, eat saffron.

Whoever is over fat, let him drink of the juice of fennel and it will reduce him.

To prevent dreaming, take the leaves of betony and hang around your neck.

bannau brycheiniog / brecon beacons

And here are a few of their medical maxims:

*The qualities of water:
it will produce no sickness, no debt,
and no widowhood.*

*The three medicines of the
Physicians of Myddfai:
water, honey and labour*

*The three victuals of sickness:
flesh meat, ale and vinegar*

*If thou desirest to die, eat cabbage
in August.*

A dry cough is the trumpet of death.

*Take not thy coat off before
Ascension Day.*

God will send food to washed hands.

At the Myddfai Community Hall and Visitor Centre is a fine display on the Lady of Llyn y Fan Fach and her medical descendants. And at the National Botanic Gardens of Wales at Middleton Hall in Llanarthne, a 'Physic Garden' has been planted incorporating herbs once used by the Physicians (a smaller version of which is being developed in the village of Myddfai, itself).

opposite, top to bottom:
Monica and Robin Barlow (Myddfai Hall trustee)
who guided me on my first visit
to the Physicians Well;

the gravestone of the last two
Physicians of Myddfai,
in the porch of the church of
St Michael at Mydffai

right:
Llyn y Fan Fach, Carmarthenshire

6.5 the battle of beliefs

**Ffynnon Isho /
St Issui's Well**
Partrishow,
nr Abergavenny
SO 2777 2238

St Issui was a hermit who established his cell in the Vale of Ewyas. His well, on the riverbank of Nant Mair ('Mary's Brook') in the beautiful Gwyrne Valley, only became curative after the saint was murdered by an ungrateful traveller for whom he had provided food and shelter, and who subsequently dumped his body into its waters. (The name Partrishow or Partricio is thought to come from the Welsh (m)erthyr [meaning 'martyr'] and Isho.) From that day on, the well became a magnet for pilgrims seeking nourishment for both body and soul.

In the eleventh century, it was recorded that a French visitor successful washed away his leprosy here and, in gratitude, was happy to pay *"a hat-full of gold"* for the first church to be built above the well.

Today, votive coins are still offered, though in less abundance, now hammered into trees as a new form of contract with the spirit world, a payment in lieu of a hoped-for gift of healing or insight.

the living wells of wales

On my first visit to St Issui's Well (a dozen or so years ago), the site was festooned with crudely-constructed crosses of all shapes and sizes, something that inspired this fine poem by Ruth Bidgood:

Patricio 2001

They have been bringing offerings
to the dark well, tying
rags to twigs in supplication, leaving
flowers to wilt in that chipped glass
uneasily perched on a dank ledge,
making crosses from bits of stick.

There seem so many of them, despite
the hiddenness of the place; as if
in a time of fear and shattering
these humble shapes are once more
valid – raw letters spelling out
helplessness, not yet
reshuffled into words of power.

Intriguingly, there now seems to be a new battle of beliefs being fought out at Ffynnon Isho as the once ubiquitous crosses are being challenged by new offerings: a profusion of 'clouties' with their pre-Christian roots. A 'clout' was traditionally a piece of cloth which, soaked in the sacred spring's waters and applied to the part of the body needing attention, is then tied to one of the trees beside the well. The belief is that, as the fabric disintegrates over time, so the ailment will disappear and the patient be cured.

right, top to bottom:
the medieval church of St Issui the Martyr, Partrishow;
Ffynnon Isho / St Issui's Well, Partrishow, 2008;
contemporary pilgrims at Ffynnon Isho

opposite:
inside St Issui's Church with its fine wall paintings, including a 'doom figure' on the back wall

bannau brycheiniog / brecon beacons

Here is Ruth and Frank Morris' warning to those thinking of removing clouts from well sites (from their 1982 book, *Scottish Healing Wells*):

The gifts become sacred to the well, or the tree. Probably the least that can happen to the thief is that he takes with the article the disease or trouble which was left in the care of the well.

6.6 ffynnon games

Ffynnon Gwyddfaen / St Dyfan's Well
Llandyfan,
nr Ammanford,
Carmarthenshire
SN 6418 1712

You would not think it when passing this sleepy rural hamlet today, but Llandyfan and its holy well were once a major pilgrimage destination, known in its day as 'The Welsh Bath of Llanduvean'. St Dyfan's Well was thought to be *"efficacious in the cure of paralytic affections, numbness and scorbutic humours"* (Nicholson, 1813, quoted in *Catholic Llandeilo: A History of St David's Parish*, by Alan Randall, 1987). Some said that the most successful cures were to be had here by drinking the spring water out of a human skull, better still that of St Teilo himself (as was also the practice at St Teilo's Well, near Llangolman in Pembrokeshire [12.13].)

In 1592, a number of pilgrims (from a reported two hundred or more present at the time at the well) were brought before the local magistrate to discourage what was then considered to be superstitious practices. And, in the early eighteenth century, similar actions had to be taken to suppress huge congregations playing an early version of football and dancing here on Sundays.

left:
Ffynnon Gwyddfaen /
St Dyfan's Well,
St Dyfan's Churchyard,
Llandyfan
The wheel was turned to lower the sluice gate to fill the pool for baptism.

opposite:
Carreg Cennen Castle,
Carmarthenshire

6.7 the security of water

**Ffynnon y Castell /
Castle Well**
Cerreg Cennen Castle,
nr Llandeilo,
Carmarthenshire
SN 665 192

Carreg Cennen's spectacular situation, perched some 300 feet above the valley of the River Cennen on a precipitous limestone crag, made it ideal to both survey the surrounding countryside as well as to discourage invaders. And the gift of water in its ancient well, set deep within a natural grotto beneath its outer ward and accessed via a dark 200-foot-long passage, was another powerful argument for the castle's establishment here.

Although the picturesque remains (privately-owned, though CADW-managed) that are visible to us today are of late thirteenth and early fourteenth century construction, the site is thought to have been in continuous occupation since the Iron Age. It regularly changed hands between the Welsh and the English between the twelfth century and its eventual and violent demolition by supporters of the Yorkist king, Edward IV, in the summer of 1462.

the living wells of wales

bannau brycheiniog / brecon beacons

There are a number of other well-spring sites in the Beacons which are being cared for by local people and organisations, replicating some of the well guardian responsibilities of earlier ages. The following are two of my current favourites:

6.8 being loved

**Ffynnon Maendu /
Maendu Well**
Brecon
SO 0390 2964

Set peacefully next to a modern housing estate north of Brecon, Maendu is a hidden gem. A wishing well for jilted women according to Francis Jones where *"maidens offered pins and wished earnestly for love"*, its waters rise up from the well, running the course of a leat and feeding a large circular bathing / baptismal pool that flows (under and over ground) to the well at the Cathedral.

Although the Grade 2 Listed wellhouse's design seems ancient – resembling that of early Irish monastic cells – an inscription on its entrance offers a date of 1754. But this was almost certainly the year of its latest major renovation.

left:

the narrow passage
leading to
Carreg Cennen Castle Well

the living wells of wales

6.9 travelling confidently

The good news here is that the Maendu Well Group have been caring for and running annual events at the

site since 2009, including litter picks, hedge laying, pond clearance and arts projects ... and they have ambitious community, structural and interpretative plans for its future.

Tŷ Ffynnon y Tafarn Newydd / The New Inn Well House
New Inn Farm, nr Cross Ash, Monmouthshire
SO 400 204

The New Inn Well House near Cross Ash in Monmouthshire is an excellent example (perhaps the best in Wales) of a community working together imaginatively to save and rebuild an important wellspring site, complete with a newly commissioned statuette of St Christopher, the patron saint of travellers. The Village Arts Building Preservation Trust (www.village-alivetrust.org.uk) was established in 2004, and – working from photographs of the building when standing – they restored the site to its original design, using traditional methods and materials. The project was completed by August 2005.

Examples like New Inn are, however, sadly, very rare. The same can be said for our drinking fountains. I Christmassed some years ago in Portugal where every fountain, in even the smallest of villages, offered refreshing clean water to the traveller. Can you think of more than a tiny handful (one even?) that are in working order today in Wales, where our supply of water is far greater than that of countries like Portugal?

It has always surprised me when travelling abroad that in places, often much poorer than Wales and with much less rainfall, drinking fountains offer cool pure water at every corner. Why is this something beyond our 'health and safety'-conscious capabilities in Wales?

While I can list very many once functioning drinking fountains now disconnected, broken and currently functioning only as litter bins, I only know of a tiny handful which still offers refreshment here, the exceptions to our unfortunate rule.

opposite:
Ffynnon Maendu / Maendu Well and Pool, Brecon
left:
ripples at Maendu Well
above:
New Inn Well House, Monmouthshire

But there is some good news. In the town of Great Malvern, two new sculptures have been created on Belle Vue Island, both led by the artist Rose Garrard, with financial support from Malvern Hills District Council and public subscription: one, the Enigma Fountain [SO 775 460] celebrates the life of local composer, Edward Elgar;

while the other, the Malvhina Fountain [SO 775 460] reflects the spiral markings on Celtic standing stones, medieval religious statuary and the Pre-Raphaelite Movement, three elements in the town's history.

And in London, the Kiosk Project is encouraging the building of attractive new public drinking fountains to challenge the £1.5bn-a-year bottled water industry and the 13 billion plastic bottles sold in the UK annually, an initiative clearly following in similar ecological footsteps to that being developed by Jacki Sime at Ffynnon Faiddog [12.21] in Pembrokeshire.

These words, written in 2014 by Robert Bevan, give the historical background to the Kiosk Project's thinking:

Drinking fountains flourished in late 19th-century London after it was realised that diseases could be waterborne. The Metropolitan Drinking Fountain and Cattle Trough Association, set up in 1859, provided some 800 fountains across the city: 'It is estimated that 300,000 people take advantage of the fountains on a summer's day', wrote Charles Dickens Junior (the novelist's son) in his Dictionary of London, 'and a single trough has supplied the wants of 1,800 horses in one period of 24 hours'. The temperance movement supported the provision, hoping the poor would find salvation in pure water rather than at the bottom of a beer glass; a surviving fountain on Clapham Common is crowned with a mythical figure of Temperance.

Yet time, neglect and clean water piped to homes have done for most of these historic fountains. Those that remain are often slimy with pigeon droppings and decomposing leaves.

above, left to right:
The Malvhina Fountain, Great Malvern;
the new Freeman Family drinking fountain, Hyde Park, London;
the re-imagined St Govor's Well, Hyde Park

Perhaps we can learn something from these (and other) initiatives which are continuing to add new layers of both utility and meaning to the lives of these once important places. Perhaps we should start making our own new, twenty-first century responses, while at the same time paying due respect to history and to tradition. Each of these interventions, though small, can add up to a revolution, as, in the words of the Roman poet, Ovid (43BC-17AD): *"Water hollows away the stone not by force but by falling often".*

A place in Wales that has done more than most to better understand and develop respect for its wellspring culture is the book town (or perhaps it should now be the 'wellspring town') of Hay-on-Wye. There are at least seven significant well sites here, three of which I will explore in some detail (while the others are recorded in smaller images at the end of this chapter [2.26, 2.29-2.31]). These springs are in various states of decay and accessibility, some are virtually lost, some are dry, others are in urgent need of repair, and one is on private land. Most have either a legend attached, a holy connection, or are reputed to have healing properties.

right:
an icon of St Canna,
painted by Nic Phillips,
on display in St Canna's Ale House,
Canton, Cardiff

6.10 the first swig

**Ffynnon Keyna / St Canna's Well
(or The Black Lion Well)**
Black Lion Green,
Hay-on-Wye, Powys
SO 2321 4240

Ffynnon Keyna lies in the riverbank at the north corner of Black Lion Green, on the eastern edge of town behind the Old Black Lion public house in Lion Street, its waters feeding directly into the Dulas Brook.

A common tale told in many areas throughout Britain (including Wales) associated with St Canna's Wells concerns a traditional arrangement to determine which one of a newly-married couple would, in future life, 'wear the trousers', as, at the end of their marriage service, the one that drinks first from the holy well would dominate. The story goes that, after the preacher's final words and the last hymn, the groom races out of the church and sprints to the well, a mile or so away. Meanwhile, the bride, sitting unflustered in her pew, reaches down into her bag, brings out the bottle of water she had filled from the well that morning, and takes the first swig!

This tradition is confirmed in a local 1908 account of an old inhabitant, who whenever hearing of a domestic squabble was reported to proclaim: *"Tom or Nell, first to the well?".*

Francis Jones suggested that this practice was carried out at Ffynnon Geneu (or Genau) [6.35] at Llangenny. In Cornwall, however, the tale was always associated with the St Keyne's Well [SX 241 579], near Liskeard.

St Keyna, Canna or Keyne may have been the twenty-fifth daughter of King Brychan of Brycheiniog, or alternatively, a Breton princess.

Either way, she is said to have been a miracle worker, once turning snakes into stone.

Even though she herself never married, perhaps the tradition of the race from the church to her well should be revived, and where better than in Hay?

bannau brycheiniog / brecon beacons

6.11 more liquid refreshment

**Ffynnon Alarch /
The Swan Well**
Hay-on-Wye
SO 2264 4206

Pure clean spring water flows straight out of the side of the elevated Swan Bank, behind the Swan Hotel, and is directed in a stone-cut swan's neck channel to its fall from an elegant spout for the waiting drinkers here.

Ffynnon Alarch has never been known to dry up, even in the most severe of winters or the hottest of summers. Locals still regularly collect water here, and it provided an essential source during the severe winter of 1962/3. In addition, it is renowned for the effective treatment of sprained wrists and ankles.

opposite:
Ffynnon Keyna /
The Black Lion Well,
Hay-on-Wye

right:
Ffynnon Alarch /
The Swan Well,
Hay-on-Wye

6.12 walk this way

Ffynnon y Cei / The Wharf Well (or **Ffynnon y Rhodfa / The Walk Well**)
The Warren, Hay-on-Wye
SO 2253 4223

Hidden down a dangerously slippery and uneven path to the river Wye, the so-called Walk (or Wharf) Well, set into the riverbank on a small stone quay, would have been part of the landscaping built by Sir Joseph Bailey in the 1870s, and, in its day, a busy part of the town.

The age of the quay (or wharf) is uncertain, though it has been suggested that it played a part in the building of the town's twelfth century church, stone for its construction arriving here by barge. It's possible that the quay (and its well) were both constructed for this purpose at that time.

It is known that the town had two medieval ferries crossing the Wye. Old Ordnance Survey maps show a footpath in the field on the other side of the river at this point, down from the Clyro road, terminating directly opposite. Today, at this tranquil spot, one can only imagine the hustle and bustle of the past as people and objects came and went, and the stories of comings and goings they would be able to tell … an ideal place, perhaps, for the creation and telling of new/old tales.

and ...

6.13: Ffynnon Priordy / Priory Well
nr Brecon Cathedral
SO 045 291

6.16: Ffynnon y Castell / Castle Well
in hills above Cwmyoy,
nr Abergavenny
SO 317 237

6.14: Ffynnon y Llygad / Eye Well ?
nr Brecon Cathedral
SO 225 422
Located *"a few yards higher up the Groves [from the Priory Well] in the side of the bank"*, it was damaged in a thunderstorm during World War One, *"sending the stones tumbling down to the reservoir leat below"*, according to Elsie Pritchard in her 1977 booklet, *Brecon, From the Struet.*

6.17: Ffynnon Padrig / Patrick's Spring
Govilon,
nr Abergavenny
SO 2635 1360
an early holy well, now an overgrown area of springs on a slope down to the canal

6.15: Ffynnon Sanctaidd / Holy well
1A Holywell Road, Abergavenny
SO 304 140
thought to have once been one of the water supplies to the Benedictine priory

6.18: Ffynnon Eglwys Sant Teilo / St Teilo's Church Well
Llandeilo
SN 627 224
Set into the outer walls of Llandeilo Church graveyard, this is another site with evidence of continuing community care.

6.19: Ffynnon Ymyl y Ffordd, Llanofer 1 / Llanover Roadside Well 1
nr Abergavenny
SO 310 084
The writing on the trough here reads, YFWCH A CHROESAW AC NAC ANGHOFIWCH WENYNEN GWENT / 'You are welcome to drink here and don't forget the Bee of Gwent' [ie. Lady Llanover]

6.22: Ffynnon Gofer / Nine Wells
Llanover Estate, Monmouthshire
SO 313 087
Access has been consistently denied by the owners to this important, probably pre-Christian site within Llanover Park, something of an irony given the important role that Lady Llanover (1802-1896) played in supporting the arts and heritage of Wales. Gofer or Gofor is thought to have been a sixth century monk from Penmon on Anglesey.

6.20: Cafn y Bwystfil / The Beast Trough
Maindiff Hospital, nr Abergavenny
SO 316 154
Rudolf Hess, the Nazi war criminal, used to walk here when he was held prisoner at nearby Maindiff Court during the early 1940s. In contrast, Maindiff's well is dedicated to being kind, especially to animals, its maxim stating that *'The righteous man regardeth the life of his beast'*.

6.23: Cafn Anifeil-iaid David Watkins / David Watkins Animal Trough
Hay-on-Wye
SO 229 425

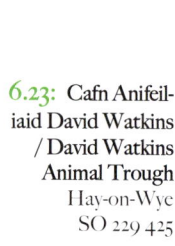

6.21: Ffynnon Ymyl y Ffordd, Llanofer 2 / Llanover Roadside Well 2
nr Abergavenny
SO 314 080

6.24: Ffynnon Faelog / St Maelog (or Meilig)'s Well
above Llowes, nr Hay on Wye
SO 193 417
This site and its tale of an irritating stone hurled by the giantess Moll Walbee from her clog while building Hay Castle symbolises the struggle between paganism and early Christianity. The saint, it is claimed, carved on the missile the elaborate cross you can see today. (For the full retelling of this legend, read *Tragic Matilda: Lady of Hay*, 2018, by Dr Peter Charles Ford [peford1@hotmail.com].)

bannau brycheiniog / brecon beacons

6.25: Ffynnon y Sgirrid / Skirrid Mountain Well
nr Abergavenny
(with Molly)
SO 333 184
According to legend, part of the hill here was broken off at the moment of Jesus' crucifixion. As a result, earth from Skirrid was thought to be especially fertile, even holy, and taken to be scattered on fields, in coffins, and in the foundations of houses and churches. Pilgrimages were regularly made to the summit and to the well, especially on Michaelmas Eve.

6.28: Ffynnon Logan / Logan's Well
nr Myddfai
SN 800 285
(with my guides, Robin and Monica Barlow)

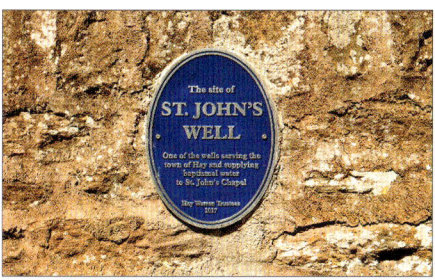

6.26: Ffynnon Sant Ioan neu Castell / St John's or Castle Well
Hay-on-Wye
SO 2298 4228
Once the source of holy water to St John's Chapel of Ease in Lion Street, now just a plaque marks the spot.

6.27: Ffynnon Anne / St Anne's Well
Trefecca,
nr Bronllys,
Powys
SO 144 321
a well with resonances of both Mother Earth and Anne, the mother of Jesus' mother, at Coleg Trefeca training / conference centre and retreat house of the Presbyterian Church of Wales

6.29: Ffynnon Fair / St Mary's Well
Hay-on-Wye
SO 2255 4212
This well is in the garden of 2 Sackville Cottages, though visible from St Mary's Church graveyard, for which it was used as a source of holy water. Reputedly, a miraculous fountain once spurted from the well when the church tower caught fire, dowsing the flames and saving the building.

6.30: Ffynnon y Dref / Town Well
Hay-on-Wye
SO 2302 4268
located near the old Nyegate or Watergate, one of the three medieval entrances into Hay, now marked with a square panel and a plaque (I am indebted to Dr Peter Ford on whose research much of my Hay knowledge is based.)

the living wells of wales

6.31: Ffynnon y Llygad / Eye Well
Hay-on-Wye
SO 2254 4222
just above the Walk / Wharf Well [6.12]

6.34: Ffynnon Syr Charles Morgan / Sir Charles Morgan Well
Brecon
SO 043 288
beside the banks of the Honddu river, a well of great significance to the town's water supply

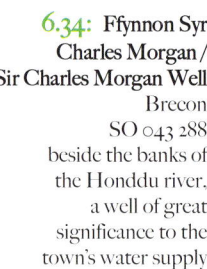

6.32: Ffynnon Goeden Bocs / Box Tree Well
above Cwmyoy, nr Abergavenny
SO 313 233

6.35: Ffynnon Geneu / St Genau's Well
Llangenny, nr Crickhowell, Powys
SO 2414 1810
The still-impressive brick and iron cistern sits today within the grounds of Pendarren House, which is run as an Outdoor Education Centre by and for Haringey Council (the well itself emerging from a hollow in the woods).

6.33: Ffynnon yr Esgob Gower / Bishop Gower's' Well
Llanddew, nr Brecon
SO 055 308
the third of the (possible) Eluned sites

6.36: Pistyll yfed Gogledd Crughywel / North Crickhowell drinking fountain
Powys
SO 214 191

Is this the site of
St Eluned's Well,
below Slwch Twmp,
nr Brecon?

7 BORDERLANDS TO ANOTHER WORLD:
gwent

It is exciting to walk the very edge of things, whether it is a cliff top or an idea.

David Adam, *Border Lands*, 1991

The lands lying alongside the lower reaches of the River Wye have always been disputed territories, infused with the turbulent and bloody history of our struggles to define who we are and how we should live, on both sides of a constantly contested front line. Attacked and settled in turn by Celtic tribes and by Roman legions, by Angles, Saxons and by Normans, the area is a rich tapestry of conflict, attack and defence, of oppression and rebellion, still marked in the landscape by a plethora of mounds, forts and castles, and the sites of numerous battles.

Although the old Brythonic kingdom of the Celts – which lent its name to modern Britain – stretched far beyond the present border, the first significant boundary between what we now know as England and Wales was the military road built by the Romans linking their chain of forts from *Isca* (Caerleon) in the south and *Deva* (Chester) in the north, in the first centuries of the Modern Era. The second, and more famous, was the 'dyke' of the Mercian King Offa, dug between the estuaries of the rivers Dee and Severn in the eighth century to resist Welsh attack.

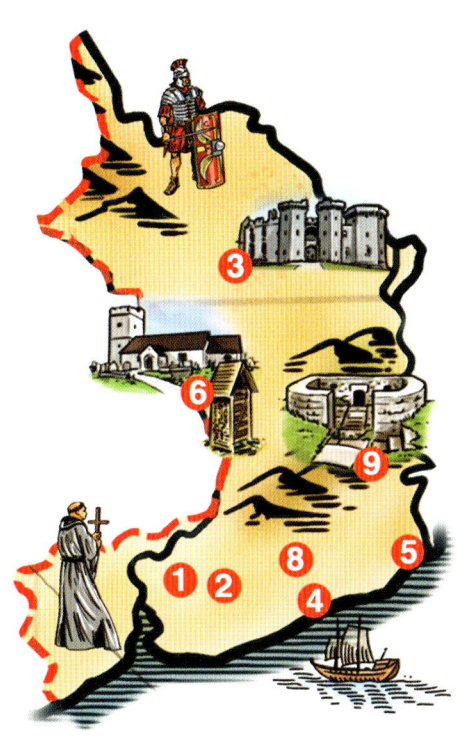

opposite:

Castell Raglan / Raglan Castle [7.3] Monmouthshire

the living wells of wales

From the late eleventh century onwards, new and even more elaborate ways to demonstrate who was in charge were introduced during the first major period of castle building in what came to be known as the Welsh Marches (from 'marca', the Latin word for 'border'), following William's Norman Conquest of 1066.

The Welsh were denied access to most of these fortresses, and severely punished if found within their walls. The loss of an arm or even death awaited those who crossed the line. In the twelfth century, the Lord of Clun offered a reward to anyone who brought him the skin of *"a wild Welshman"*. It is ironic, then, that many of our most impressive physical monuments in Wales – our great castles, and our church and monastic buildings upon which much of our tourist industry is now based – are the products of oppression, constructed by Marcher Lord or Benedictine monk, to undermine local power and belief systems, *"a magnificent symbol"* in the words of Thomas Pennant (1726-1798) *"of our subjection"*.

The struggles to define the contested territories of the borderlands were reflected in the explanations of the true meanings of our springs and wells, similarly set within a battlefield of interpretations, constantly changing over time.

Ancient traditions included the belief that sacred springs issued from a supernatural underworld, the spiritual womb of Mother Earth, before flowing through the world's rivers to the sea. Celtic mythology places the Well of Wisdom at the very centre of its 'OtherWorld', the spiritual source from which all waters, and life itself, is created.

In pre-Christian times, natural springs would have had a magical significance, not only as an element essential to all life but, just as importantly, as a place where the most powerful of nature spirits resided and where a dialogue with other realities was possible, *"borderland places"* in the words of Janet and Colin Bord, *"where this world and the hidden Otherworld meet"* (from *Sacred Waters: Holy Wells and Water Lore in Britain and Ireland*, 1985).

left:

Offa's Dyke
at Garbett Hall,
nr Knighton

opposite left:

armour store, National Roman Legion Museum, Caerleon (thanks to National Museum Wales)

opposite right:

the amphitheatre at Isca Augusta at Caerleon; the remains of the small bath-house, situated next to the amphitheatre

7.1 rome's state-of-the-art leisure centre in wales

Baddon Rhufeinig Caerllion / Caerleon Roman Baths
Isca Augusta, Monmouthshire
SO 340 906

On the river Usk at Caerleon, a little way north-east of Newport, is the only still visible Roman legionary barracks (or *castra*) in Europe, the headquarters of the Second Augustan Legion between 74 and 300 AD. The name Caerleon came from the Welsh for 'fortress of the legion', although the Romans called it *Isca*, from Wysg, the Welsh name for the river.

The *Isca Augusta* site is world famous for its amphitheatre (thought in the past to have been the 'Round Table' of King Arthur), its huge fortress baths (even larger than those of *Aquae Sulis* [Bath]) and its extensive military barracks, as well as the recently discovered remains of a major Roman harbour on the river.

7.2 bath time

**Baddon Rhufeinig Caerwent/
Caerwent Roman Baths**
Venta Silurum, Monmouthshire
SO 470 907

The pacification of the Silures in south-east Wales took more than twenty-five years of bloody military endeavour against fierce local resistance. Following their surrender in 74/75 AD, however, the Roman victors built an impressive walled city at a place now known as Caerwent. By the year 200, *Venta Silurum* – or the 'market of the Silures' – had become the largest Roman civilian settlement in Wales, and the administrative capital of the tribe, now granted a form of local government, a partial devolution a little perhaps like Wales' relationship with the British state for most of its modern life.

Caerwent today illustrates better than anywhere else the way in which civilisations have built, layer upon layer, upon the constructions of their predecessors. When the Romans who had themselves built upon Silurian foundations left, the settlement fell into decay until it became the site of a monastery built by the Irish St Tathan, then later that of a small Norman castle. And, even today, we continue to build upon the stones of the past as the modern day launderette in Caerleon sits, appropriately perhaps, on top of the site of the original Roman bath-house.

opposite:

bather at *Isca Augusta*, Caerleon
(thanks to Cadw, Welsh Government for permission to photograph)

above:

the Caerwent launderette, built on the site of the Roman bath-house

When the Romans eventually departed these shores in the early years of the fifth century, bath-house culture declined in Britain and with it the reliance upon Roman deities.

Tensions were increased in the dark years that followed by political strife and instability, and wave upon wave of new, less sophisticated invaders.

In its earliest days, Christianity frowned upon those who continued to take recreational baths for pleasure; some even believed that the devil resided in thermal waters:

Bathing is not absolutely forbidden ... If you are ill you need it; so it is not a sin. If a man is healthy, it cossets and relaxes the body and conduces to lust.

Barsanuphius of Gaza, a sixth century Palestinian hermit who is said to have lived in absolute seclusion for fifty years

He who has bathed in Christ has no need of a second bath.

the words of the fourth century ascetic, Saint Jerome

Bathing now, in the eyes of those who espoused the new faith was only acceptable as long as it wasn't enjoyable. There are many tales of early Christian ascetics spending large parts of their lives in freezing waters.

For those unwilling to brave the cold for god, being dirty was the next best thing, as an alternative spiritual triumph over the body.

Much later, even 'science' suggested that a layer of dirt on the skin would protect against infection and disease. This admonition not to over-emphasise the cleanliness of the body to the detriment of the soul – completely antithetical to Roman bath-house thinking – was clearly understood as, more than ten centuries later, Queen Elizabeth I (1533-1603) is reported to have claimed that she took a bath once a month, 'whether she needed to or not'!

opposite:
Raglan Castle

the power and the glory: watering three monmouthshire castles

7.3 riches to rags

Ffynhonnau Castell Rhaglan / Raglan Castle Wells
Monmouthshire
SO 4144 0835

hundred rooms filled with festive fare, / its hundred chimneys for men of high degree

the poet Dafydd Llwyd ap Llywelyn ap Gruffudd (c.1400–c.1490), writing about Raglan Castle

Although its foundations probably date back to the time of the Norman invasion of Gwent in the late eleventh century, the inspiring castle building we see at Raglan today was begun in 1435 by Sir William ap Thomas, the fifth son of a minor Welsh gentry family who was later to be honoured by Henry VI as 'the blue knight of Gwent'.

Significantly added to by William's son, Baron Herbert (who, as a major supporter of the House of York, was to become the most powerful Welshman of his day), and after him by the Bloet family, it was the Somersets (Earls of Worcester) who made the last sumptuous additions to the castle, including its fine 'Renaissance' gardens, complete with marble statues of Roman emperors.

gwent

the living wells of wales

Henry Tudor spent his childhood at Raglan, and Charles I was entertained here on many occasions. During the English Civil War (1642-1651), the castle strengthened its defences and held out for the king against the New Model Army, until it eventually fell during the siege of 1646.

In later centuries, like so many other tumbled ruins, it was used as an easy source of building materials for new constructions.

At the height of its opulence, Raglan Castle was graced with two fine wells – one in the Great Tower (the most

In 1663, Edward Somerset, the second Marquis of Worcester, who grew up at Raglan Castle, wrote a book about great inventions, one of which he himself had designed: the 'water commanding machine', probably the world's first practical steam pump which could spout water from the

The castle was damaged by bombardment, and the victorious Parliamentary forces set about demolishing the palace-fortress, stripping the lead from the roofs, destroying the forests and the water gardens, and burning the library which housed one of the finest collection of Welsh manuscripts and books.

secure area) and one in the Pitched Stone Court. It also had an ornamental marble fountain known as 'The White Horse' in the aptly-titled Fountain Court, whose waters were piped from a high spring at Tregaer a mile away.

Raglan moat as high as the top of the Great Tower. When the Civil War destroyed Raglan, it wiped out much of the family's wealth, and forced Edward to cross yet another border, this time between vast riches and poverty, dying deep in debt.

7.4 indoor plumbing

**Castell Cil-y-Coed /
Caldicot Castle**
Monmouthshire
ST 4866 8852

This motte and bailey structure is the oldest part of the castle, built as a stronghold by English barons installed by the Normans in the thirteenth century to hold in check the people of the Gwent Levels.

above and opposite,
left to right:

the well in the Great Tower,
Raglan Castle;
all that remains of
*"The Fountaine trim,
that runs both day and night"*
(Thomas Churchyard from his poem,
'The Worthines of Wales', 1587);
the well in the Pitched Stone Court,
Raglan Castle

Two shaft wells served the needs of Caldicot Castle, one sunk into the green of the inner ward, the other more unusually within the castle's thirteenth century keep, an early example of indoor plumbing!

centre:

the well in the Caldicot Castle's
Keep Tower

above:

the Keep and walls,
Caldicot Castle

the living wells of wales

7.5 to drink or not to drink

Ffynhonnau Castell Casgwent / Chepstow Castle Wells
Monmouthshire
ST 5342 9415

The first fortifications at strategically-placed Chepstow Castle used masonry from the nearby Roman town of Caerwent [7.2]. And, like at Caldicot [7.4], it was constructed to secure the border with Wales, and was also served by two water sources: the 7m deep shaft well inside the lower bailey just outside the entrance to the Marten's Tower; and an innovative source with a fascinating story to tell, set below the castle walls at the bottom of the sheer cliffs on the banks of the River Wye.

This so-called 'sub-tidal cistern' is thought to have been the original source of water for the castle, on which the first building work began in 1067 (the other well being of twelfth century construction). The beautifully made circular stone structure, which today sits in the estuary silt below the cliffs beside the river, was first revealed by the eccentric Dr Orville Owen of Detroit, Michigan in his excavations of 1909 and 1911 (although its presence was known a century before his and his partner Dr Prescott of Boston's efforts). Dr Owen was an incredible fellow.

He had undertaken a detailed study of Shakespeare's plays and those by many other Elizabethan dramatists and poets and came to the conclusion that all had been written by Sir Francis Bacon, who he believed was the illegitimate son of Queen Elizabeth I and Robert Dudley, the Earl of Leicester.

Led, he thought, by the spirit of Bacon himself, Owen claimed that the collected works contained a message, and he developed a fantastical machine on which all of the texts were cut up and pasted which he claimed, when rotated, provided messages from Sir Francis himself.

One of these revealed that the original manuscripts of Shakespeare's plays were hidden in a cave below Chepstow Castle in sixty-six lead-lined, iron-bound boxes, sealed within a masonry and concrete chamber.

Not surprisingly, Dr Owen didn't find the manuscripts but he did stumble upon a masonry and concrete chamber that turned out to be the original water source for the castle. A constant flow from a spring in the cliff face filled the cistern, and its pure waters were raised some 27m up to the castle.

opposite:

a visitor from the past at the well on the green at Caldicot Castle

left:

the position of the 'sub-tidal cistern' well on the banks of the Wye below Chepstow Castle

the living wells of wales

above:

Bowlore History & Legend
Medieval Display Group
(www.bowlore.com)
at the well in the lower
ward of Chepstow Castle

7.6 respect

Ffynnon Sannan / St Sannan's Well
Bedwellty,
nr Blackwood,
Monmouthshire
SO 168 004

The housing at St Sannan's Well in Bedwellty is unique in being constructed using wicker over its simple rectangular pool. Surrounded by the shading of trees and with two new wooden benches, this is a beautiful spot at which to revere the waters, and perhaps also St Sannan himself.

Sannan is believed to have been a sixth century Irish bishop who travelled widely, was a good friend of Dewi Sant, and credited by some as being the father of St Winefride.

right:
the simple wicker-covered
Ffynnon Sannan
at Bedwellty

7.7 the white hart

Ffynnon Gybi / St Cybi's Well
Llangybi,
nr Newport,
Monmouthshire
ST 3746 9666

St Cybi and his company are said to have arrived here from Cornwall in the sixth century, coming ashore from the river Usk. Edelig, the local king, initially tried to eject them but, after being struck blind and his horse felled, the pagan leader had second thoughts and relented. He was rewarded with the return of his sight (and of his horse) and, in gratitude, gave the saint a hand bell and land upon which to build his churches.

The well itself here is said to have erupted at the spot where the saint struck his staff to mark where his first hermitage would be built. This was Llangybi's main water source until 1951 when it fell into steep decline, described by later visitors as merely a pile of toppled stones. Happily, the well was restored by Llangybi Fawr Community Council (with financial help from CADW) and re-dedicated by the Bishop of Monmouth on 21 September 2007. The Council's efforts in repairing the well and re-establishing the site as a focal point for the community were rightly rewarded by an Usk Civic Society Award.

Ffynnon Gybi and the public house above it are now believed to have been the inspiration for TS Eliot's poem 'Usk', which had baffled critics for decades, not recognising that the 'white hart' in question was the name of the hostelry (constructed in the early 1500s, occupied in turn by Henry VIII and Oliver Cromwell, and visited by Eliot in 1935), rather than the animal:

Do not suddenly break the branch, or
Hope to find
The white hart over the white well.
Glance aside, not for lance, do not spell
Old enchantments. Let them sleep.
'Gently dip, but not too deep',
Lift your eyes
Where the roads dip and where the roads rise
Seek only there
Where the grey light meets the green air
The Hermit's chapel, the pilgrim's prayer.

gwent

opposite:
the White Hart village inn, Llangybi

left:
Ffynnon Gybi / St Cybi's Well, Llangybi

7.8 mint condition

Ffynnon y pentref Llanfair Discoed / Llanfair Discoed village well
nr Chepstow,
Monmouthshire
ST 4478 9266

I would have struggled to find this wonderful village wellspring site if not taken there by Keith Gibbs, the landlord of the excellent Woodlands Tavern. Keith told me that the two ladies who lived in the cottage above the well, and survived to ripe old ages, exclusively using this water source for the whole of their lives.

With its minty aroma, water falls from the well-cared-for spring at Llanfair Discoed into the tiny Llanfair Brook, then feeds the Nedern Brook near Caerwent.

right:
Llanfair Discoed village well sign

7.9 the mother of the world

**Ffynnon Rhinweddol /
The Virtuous Well**
(or **Ffynnon Anne / St Anne's Well**)
Trellech, nr Monmouth,
Monmouthshire
SO 5030 0510

... the traditional pagan worship of mother Goddesses at holy wells, the natural interpretation of the well as a secret entrance into the body of the Earth Mother or even as her womb, the belief in the life-giving or pro-creative powers of water – all combine to instil in people the certainty that the holy well was the source of fertility.

Janet and Colin Bord
from *Earth Rites: Fertility Practices in Pre-Industrial Britain*, 1982

Although Christianised to St Anne – the apocryphal mother of the Virgin Mary and, therefore, the grandmother of Jesus (though never mentioned in the New Testament) – the Virtuous Well in Trellech is likely to have had much earlier origins. Anne is revered in the Islamic, as well as the Christian, faith. She is the patroness of un-married women, housewives, women in labour and those who want to be pregnant; and of grandmothers, educators and teachers. In addition, she has become the patroness of horse riders, cabinet-makers and miners; and of sailors as a protectoress from storms.

Many pagan gods and goddesses were co-opted by the Christian church as saints for their new faith. Demeter, the Greek goddess of festivals became the male warrior saint, Demetrios; Aphrodite became the 'repentant whore' St Aphrodite; the Roman god Mars was transformed into St Martin; and the protector of sailors, the Roman Gemini blended seamlessly into St James, the patron saint of pilgrim travellers. New churches were built upon the foundations of pagan temples by the disciples of the new faith, often at sacred crossroads and springs, sometimes retaining the original pagan circles of stone for their new boundary walls. Phallic carvings were re-chiselled into Christian crosses, and many old festivals, dates and ceremonies continued in the ecclesiastical calendar, little altered.

A belief in a Mother Goddess with responsibilities for birth and fertility is at the sacred centre of all early civilisations. St Anne is thought to have originally been attributed to the variously named Danu, Annis, Anu, Britannia, Andraste, Modron, or Matrona the Celtic mother goddess of rivers, springs, magic, wisdom ... and new beginnings. The well with Anne's name at Trellech is also known as The Virtuous Well.

Trellech is a fascinating place, and the location of three so-called 'mysteries'.

The first of these are three monoliths known today as 'Harold's Stones', though clearly erected well before King Harold, a political re-dedication like that observed at so many well-spring sites. Nobody really knows whether these phallic pillars were ceremonial in nature, the location for fertility rites or of cosmic observations.

The second mystery is the Tump Turret, 40ft high and nearly 400ft in circumference. It was once thought to have been the cemetery of King Harold's men, slain in battle, or, alternatively, the burial place of plague victims. It is more likely, however, to be the remains of the motte and bailey castle of the De Clare family, who built a string of Norman keeps in this area. As the interior has never been explored – there is said to be a curse against anyone who disturbs the mound – it too retains its secrets.

The final 'mystery' is the (medicinal, and therefore) Virtuous Well. Situated in a field on the eastern edge of the village beside the Tintern road, it is said to mix water from four separate springs, three of which contain iron, and each offering a cure for a different complaint. A writer in the 1600s claimed that if the waters were drunk in the morning on an empty stomach, they would cure *"scurvy, collick and distempers"*. Its speciality, however, seems to have been the relief of eye ailments and *"complaints peculiar to women"*.

There is a theory that the water which emerges here runs first under Harold's Stones, and that the well may originally have been used in Druidical ceremonies. Others have claimed that fairies dance around the well on Midsummer's Eve, and drink its water from harebell cups at sunrise.

opposite:
Llanfair Discoed village well

left:
Harold's Stones, Trellech;
one side of the stone sun-dial in St Nicholas' Church in Trellech which depicts Harold's Stones

A story is told at Trellech of a local farmer who dug up the fairy ring around the well, claiming that he *"didn't like all them silly tales"*. The following day when he went to draw water, he found the well was completely dry, but for him only; all of the other villagers were able to fill their buckets as usual. The man tried to collect water repeatedly, even waiting expectantly behind others who left with full pails, but as soon as he dipped his pail into the well, the waters receded and he was left with nothing. This went on for many days until, one morning, the farmer met with a little old man who he had never seen before, sitting on the wall of the well. The stranger told him that he had upset the fairies and that he should replace the turf he had removed. This he did and his bucket filled with the life-giving waters.

Anne's was also an important wishing well. The petitioner would be required to throw a small metal object into the waters and count the number of bubbles that resulted, their rapidity or otherwise determining how quickly the wish would be granted ... and, no bubbles at all meaning that the wish had been denied. On other occasions, young girls anxious to know how long they would have to wait until their wedding day, would drop a white stone into the water and wait for a message from below, each bubble, it was said, counting as one month.

opposite and above:
St Anne's
or the Virtuous Well,
Trellech

left:
Ffynnon Rhinweddol /
The Virtuous Well's
depiction in the
Trellech sun-dial

the living wells of wales

and ...

7.10: Ffynnon Castell Brynbuga / Usk Castle Well
nr Pontypool
SO 375 014

7.11: Ffynnon Castell Gwyn / White Castle Well
nr Abergavenny
SO 3797 1677

7.12: Ffynnon Gwladys / St Gwladys' Well
Basseleg, nr Newport
SO 254 877

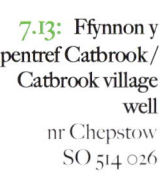

7.13: Ffynnon y pentref Catbrook / Catbrook village well
nr Chepstow
SO 514 026

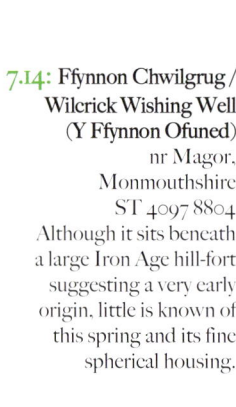

7.14: Ffynnon Chwilgrug / Wilcrick Wishing Well (Y Ffynnon Ofuned)
nr Magor, Monmouthshire
ST 4097 8804
Although it sits beneath a large Iron Age hill-fort suggesting a very early origin, little is known of this spring and its fine spherical housing.

7.15: Ffynnon Cynheiddon / St Cenedlon's Well
Rockfield / Llanyronwy, Monmouthshire
SO 482 148

gwent

7.16: Ffynnon Tewdric / St Tewdric's Well
Mathern, nr Chepstow
ST 5227 9117
RS Thomas once observed that in the borderlands *"the scent of dead heroes and dead saints"* often intermingled. King Tewdric, called out of spiritual retirement by his son and heir Meurig to defeat the pagan Saxons, died in the attempt, after which two stags emerged from the forest and drew the wounded king to his final resting place at Mathern.

7.17: Cafn ymyl y ffordd Hendre / Hendre roadside trough
opposite Rolls Golf Club entrance, nr Rockfield
SO 456 147

7.18: Ffynnon ofuned pentref Tredynog / Tredunnock village wishing well
nr Caerleon
ST 3792 9478

7.19: Ffynnon y dref, Trefynwy / Monmouth Victorian town well
SO 504 124

7.20: Cafn ochr y ffordd, Ynysgynwraidd / Skenfrith roadside trough
nr Raglan
SO 459 202

7.21: Ffynnon goffa, Ynysgynwraidd / Skenfrith memorial well
nr Raglan
SO 459 203

8 A WOUNDED LAND:
y cymoedd / the valleys

The South Wales Valleys is, arguably, the area of Wales that has experienced the greatest degree of disruption and change, particularly over the past two hundred years.

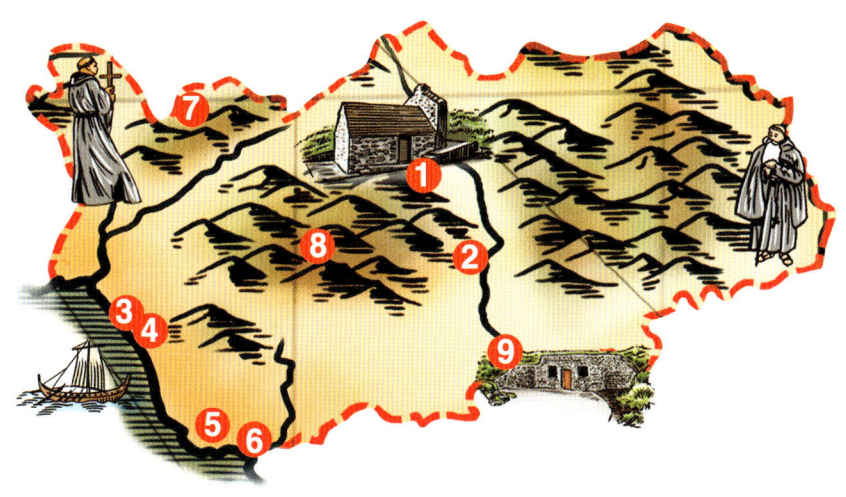

The exploitation of coal on an industrial scale from the mid 1800s onward turned small rural farming communities into over crowded urbanised centres almost overnight. Thousands of workers were attracted to the area (speeded by the development of the railways, and the building of packed ribbons of homes to shelter them and their families), releasing the floodgates to dangerous, often lethal working conditions and the despoliation of the land.

Today, following the closure of the pits and the land reclamation schemes of the late 1980s and early '90s, the quieter, greener landscapes are slowly returning, though the massive scars in the people and on the land are still clearly visible, in a historical trajectory which in many ways parallels that of our seared springs and holy wells throughout Wales.

opposite:
Tarren Deusant [8.2]
nr Llantrisant,
Rhondda Cynon Taff

8.1 water, wood and fire

Ffynnon Fair / Mary's Well
Penrhys,
Rhondda Cynon Taff
ST 004 944

These days the view below is no longer of tranquility and woodland but a valley full of industry and housing estates; the old pilgrim's route has been replaced by a new road and one has to use a certain amount of imagination to recapture the atmosphere of olden times.

Audrey Doughty,
Spas and Springs of Wales (2001)

Initially an area in which to graze livestock and later to farm, the presence of the holy well and the miraculous appearance of the Virgin and Child statue here jolted Penrhys Hill – straddling high above the Rhondda Fawr and Rhondda Fach valleys – into international popularity ... and later notoriety. New buildings were erected to service the growing numbers of pilgrims as Penrhys became a must visit destination for believers.

The holy well at Penrhys would have pre-dated all of the other important buildings here, being a centre for pagan worship long before Christianity arrived in Britain. The small stone beehive-hut-like structure we see today is known as Ffynnon Fair or Mary's Well. The spring was said to be efficacious in curing many ailments, including rheumatism, 'king's evil' and disorders of the eyes. Penrhys was known colloquially as a 'pin well'. The person hoping to be healed here would, after taking the waters, cast a pin into the well; if it became discoloured, it was a sign that their petition had been granted.

The shrine of the Virgin and Child at Penrhys was one of the most important in South Wales, second only to that of our national saint at St Davids. Pilgrims came, according to the poets, *"over land and sea"* to worship at the statue of Jesus and his mother, richly painted in white, blue and gold. The Virgin, it was said, gave sight to the blind, made cripples walk, the deaf to hear, and even raised the dead.

According to tradition, the sculpture had miraculously appeared in an oak tree as *"a gift from heaven"*, and a team of oxen had been unable to drag it from the branches. The statue only allowed itself to be moved when a shrine and chapel were built to house it on land belonging to the monks of Llantarnam, alongside a lavish hostel for pilgrims, and a network of roads and bridges to ease access.

Penrhys' popularity eventually led to its downfall, however, when the shrine was targeted for destruction during Henry VIII's Protestant Reformation which sounded the (albeit temporary) death knell for Catholicism in Britain. Bishop Latimer had written to Thomas Cromwell suggesting the elimination of a number of shrines of Our Lady, believing them to be a focus of idolatry, and thus *"the devil's instrument"*, and in 1538 Cromwell instructed William Herbert to remove the effigy as *"secretly as might be"* at dead of night to avoid an anticipated local uprising. On 26 September 1538, the Penrhys image was publicly burnt in London.

left:
Lee Williams' painting of the Virgin and Child statue
opposite left:
rusting derelict car, Ffynnon Fair, Penrhys
opposite right:
the 2008 *Pererinion Penrhys Pilgrims Festival* Service in front of the 1953 statue

y cymoedd / the valleys

But the stones and the significance of Ffynnon Fair could not be so easily destroyed, and the healing well continued to be used.

In 1947, some four thousand Catholics revived the tradition of pilgrimage to St Mary's Well.

In 1953, a new statue – carved this time out of Portland stone – was erected on Penrhys and blessed by Archbishop McGrath. A year later, Rev PJ O'Reilly Gibbons, the parish priest at Ferndale, organised another pilgrimage for an estimated 25,000 people.

the living wells of wales

above, left to right:

the lower well at Penrhys,
lying a few metres below the main well;
inside the Ffynnon Fair well-house;
Ffynnon Fair and the Rhonnda Valley

opposite right:

procession to the 2008 *Pererinion Penrhys / Pilgrims Festival* Service

y cymoedd / the valleys

The Church in Wales organised its first visit to the shrine in May 1976, and the following year 2,000 people attended the first pilgrimage of the sick to the statue and the holy well since the Reformation. Today, pilgrimages to Penrhys are once again commonplace.

Penrhys has a unique story to tell – of destruction, resilience and renewal – its significance as a major European religious centre stretching back into the mists of time. The sixteenth century bard, Lewys Morgannwg, spoke of there being *"nine heavens in one meadow"* at Penrhys, and it was this phrase that sparked the initial inspiration for the *Pererinion Penrhys / Penrhys Pilgrims Festival* of 2008 to mark four hundred and seventy years since the destruction of the Penrhys Shrine and the confiscation and burning of the Mother and Child statue, as well as the fortieth anniversary of the completion and occupation of the Penrhys estate ... and to celebrate the survival and enduring importance of both.

the living wells of wales

8.2 the womb of the earth

**Tarren Deusant /
The Knoll of Two Saints**
Castellau, nr Llantrisant,
Rhondda Cynon Taff
ST 0520 8721

despite even the influence of Christianity in most recent times, the Great Goddess has never yet left the landscape of Europe

Michael Everson,
from *Tenacity in religion, myth, and folklore*, published in *Journal of Indo-European Studies* 17 (1989)

Unlike the detailed history and layers of myth retained at the Penrhys holy well, nobody is really quite sure about Tarren Deusant. Are the carvings of the heads here Celtic in origin, or are they later? And what was their purpose?

Tarren Deusant means the 'knoll', 'cliff' or 'rock of the two saints'. Originally, there were just two heads carved in low relief here, but over time others have been added (there are at least eight, now), together with a confusion of crosses and graffitied initials. Were these petroglyphs part of the Celtic Cult of the Head or, as their naming suggests, representations of Christian saints? If the latter, which two saints do they represent, and what was their association with this area?

What does seem clear, however, is that the original attraction of this site was the unearthly amber-coloured outcrop of rock around which the other contributions have been added over time, standing as it does beside a spring emerging from the bottom of the cliff.

Natural features in the landscape like these had a meaning for our distant ancestors that we have mostly lost or forgotten. Known locally as the 'Druid's Altar', this was most likely a centre of powerful earth magic, a place where the veil between daily existence and a deeper, more profound experience was possible, another 'thin place' that allowed a measure of access to other realities. Certainly, it is difficult to find an alternative symbol of Christian significance to explain the veneration of this strange stone, the crosses I assume having been added in an attempt to dilute its original pagan powers.

It has been suggested that the stone itself represents the female genetalia, offering a place where one could symbolically return to the womb of the earth.

Naturally occurring – rather than being the creation of a shaman, a priest or an artist – Tarren Deusant would have had an extra significance, added to here by the life force issuing from the body of the Earth Mother at its sacred spring.

opposite:

some of the *Penrhys Pilgrims / Pererinion Penrhys Festival* events, inc. Carlton Bunce and musicians performing a specially-commissioned Penrhys play; music from Pavane Early Music Consort, and Robin Williamson; Oblivion rock band; the launch of Lee Williams' new *Mother and Child* painting; the new Penrhys community sculpture; and Nicaragua Solidarity Campaign Cymru launching their *All Water Is Sacred* campaign inside the Ffynnon Fair well-house

y cymoedd / the valleys

There are many wells throughout the Margam Estate between Bridgend and Swansea. Here I will explore one which has been visible for a very long time, and one which is only now being slowly revealed.

8.3 hidden away

Ffynnon Gyffyr / Monks' Bath-house
Margam Park,
Neath Port Talbot
SS 803 869

Located on the west bank of the Afon Cwm Bach, off a forestry path above Margam Abbey, this isolated fourteenth century site was probably a medieval baptistry, for those who worshipped at the chapel on Hen Eglwys above [see 8.4], the presence of the local 'un-washed' being un-welcome at the abbey and church below.

It is believed that this medieval bath-house was built over a medicinal spring known as Ffynnon Gyffyr. This was a 'cloutie' or rag well where those in search of assistance would soak their cloths in the sacred waters, apply them to the part of the body needing relief, then hang them onto an adjacent tree or bush to await the relief of the pain or problem as the rag disintegrated.

opposite and left:
Tarren Deusant
at Castellau,
nr Llantrisant,
with two of the
'saints' heads

the living wells of wales

below:

the exterior and interior of the Monks' Bath-house at Margam Park

8.4 revealed

Ffynnon Mair / Mary's Well
Capel Mair ar y Bryn,
Margam, Neath Port Talbot
SS 797 866

The Rev William Thomas (1760-1799), who was born at Eglwys Nunydd farm a mile from Margam House, wrote an account of his visit to Margam Abbey in 1787:

In the noble wood above the house stands the roofless walls of an ancient church with traces of a churchyard enclosure around it. There is a niche near the altar for the Statue of the Virgin, to whom it is dedicated.

In the churchyard and near the large door of the church or chapel is a well by the foot of an ancient tree which might probably be used in early times for the baptismal ceremony or as holy water for aspersion, called Ffynnon Mair – Mary's well.

For the past few years, the Friends of Margam Park, led by Keith Edger and supported by the Glamorgan-Gwent Archaeological Trust, have been excavating a site a little to the north of the ruins of the fifteenth century Hen Eglwys chapel (or Capel Mair) on the hillside of Craig Fawr overlooking Margam Abbey. The summer of 2018 saw major progress being made, with the clear outline of the holy well revealed.

above:

the Ffynnon Mair dig,
September 2018,
with the Friends of Margam Park
(Peter Nash, Doreen Nash,
David Harris, Keith Edger
and Geoffrey Lewis-Jones)

the living wells of wales

8.5 this neck of the woods

**Ffynnon Gollwyn /
St Collwyn's Well**
The Collwyn,
Pyle,
Bridgend
SS 823 824

*Yn y Rhodd Duw gwyn heb
   gwyno-ffynnon
Er Ffiniant I'm puro.
Iechyd I'm bryd o fewm bro
Amylgwyd wrth demi Iago.*

('Blessed God gave me the fountain freely as a gift / To make me pure. / My face is now healthy / In that place near the temple of James.')

the bard Dafydd Benwyn from Llangeinor, writing about St Collwyn's Well in 1580

It's doubtful that a saint called Collwyn gave his name to this site (or that he even existed), although there was an early seventh century St Collen who was said to have been the grandson of King Arthur.

left:
the littered path to
Ffynnon Gollwyn /
St Collwyn's Well,
Pyle

right:
Ffynnon Gollwyn /
St Collwyn's Well

opposite:
the well-house gate,
Ffynnon Fawr / The Big Well,
Nottage, nr Porthcawl

A fascinating character, he fought with pagan leaders and chased away fairies, though he didn't seems to venture anywhere near this neck of the woods. The Welsh words collen and llwyn mean 'hazel' and 'grove', an appropriate description of this densely wooded gorge of the river Kenfig. St James' Church in Pyle was no doubt constructed above the sacred well and grove to fight against the old spirits and beliefs.

The site – said to have been a healing well, as illustrated by Benwyn's account above – certainly still has a strongly pagan feel, recalling the sacred groves and springs so prized by Druids and their followers (though the place today, littered and neglected, is far from seen in this light by local people).

8.6 a necessary blessing

Ffynnon Fawr / The Big Well
Nottage, nr Porthcawl,
Bridgend
SS 822 781

Today, set uncomfortably beside the roundabout at the junction of the A4106 and A4229 roads a little to the north of Porthcawl, this well is thought to have been an ancient site, although its last building phase was in the early nineteenth century.

A bi-lingual plaque with a verse with typically Victorian sentiments here reads:

Mae dwr yn fendith angenreidol
Rhoddes Duw inni ar lawr:
Cofiwyn 'Awdur Pob Daioni'
Wrth yfed dwr o'r Fynnon Fawr.

Water as a necessary blessing
Which God has given us on earth;
Let us remember 'The Author of all
  Goodness'
As we drink from Fynnon Fawr.

y cymoedd / the valleys

8.7 a real stinker

**Ffynnon Ddrewllyd /
The Stinking Well**
Cwm-Twrch Isaf,
nr Merthyr Tydfil
SN 764 104

Ffynnon Ddrewllyd – the 'Stinking Well' – is another which got its unappealing name from the strong presence of sulphur in its waters. It was popular with the Victorians who drank, washed and bathed in it. In the 1870s, a Dr D Thomas sent samples for analysis to confirm the efficacy of its sulphur compounds and iron salts for the alleviation of rheumatism, gout, skin troubles, blood impurities, and diuretic and urinary complaints.

This is one of the few wells in Wales whose very real medicinal attributes were not (as far as we can tell) claimed and named for Christianity. The grassy area in front of the well – known locally as Maes-y-Ffynnon – became a focus for community activities, for choir practices, religious meetings and political gatherings, as well as the annual Cwmtwrch Eisteddfod.

The well was restored in 1920, and again in April 1993 by Ystalyfera Community Council (with the help of grants from the Prince of Wales Trust and Dŵr Cymru), the latter renovation being, it must be said, with its profusion of intrusive plaques and its aluminium handrails, a real stinker!

opposite:
Ffynnon Fawr /
The Big Well,
Nottage,
nr Porthcawl

right:
the unsympathetic restoration
of The Stinking Well
at Cwm-Twrch Isaf
has not deterred
water gatherers

the living wells of wales

y cymoedd / the valleys

8.8 not so sweet wells

**Ffynnon Mogwai /
Sweetwells**
Pont-y-Rhyl, Garw Valley,
Bridgend
SS 908 892

Sweetwells, whose waters reach the road through two beautiful waterfalls, served the people of the six-mile-long, dead-end Garw Valley and, in particular, the row of terraced houses which takes its name.

Nearby is the site of the Lluest Colliery. One can imagine miners filling up their bottles here before a shift and slaking their thirst after hours underground. Today, there are few reminders of the mining industry left in the landscape here. The Lluest Colliery disaster site where nineteen men and boys lost their lives in August 1899 is marked by a coal dram and a simple plaque (though there are some fine new ceramic sculptures dotted throughout the valley which remind of the hardships of mining life).

Little respect is currently being shown for the impressive Sweetwells falls. I live in the Garw Valley and regularly move the rubbish dumped by people who I can only assume are unaware of their importance (although their continuing beauty should be clear to all).

opposite:
the blood red waters of Ffynnon Ddrewllyd

right, top to bottom:
Ballarat Colliery sculpture above one of the Garw Valley's new lakes;
the coal dram memorial to the Lluest Colliery dead, Garw Valley;
Lluest Colliery oral history wall sculpture

left:

one of the two Sweetwells waterfalls, Garw Valley

opposite:

Sweetwells regularly used as a site to dump rubbish;

the author's mother and late father at Taffs Well

y cymoedd / the valleys

8.9 in hot water

Ffynnon Dwym / Hot Well
(or **Ffynnon Taf / Taff's Well**)
nr Tongwynlais,
Rhondda Cynon Taf
ST 002 945

The Ffynnon Dwym hot springs are warmed geothermally from deep within the earth. At a constant twenty-one degrees centigrade, the waters travel on their slow, twenty-five kilometre journey from their source, at perhaps just a few metres a year, through warming cracks in the earth.

Taff's Well's curative properties were recognised as far back as Roman times, attested to by the discovery of Roman masonry when a flood in 1799 washed away part of the floor. In later times, crutches were regularly left behind here in recognition of the water's ability to cure rheumatism and lameness within a month of bathing.

Ffynnon Dwym also seemed to have had stimulating properties for those of fit body and mind, offering protection from future illnesses, too. During the nineteenth century, young people assembled here on the eighth Sunday after Easter and *"dipped their hands in the well, and scattered drops of water over one another, and then repaired to the nearest green space to spend the remainder of the day in dancing and merriment."* (Francis Jones)

Jones also tells us that a *"corrugated iron structure"* was erected over the well *"to preserve the modesty of the bathers. When a man bathed it was customary to hang a pair of breeches outside to indicate the sex of the bather within: women hung up an essentially feminine garment."*

Taff's Well is believed by some to be haunted by a grey and slender female ghost, longing to be released from her bondage by a man who had to hold her tightly by the hands and make no sound, an instruction that was invariably disobeyed.

Following the decline of the Welsh spa industry, Taff's Well was neglected, though local people built an open-air swimming pool on the site, fed by the warm spring water, which was still in use in the late 1950s.

the living wells of wales

I reported in my first book on Welsh wellsprings (*Holy Wells: Wales*, 2008) that the site was *"once again in a very poor state of repair, regularly vandalised, a favourite haunt for the graffiti artist, and closed to the public"*. You should be careful what you wish for. On a recent visit, Ffynnon Dwym was open but its renovation was overpowering and inappropriate – with huge metal girders enclosing the historic well, a metal safety fence, and a huge blue metal box with two buttons (English and Welsh) to play the commentaries, neither of which worked!

The spirit of the place had been entirely lost amid this and the three very large, well meaning interpretative panels at its entrance.

A lot of money has clearly been spent here with the laudable aim of making the site accessible once more ... but nothing of the early importance and uses of the site is suggested in the new design. For me, it now has more than anything else the spirit of the caging of a once-powerful animal, or, perhaps, more appropriately to this site, of a ghostly woman held tightly forever.

and ...

y cymoedd / the valleys

opposite:
exterior and interior of Taffs Well, today

8.10: Ffynnon Castell Caerffili / Caerphilly Castle Well
ST 156 872

8.13: Ffynnon Dôl yr Ogwr / Ogmore Down Well
Pant Mari Flanders, nr St Brides Major, Bridgend
SS 882 757

8.11: Ffynnon Dewi / St David's Well
Moor Lane, Nottage, nr Porthcawl, Bridgend
SS 821 786
St David himself was thought to have visited this holy well which gained a reputation for cures for rheumatism and internal disorders.

8.14: Ffynnon a Phwll Bedyddio, Corntown / Corntown Well and Baptismal Pond
nr Bridgend
SS 919 775

8.12: Ffynnon Ciwg / St Ciwg Well
nr Pontardawe, Neath Port Talbot
SN 724 056
Johnny and the late Jenny Morris before their renovation of this once-important wellspring site

8.15: Ffynnon Ioan Fedyddiwr neu Ffynnon Sandford / St John the Baptist or Sandford's Well
nr Newton Church, nr Porthcawl, Bridgend
SS 836 774
It is claimed that when the tide is out on nearby Newton Beach the well is full, and vice versa.

9 GETTING AND SPENDING:
caerdydd a bro morgannwg / cardiff and the vale of glamorgan

The world is too much with us; late and soon,
Getting and spending, we lay waste our powers;
Little we see in Nature that is ours ...

William Wordsworth (1770-1850), from his poem,
The World Is Too Much With Us

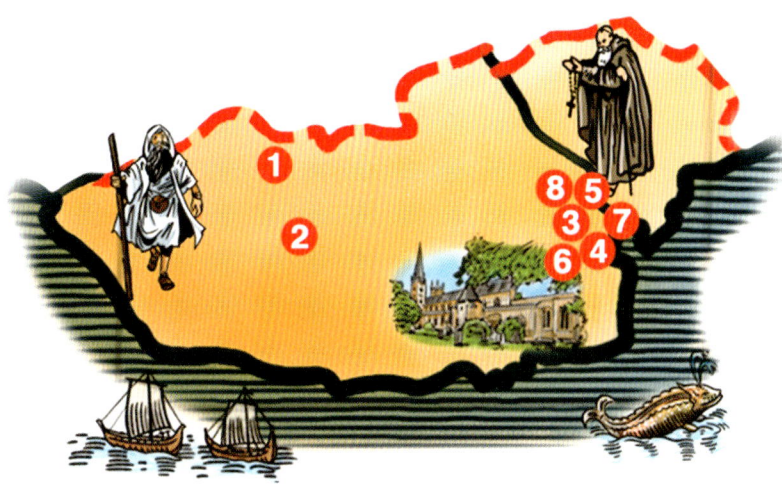

Cities and large towns often overwhelm our once-sacred places. This is more true, it seems, with regard to wellsprings than any other sites with a religious resonance, fragile as they nearly always are.

opposite:
Ffynhonau y Pentre 1 /
Salmon's Well 1 [9.1]
Penllyn,
Vale of Glamorgan

the living wells of wales

9.1 a gift from god (and dr salmon)

Ffynhonau y Pentre / Salmon's Wells
Penllyn, nr Cowbridge,
Vale of Glamorgan
SS 973 767

The waters here have been used by local people for at least six centuries, until a piped supply became available to the village of Penllyn in 1937. The site received its name – not, as might be expected, from the presence of a fortune-telling fish – but from the time when, in 1883, Dr William Salmon (the occupant of Penllyn Court) repaired wellheads 1 and 2, paved their frontages, and improved the area's drainage.

Although an inscription above the entrance to wellhead 1 reads *Dŵr Rhudd Yr Hollalluog Dduw* ('Water, the Gift of Almighty God'), the wells fell into disrepair after 1940, to be completely covered by trees and bushes.

But Grade 2 Listed as an Historic Site in April 1998, and restored and landscaped in 2000 as part of a Community Millennium project, the three wells here are today once again being cared for by local people.

caerdydd a bro morgannwg / cardiff and the vale of glamorgan

opposite:

the fourteenth century
Ffynhonau y Pentre /
Salmon's Well 1,
plus Well 2
in the background

clockwise from top left:

Salmon's Well 2;

Salmon's Well 3,
created in 1911
to meet extra need;

changes in the niche
at the back of Salmon's Well 2,
with the latest addition
of a pagan *sheela na gig*

9.2 turning heads

**Ffynnon Santes Anne /
St Anne's Well**
Llanmihangel,
nr Llandow,
Vale of Glamorgan
SS 9811 7190

A Grade 2 Listed site – which demonstrates that listing never guarantees care, or even survival – this well in Llanmihangel, set between the Grade 2* Listed parish church of St Michael and the fourteenth century Grade 1 Listed Llanmihangel Place manor house, and predating both, is today entirely neglected.

Like the Virtuous Well at Trellech in Monmouthshire [7.9], it was dedicated to St Anne, the mother of the Virgin Mary.

The water from this well, accessed down a series of steps within the church graveyard, did not emerge from a mouth, like that at Tremeirchion [4.7], but from the breasts of the saint, carved into a small stone tablet.

Today, forgotten, overgrown and unloved, its waters no longer flow and its sculpture is obscured.

above left:
St Michael's Church, Llanmihangel

above right:
St Anne's Well, Llanmihangel, 2008 and 2018

opposite, left to right:
a temporary resident of what's left of Canton Drinking Fountain (junction of Llandaff and Romilly Roads), Cardiff;

Ffynnon y pentref, Llandaf / Llandaff Village Well, Cardiff Road, Cardiff, with its fine carvings of frogs, lizards and fish

The sad neglect of St Anne's Well is paralleled by many historically and spiritually important sites in our more highly populated areas. Two of the saddest examples of our amnesia and neglect in Cardiff are the remains of the **Ffynnon Yfed Treganna / Canton Drinking Fountain** [9.3 / ST 164 770], and the fine **Ffynnon ymyl y ffordd Dinas Llandaf / Llandaff City roadside well** [9.4 / ST 155 777].

One of my favourite pastimes is to stand next to the Llandaff well-house on the main road in Llandaff and stop passers-by to ask if they know where the well is, the responses almost always being – even from locals of many years – *"No, I don't think there's a well round yer, love!"*.

the living wells of wales

9.5 not so miraculous

Ffynnon Sant Teilo / St Teilo's Well
Llandaff Cathedral, nr Cardiff
ST 155 780

St Teilo was the second Bishop of Llandaff, in the sixth century, and was one of the three Welsh saints to whom Llandaff Cathedral was originally dedicated (the others being Dyfrig and Euddogwy).

Ffynnon Sant Teilo was believed to possess miraculous healing powers. His largely neglected well site today clearly needs its own miracle or two …

9.6 the dairy cross

Ffynnon y Llaethdy / The Dairy Well
Llandaff Cathedral, nr Cardiff
ST 156 782

This fine cross now sited within Llandaff Cathedral is all that remains of the Dairy Well in Llandaf. Said to have once sat next to the well in the well-house shed, it was rediscovered by the Bishop of Llandaff in April 1870.

caerdydd a bro morgannwg / cardiff and the vale of glamorgan

We are very lucky in Cardiff to have the National Museum of History at St Fagans (better known from its opening in 1948 as the Welsh Folk Museum). Situated on the outskirts of Cardiff, it was the UK's first national open air museum and is today Wales' most popular heritage visitor attraction (even winning *Which? Magazine*'s favourite UK visitor attraction accolade in 2011). Its aim is to re-erect and protect often threatened historically important buildings to represent the rural, religious and industrial architecture of Wales on one site. The two wells here have not, however, been moved from another place; indeed, one of them provided the name for the whole area.

9.7 not cool

Ffynnon Fferm Llwyn-yr-eos / Llwyn-yr-eos Farm well
National Museum of History,
St Fagans, nr Cardiff
ST 115 771

The Lwyn-yr-eos farmhouse is the only major building (apart from the castle) within the vast St Fagans complex which is in its original location. The current house was built in 1820 and the farm specialised in diary produce.

On the green in front of the building is an attractive, well-cared-for well, though there is no information about it available. An attendant thought it might have been a 'dairy well'. These were places where milk and cheeses were kept fresh in the constantly cooling waters of most wellsprings. This would certainly reflect the main work of the families here, although it is doubtful that such a large, finely-built structure would not also have been the main water source for the farm itself.

opposite,
clockwise from top left:
St Teilo's Well,
nr Llandaff Cathedral;

Llandaff Cathedral;

The Dairy Well Celtic Cross,
Llandaff Cathedral;

St Teilo's Chapel,
Llandaff Cathedral;

frieze of St Teilo
by Frank Roper, 1966,
Llandaff Cathedral

right:
Llwyn-yr-eos Farm Well
(and kitchen),
St Fagans, nr Cardiff

the living wells of wales

9.8 selling wales short

**Ffynnon Sant Ffagan /
St Fagan's Holy Well**
National Museum of History,
St Fagans, nr Cardiff
ST 118 772

Despite the great care the National Museum Wales (NMW) shows for the buildings it preserves and illuminates at St Fagans, the same cannot be said for the very well that gave the place its name.

St Fagan's Holy Well is located in the formal gardens opposite St Fagans' sixteenth century castle, beside one of its fishponds. Now barely visible and with nothing to suggest its existence, either at the site itself or in any of the St Fagans' literature, we are missing an opportunity here .... and selling Wales short.

Cardiff Council's *St Fagan's Conservational Area* report highlighted the historic importance of the well site in 2007:

"The village of St Fagans was first established as an important location during medieval times, when the Norman conquerors built a motte and bailey castle to control the crossing of the river Ely.

Nothing of the original Castle now remains, with the exception of the Holy Well of St Fagan ..."

Cardiff Dowsers' Group has written more recently to NMW to request action, suggesting that work on the site would fit well within the stated aims of a National Museum of History.

Sacred springs and holy wells tell an essential part of the story of the lives of the people of Wales, and, as such, should surely be better represented at our National Museum, especially given the huge opportunity offered by the survival here of this ancient sacred site.

above, left to right:
St Fagan's Castle from
St Fagan's Holy Well;
Ffynnon Sant Ffagan;
the well site viewed
from St Fagan's Castle

caerdydd a bro morgannwg / cardiff and the vale of glamorgan

and ...

9.9: Ffynnon Llyswyrni / Llysworney Well (and pond)
Vale of Glamorgan
SS 962 741

9.12: Ffynnon Saint-y-Brid / St Bride's Major village well and pond
Pwll y Mer,
Vale of Glamorgan
SS 896 745

9.10: Pwmp pentref y Bontfaen / Cowbridge village pump
Vale of Glamorgan
SS 995 748

9.13: Pwmp Eglwys Sain Nicolas / St Nicholas Church pump
Vale of Glamorgan
ST 090 744

9.11: Ffynnon Croes Ham / Ham Cross Well
Llantwit Major,
Vale of Glamorgan
SS 966 694
(Visit while here St Illtyd's Church and its fine collection of ancient stones, see [10.5].)

9.14: Ffynnon Castell Caerdydd / Cardiff Castle Well (outer),
Sophia Gardens,
Cardiff
ST 180 766

the living wells of wales

9.15: Ffynnon Castell
Coch / Castell Coch Well
nr Cardiff
ST 131 825

9.18: Pistyll Yfed
Caeau Llandaf /
Llandaff Fields
Drinking Fountain
Cardiff
ST 161 777

9.16: Ffynnon Gattwg /
St Cadoc's Well
Pentyrch,
nr Cardiff
ST 104 817
(the probable site)

9.19: Pistyll Yfed
Gerddi'r Faenor /
Grange Gardens
Drinking Fountain
Cardiff
ST 180 749

9.17: Pistyll Yfed
Parc Buddug /
Victoria Park
Drinking
Fountain
Cardiff
ST 155 769

9.20: Pistyll yfed
Canolfan Ddinesig
Caerdydd / Cardiff
Civic Centre
drinking fountain
The Friary,
Cardiff
ST 183 767

caerdydd a bro morgannwg / cardiff and the vale of glamorgan

9.21: Ffynnon Llandennis / St Dennis' Well
Roath Park, Cardiff
ST 184 806

10 CHRISTIANITY-SUPER-MARE:
abertawe & phenrhyn gŵyr / swansea & the gower peninsula

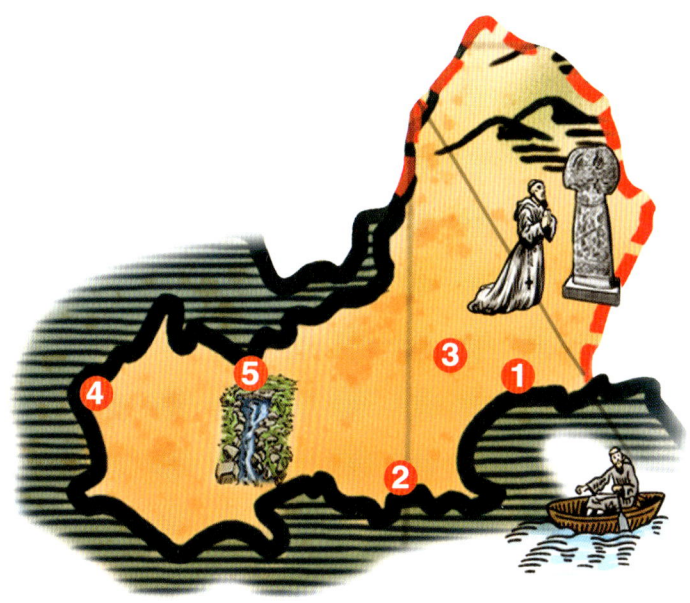

The city of Swansea and the Gower Peninsula are in their different ways dominated by the sea, the former because of its once important port, the latter with its world famous tourist attracting beaches and surf.

Few, however, are aware of its wellspring riches.

opposite:

Ffynnon Bedr /
St Peter's Well [10.2]
nr Caswell Bay,
Gower

the living wells of wales

10.1 shut too, in a tower of words *

Ffynnon Castell / The Castle Well
Swansea
SS 658 933

One of the Swansea Castle prison's most famous – and certainly most fortunate – inmates was Welsh freedom fighter, William Cragh. Sentenced to death for his part in the attacks on Swansea and Oystermouth Castles in 1287, he survived hanging, twice. In the early 1930s, when Dylan Thomas worked as a reporter for the *South Wales Daily Post*, its offices and printing presses occupied the Castle courtyard, here. Thomas wrote of his own escape: *"I didn't stay long. I sought my own freedom to write poetry"*.

Hidden for many years, the site of Swansea Castle's well has been attractively remodeled by the city council, crowned with a metal disc sunk into the courtyard floor. In both of our languages, it reads *"And Abertawe town of war, broken towers, and today there is truly peace"*.

* Dylan Thomas, from his poem, *Especially when the October wind*

right:
the site of the Swansea Castle well

opposite near:
Swansea Castle;
the well covering

opposite far:
the reconstructed roundhouse
in Bishop's Wood;
St Peter's Chapel remains

abertawe & phenrhyn gŵyr / swansea & the gower peninsula

10.2 eternal waters

**Ffynnon Bedr /
St Peter's Well**
Bishop's Wood,
Caswell Bay, nr Murton,
Gower
SS 5904 8837

St Peter's well is very firm walled and stone benches and pavement belonging to it. it never friezeth. it continueth the stream be the weather wet or dry.

local historian, Isaac Hamon, writing in the late seventeenth century

The tumbled ivy-clad medieval stone ruins of St Peter's once-elaborate chapel and priest's house contrast starkly with the two springs here that burst out of the hillside promoting an explosion of greenery, and continue to flow to the sea ... never drying and demonstrating silently, without ostentation, the transience of our human constructions beside the quiet eternal power of nature.

the living wells of wales

abertawe & phenrhyn gŵyr / swansea & the gower peninsula

10.3 pumping iron

Ffynnon pentref Murton Green / Murton Green village well
Gower
SS 586 893

Murton sits between Bishopston and Newton on the Gower, and its large public green is the home to one of the finest village wells in Wales, complete with well-house, metal pump and swirling pool.

10.4 the surfing church

Ffynnon Cenydd / St Cenydd's Well
Llangennith, Gower
SS 429 915

Another fine village well is that at Llangennith on the far west of the Gower Peninsula (best known today as a centre for surfers), but this one is said to have had its origins in the visit of an early saint, Cenydd (or Cynydd, Cenna, Kynyd or Keneth). His church founded here in the sixth century was originally established as a hermitage, though its early buildings were destroyed by Vikings in 986. The present Norman structure was built in the late eleventh and early twelfth century, and is now the largest church on Gower.

As well as the striking Ffynnon Cenydd, another of the great attractions of Llangennith is its ancient St Cenydd's Stone. An Early Christian (probably ninth century) sculpted carving with intricate Celtic knotwork, it was possibly used as a coffin lid or as the base of a Celtic standing cross. It used to lie on the chancel floor and was said to mark the site of the saint's tomb.

Ironically, despite the floor being raised by some four feet in the early 1880s to counteract the ingress of water from the springs below, the church still suffers from rising damp!

opposite:
the two springs and water tank, St Peter's Well, Caswell Bay

left below:
On one visit many years ago, the whole area surrounding St Peter's Well and chapel was festooned with strange ceramic heads.

above:
Murton Green Village Well, Gower

the living wells of wales

above:

St Cenydd's Stone, Llangennith Church; Since 2008, it has been displayed within a recently rediscovered neo-gothic alcove on the south side of the chancel arch.

above:

St Cennydd stained glass window (1945), Llangennith Church The full display shows Cenydd and David on either side of the risen Christ.

above, top to bottom:

Ffynnon Cenydd / St Cenydd's Well, through the lych gate of Llangennith Church;

the fine carvings on the lych gate of Llangennith Church illustrating the life of St Cenydd (created in 1962, by ship's carpenter, William Melling)

opposite:

St Cenydd's Well, Llangennith

abertawe & phenrhyn gŵyr / swansea & the gower peninsula

10.5 cradles of celtic christianity

Ffynnon Illtud / St Illtyd's Well
Llanrhidian, Gower
SS 498 924

The most famous site associated with the fifth century St Illtyd is, of course, that of his monastery and college of divinity – thought to have been the earliest such centre of learning in Britain and the cradle of Celtic Christianity – at Llanilltud Fawr / Llantwit Major) in the Vale of Glamorgan. Such was his importance in South Wales (and beyond), however, that numerous churches, chapels, settlements and other objects venerating his life through the remembrance of his name are to be found throughout the old areas of Glamorgan, Brecknockshire, Carmarthenshire and Pembrokeshire, as well as on the Gower.

Illtyd (or Eltut, and, in Latin, Hildutus) was also known as Illtud Farchog ('Illtud the Knight') for his prowess in battle, serving it is claimed both King Arthur and King Poulentus in his wilder early years. Following an encounter with St Cadoc, however, when he and his hunting party were swallowed up by the earth in punishment for their selfishness, Illtyd (being the sole survivor) changed his ways (including forsaking his wife, Trynihid) and became a hermit.

the living wells of wales

One of the founding fathers of Welsh monasticism – based upon the ascetic principles of the Egyptian, Syrian and Palestinian desert fathers – Illtyd's pupils were said to have included St Patrick, Taliesin the poet, and even St David.

Well versed in the scriptures, in Greek and Latin, as well as in the arts and sciences of literature, philosophy, theology, geometry, rhetoric, grammar and arithmetic, he was believed to have had the power to see into the future and – almost a prerequisite for people of significance of the time – to have been related to King Arthur. Some tales claimed that he was one of the three – alongside Cadoc and Peredur – entrusted with the custody of the Holy Grail … which has led some to even equate Illtyd with Sir Galahad.

Illtyd was thought to have lived as a hermit at Llanrhidian. The sea often flooded his cell, undeterred by the mounds of mud and stones he regularly pilled up to try to keep himself safe and dry. Eventually, it is said, he asked an angel for assistance and the sea subsided. In thanks, he stuck his staff into the ground and a spring gushed forth, creating this holy well with its curative properties.

In later years, Ffynnon Illtyd was known by locals as a 'milk well' because milk was said to flow from it instead of water.

abertawe & phenrhyn gŵyr / swansea & the gower peninsula

below:
the sixth to eleventh century sacred stones beautifully-displayed at the recently-restored Galilee Chapel in St Illtyd's Church, Llantwit Major

below:
the Houelt Cross in the Galilee Chapel of St Illtyd's Church

opposite:
St Illtyd's Well at Llanrhidian, in the garden of the private Bay Tree House across the path from the church he shares with St Rhydian, is a simple though affecting site, well-maintained by the present, always welcoming owner (and his dogs).

the living wells of wales

and ...

10.6: Ffynnon Sanctaidd / Holy Well
nr Reynoldston, Gower
SS 497 899
Near Ffynnon Sanctaidd is Arthur's Stone, a Neolithic burial tomb dating back to 2500 BC, and its wild horses. (Laura, one of my daughters, and I once sat on Arthur's Stone and watched as a mare give birth here, the foal up and running within minutes.)

10.8 Ffynnon y Felin / Mill Well
Parkmill, Gower
SS 543 893
and its nearby interesting heritage centre

10.7: Ffynnon Kithen / Kithen Well
nr Parkmill, Gower
SS 538 896
Little now remains here, although a visit is worthwhile for the so-called 'Giant's Grave' Neolithic long barrow tomb, nearby.

10.9: Ffynnon y Drindod neu Ffynnon Cenydd / Trinity Well or St Cenydd's Well
Ilstone, Gower
SS 553 895
The medieval Trinity Well sits within the remains of Ilston Chapel, an important site in the history of the Baptist Church in Wales. A June 1928 stone tablet here reads: *"To commemorate the foundation in this valley of the first Baptist Church in Wales, 1649-60, and to honour the memory of its founder, John Myles. This ruin is the site of the pre-Reformation Chapel of Trinity Well and is claimed by tradition as a meeting place of the above Cromwellian church."*

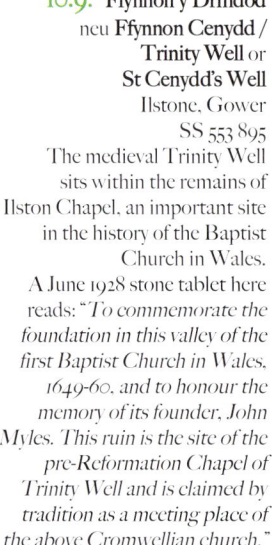

abertawe & phenrhyn gŵyr / swansea & the gower peninsula

another image of
Ffynnon Illtud
and its well guardian dogs,
Llanrhidian, Gower
[10.5]

11 RITES AND WRONGS: sir gaerfyrddin / carmarthenshire

Some wellspring sites offer pleasant walks, along rural lanes or clifftop paths, or along beaches when the tide is out, like St Anthony's at Llansteffan here, or St Dwynwen's on her island off Anglesey.

Some, though, require long hikes, or drives along dangerously narrow lanes, choppy boat journeys, climbs up mountains and hills, fights through head-high overgrowth stung by nettles and scratched by brambles, wades through boggy fields ankle-deep in mud, drops over cliffs, and, on occasion, being menaced by bulls, and sometimes even by farmers.

Others are even more of a struggle to experience. I have already mentioned being repeatedly denied access to Ffynnon Gofer on the Llanover Estate near Abergavenny [6.22]; and the issues surrounding Trefriw Wells and Spa [4.1], and Ffynnon Fair at Trefnant [4.2]. Sadly, as well as the glories of places like St Anthony's Well and Capel Erbach in Carmarthenshire, there is also a spiritually important site newly denied to us, here.

opposite:
Ffynnon Antwn Sant /
St Anthony's Well [11.1]
Scott's Bay,
nr Llansteffan

11.1 a welcome change

**Ffynnon Antwn Sant /
St Anthony's Well**
Scott's Bay,
nr Llansteffan,
Carmarthenshire
SN 346 099

It is thought that the sixth century Welsh hermit, Antwn, took his name from the first Christian hermit, St Anthony of Egypt (c.251-356), whose ascetic teachings had a massive influence on the early Celtic Christian church in Wales.

The Welsh Anthony settled at this tranquil spot on the wide Tywi estuary of Carmarthen Bay and probably used the sacred waters here to baptise his new converts to Christianity. Since that time, it has become famous for its healing properties, and as a wishing well for lovers.

I have made many visits to this beautiful spot, and each time something has changed. At my first visit, a ladle had been provided but with a warning printed along its long handle threatening a 'triple curse' on anyone who stole it; it wasn't there on my next visit! Once, quite recently, Tibetan prayer flags had been hung up around the well, and fresh flowers nearly always grace the Anthony statue.

Scallop (and other) shells are still left as votive offerings, the symbols of pilgrimage after St James, one of Jesus' disciples, was said to have used one on which to travel to Spain in the first century. Pilgrims followed his lead, using them to scoop water and as a simple plate for food, as well as to signify their poverty.

St Anthony has now become the patron saint of all Welsh pilgrims.

left, top to bottom:

the walk to Ffynnon Antwn Sant along Scott's Bay, named after Robert Falcon Scott 'of the Antarctic';

the long-handled ladle left for pilgrims' use at Ffynnon Antwn, with its inscription, *'Never deprive others of my use, for surely, a three-fold retribution shall the keystone loose!'*;

Tibetan prayer flags at St Anthony's Well, 2018

opposite:
the interior of Ffynnon Antwn Sant

sir gaerfyrddin / carmarthenshire

11.2 prophet and loss

**Ffynnon Geler /
St Celer's Well**
Plas Geler, nr Llangeler,
nr Llandysul, Carmarthenshire
SN 3740 3938

My original text for this section included the following words: *"Another kind of welcome awaits you at St Celer's Well, at Plas Geler near Llandysul, where the Russian Orthodox Mission of St Celer of Dyfed is run by the energetic and inspirational Nicole Xenia."* Then I heard that Sister Xenia had died. On 18 October 2018, she was taking her daily walk along her driveway past St Celer's Well. She was found there by the postman the following day.

It is said that the early Christian St Celer lived in caves and woods here and would have used this spring, which made the place a focus for pilgrimage and healing. The Welsh naturalist, linguist and antiquary, Edward Lhuyd (1660-1709) wrote that the site was visited by *"such a concourse of people that no fair in Wales can equal it in multitude"*. Frequented by the infirm in summer (particularly between 21 and 29 June), sufferers after bathing were said to have to lay down on a flagstone in the churchyard, and if they managed to sleep they were certain to be cured.

the living wells of wales

This is a little of what Father Vladimir, who gave Nicole's eulogy at her funeral on 2 November, said:

"Many of you expressed your surprise, 'I always thought she was immortal!' ... but many of us also knew of her mortality: her broken bones, her trouble breathing, her numerous aches and pains – some things she did her best to hide from us.

However, as one person pointed out, all deaths are sudden ... She was active and in motion, up until the moment that she wasn't ..."

Nicole did not complete her walk beside St Celer's Well. She did not wake from her last sleep, and her loss is strongly felt ... by her family, her friends and by those very many people she inspired during the eighty-seven years of her life. What has also been lost is another dedicated well guardian who fully understood the deep-rooted spiritual significance of this sacred place.

left:
Ffynnon Geler,
Plas Geler, nr Llangeler

above:
Sister Nicole Xenia
beside Ffynnon Geler,
June 2018

sir gaerfyrddin / carmarthenshire

11.3 open

Capel Erbach / Erbach Chapel
nr Porthyrhyd,
Carmarthenshire
SN 5295 1472

There are two very special wellsprings in the Porthyrhyd area of Carmarthenshire, though little is known of their origins or histories.

The well which runs under the altar down through the centre of the chapel at Capel Erbach was efficacious in the relief of sprained ankles or broken limbs when they were held under its cooling stream.

Both emerge from within elaborate cathedral-like chapels which would have been built most probably over pagan water worship sites, around the late thirteenth century.

Impressively constructed in similar styles less than a mile apart from one another, currently they have two very different stories to tell.

Such an elaborate architectural structure for only such simple gains seems unlikely however, suggesting other explanations yet to be fully unearthed.

above left:
Capel Begawdin
above left:
Capel Erbach

From the evidence of objects excavated from the drain, offerings of quartz pebbles were favoured, traditionally popular gifts for the Earth Goddess.

the living wells of wales

Though Capel Erbach is on private land, the owners here – if asked nicely – are happy to allow visitors to share the glories of their impressive site. But, as I have already intimated, not all wellsprings offer such a warm welcome.

11.4 closed!

**Ffynnon Capel Begawdin /
Begawdin Chapel Well**
Wern Las,
nr Porthyrhyd,
Carmarthenshire
SN 5115 1471

Lying within a deeply wooded area, a visit to the magical Capel Begawdin was always worth the climbs over fences, walks across fields and, more often than not, the trudges through deep mud to reach its enigmatic pull and promise.

These photographs were taken many years ago, when Capel Begawdin was owned by a woman who understood the importance of allowing access to the once important sacred site on her land.

Sadly, the present owner has very different ideas and forbids entrance to all, even denying on my most recent visit, the very existence of the site.

opposite:
Capel Erbach

above:
Capel Begawdin

the living wells of wales

left:

Ffynnon Capel Begawdin

As I have written before regarding Ffynnon Fair near Trefnant [4.2], it is my strongly held view that access to our heritage should be open to all – as it is in Scotland – and not just to those who have the resources to be able to purchase the land upon which it stands. Not only is this important for our visits but, more significantly, to ensure that the proper care and protection is being given to these often fragile places.

Capel Begawdin and Capel Erbach are two of the greatest architectural wellspring relics in Wales. They contain important aspects of what we as a people have been and are; they are part of our identity and, as such, we should not allow our access to them to be restricted by the privileges of land ownership.

sir gaerfyrddin / carmarthenshire

and ...

II.5: Dwlch i Dduw
nr Llanon,
nr Llanelli
SS 538 068

II.6: Ffynnon yn
Ddragau /
The Well of Tears
Bancyfelin,
nr Carmarthen
SN 340 156

II.7: pistyll ymyl
y ffordd /
roadside fountain
Five Roads,
nr Llanelli
SS 489 054

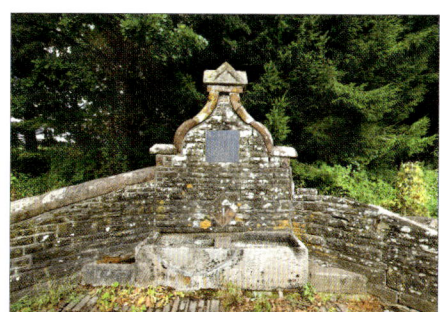

II.8: cafn ymyl
y ffordd /
roadside trough
Five Roads,
nr Llanelli
SS 491 055

II.9: pistyll goffa
Rees Goring
Thomas / Rees
Goring Thomas
memorial fountain
Llanon,
nr Llanelli
SN 540 084

II.10: 'Ogofdy Hygrea' /
'The Grotto of Hygrea'
Pont Felin Gât,
National Botanical Garden
of Wales, Llanarthne,
nr Carmarthen
SN 516 178
a chalybeate spring which
is currently undergoing
a major restoration

12 PUSHED TO THE MARGINS:
sir benfro / pembrokeshire

opposite:

Ffynhonnau Sain Gofan /
St Govan's Wells [12.6]
nr Bosherston,
Pembrokeshire

If I were called in
To construct a religion
I should make use of water.
Going to church
Would entail a fording
To dry, different clothes;
My litany would employ
Images of sousing,
A furious devout drench,
And I should raise in the east
A glass of water
Where any-angled light
Would congregate endlessly.

'Water' by Philip Larkin (1922-1985)

Although there are holy wells to be found throughout the British Isles, they are, it seems, most numerous in those places on the margins: in Cornwall, in Scotland, in Ireland ... and, here in Wales. In addition, within these countries, it is in the furthest-off places – the far west or the far north, or on our isolated islands – that the most special sites are usually to be found.

the living wells of wales

The fact that Wales is blessed with more than its fair share of spiritually significant holy well and other sites is no geographical coincidence. As the things that really should matter are pushed to the peripheries, it is only at these extremities – the distant places, furthest from what is considered to be real, to be of most import within a world which prioritises the superficial and celebrates the trivial and the temporary – it's only here that ideas like those contained deep within these ancient well pools are remembered, and survive, until they are once again deemed useful.

Like the sites along the arm of the Llŷn Peninsula which all led towards Ynys Enlli, the island of the saints, the ultimate destination of pilgrim visitors to most wellsprings throughout Pembrokeshire was and is the holy city of St Davids.

In the sixth century, Non gave birth here to Dewi Ddyfrwr ('David the Water Drinker'), whose early monastic community, built in a grassy hollow a short distance from the sea, gradually evolved into a cathedral, its founder eventually becoming the patron saint of Wales, Dewi Sant, attracting pilgrims from throughout Britain and beyond. Most of Pembrokeshire's wells, then, would have developed their importance through this 'faith-tourism', two trips to St Davids being equal to one to Rome, and three trips to one to Jerusalem.

The holy wells here would have been convenient stopping places for both physical and spiritual recuperation for pilgrims on their trails north and south to St Davids, following in the saint's footsteps to one of the great historic shrines of Christendom.

Although Pembrokeshire is rich with sacred spring and holy well sites, few people know of their locations and the tales associated with these once-magical places. There are still regularly visited wellspring sites here – at St Non's [12.17] near St Davids, St Govan's [12.6] near Bosherston (although people often fail to spot either of his two holy wells, there), and, to a lesser extent, the three wells below the church at Gumfreston [12.1] near Tenby. These, however, are very much the exceptions to the rule, as most are neglected and unloved, and in danger of disappearing altogether. Most are unmarked and have no interpretation; and few of us still remember the rich library of powerful stories – usually associated with their origins and usage – that they still can tell us.

left and opposite:
stained glass windows
of St Non and St David,
St Mary's Church,
Strata Florida

12.1 let the new year in

Ffynhonnau Sanctaidd Gumfreston / Gumfreston Holy Wells
St Lawrence Church,
Gumfreston,
nr Tenby,
Pembrokeshire
SN 109 011

All three wells below Gumfreston's fourteenth century church of St Lawrence have for many centuries been held to possess great medicinal properties, each one – though closely grouped – providing distinctly different water, offering a different remedy to the sick. The highest well, of pure water, was believed to cure ailments associated with the legs (and is in the shape of a leg); the middle (arm-shaped) well was of chalybeate and assisted the hands and the arms; and the lower circular bubbling pool was sulphurous and brought sight to blind eyes.

Francis Jones tells us of the custom in Gumfreston and the other wells of South Pembrokeshire of 'New Year's Water', which children drew and carried to local houses to sprinkle on their residents' front doors with sprigs of evergreen or box. The song they sang has clear pagan as well as Christian resonances, the 'fair maid' representing both the Virgin Mary as well as the Earth Goddess:

Here we bring new water
   from the well so clear,
For to worship God with,
   this happy new year;
Sing levy dew, sing levy dew,
   the water and the wine,
With seven bright gold wires,
   the bugles that do shine;

Sing reign of fair maid,
   with gold upon her toe,
Open you the west door,
   and turn the old year go;
Sing reign of fair maid,
   with gold upon her chin,
Open you the east door,
   and let the new year in.

the living wells of wales

Coflein (the online database for the National Monuments Record of Wales) confirms what I have always felt on my many visits here, that the *"proximity of the wells to the church suggests this is an example of a Christian site chosen in the Dark Ages to absorb an earlier pagan well-cult".*

The site and the church were for many years cared for by a dedicated and knowledgeable couple, Trevor and Chris Silverman. Sadly, however, Trevor has recently died and Chris has moved away, a huge double loss for Gumfreston and for Wales.

What follows is part of the 'Appreciation' I delivered at Trevor's funeral at St Gwyndaf's Church, Llanwnda [12.15] on 26 January 2018:

I think I first crossed paths with Trevor in 2005.

I was researching my first book on the holy wells of Wales, and the two things that immediately struck me about him were his knowledge of the subject (particularly of the wellsprings throughout Pembrokeshire), but, more significantly I think, his willingness to share his research and, indeed, his passion. (I'm not sure I would have gotten that first book to print without him.) And this generosity continued throughout all the years I knew him.

Fraser, in his 1890 book The Golden Bough *wrote that "Every man is more or less his own magician", and Trevor was certainly one of these, making things appear that we'd forgotten about, and revealing new treasures in words and in the soil.*

And, as well as revealing, protecting, making accessible and publicising the holy well at Porthclais [12.18], *he provided a similar service here at Llanwnda and at Gumfreston, where he played his part in the equally inspiring example of contemporary well guardianship in Chris' always profoundly moving Easter Sunday services, when the three nails of Christ's crucifixion were thrown into the three wells, powerfully mirroring, in the process, the tradition of casting medal objects into waters thought to be sacred, in pre-Christian days.*

left:
the 'Ceremony of the Nails', Gumfreston Holy Wells, Easter Sunday 2006 (including Chris and Trevor Silverman, and the author's mother and late father amongst the small congregation)

opposite, clockwise from the left:
Gumfreston Holy Wells; St Lawrence's Church, Gumfreston; Some of the American pilgrims I guided on a tour of the holy wells of Wales in May 2018, singing inside St Lawrence's Church (left to right: Constance Pepin, Tom Kurz, Kathy Keleher)

sir benfro / pembrokeshire

the living wells of wales

right:
the Gumfreston
Eye Well
(Note the three nails
ready to be thrown
into the waters.)

below:
the author's mother at
Gumfreston Wells

Many writers have been inspired by their visits to Gumfreston, and to the other Pembrokeshire wellspring sites.

Here is a poem written by Tony Curtis, from his 2007 collection *Crossing Over*.

At Gumfreston Church

At Gumfreston Church
That evening, after a hard, hot drive,
The dark lane's coolness of trees
Was like water walked into,
Calm and quiet – no traffic,
Deep shadows,
All the gulls out at sea.

Augustus and Gwen's father
Walked the two miles from Tenby
Every Sunday to play the organ here.
I search for his headstone and find no-one
But Ken Handicott the grocer
I worked for one school summer holiday
Forty years ago.

They leave the church door unlocked:
There is no congregation but the curious passing folk.
And inside is the simple splendour of stone font,
Low wooden roof, draped altar,
Norman-built
On earlier significance – St Teilo, St Bridget.
The place shivers in the dusk
And moves into another night.

Here were the early missions, saints and sinners
Crossing the Irish Sea, moving east
With their crosses and swords.
Here was a quay, a village the river Ritec
Joined to the sea that led to the world.

And here, behind the church, before the woods
Where the Magdalens brought their lepers,
Still flow the three springs of purity
And healing, coming to us from a depth.
Water that plays the oldest music.

Without thinking
I take a handful
And with wet, cool fingers
Cross myself.

12.2 on the arm of pembrokeshire

Ffynnon Ddeiniol / St Deiniol's Well
Penally, nr Tenby,
Pembrokeshire
SS 117 993

There are three wells currently to be seen at Penally, all connected to the Abbey (now a fine restaurant and hotel). The most significant, the Grade 2 Listed St Deiniol's Well stands in front of a private house, across the narrow lane from the still-impressive ruins of St Deiniol's Chapel in the grounds of Penally Abbey. Water from the well still flows down to the edge of the chapel.

Deiniol began his saintly life as a hermit *"on the arm of Pembrokeshire"*. After a long pilgrimage to Jerusalem, he came home, bringing with him, it is said, a jar containing water from the River Jordan. Finding that the local water supply had dried up, he thrust his staff into the earth and poured the precious water around it. The staff became a tree and a spring bubbled up from the ground, the site thenceforth becoming a focus of pilgrimage and for the curing of diseases.

sir benfro / pembrokeshire

12.5 care and repair

**Ffynnon Porth Lliw /
Port Clew Holy Well**
Freshwater East, nr Tenby,
Pembrokeshire
SN 0207 9861

I was guided to this evocative site, recently re-dedicated by Fr Gildas of Caldey Island, by the joint landowner (and consultant geologist), Sid Howells. While Mr Howells is open to people visiting both the well and the nearby ruins of its medieval chapel (dedication unknown), he asks that visitors contact him (or his neighbour) first, to act as guide. While I initially viewed this as an imposition, the well is not easy to find and Mr Howells is very knowledgeable and entertaining, suggesting other points of interest, including a sunken 'pilgrims' lane', pagan / saints' 'burial mound', the chapel orchard, etc., en route.

In 2009, Dyfed Archeological Trust worked at the site and found evidence of early medieval building structures, and cist burials, including some human skeletal remains. Their Report suggested that the site was occupied from 550 AD onwards, with the current chapel being built in the thirteenth century, but on these much earlier foundations.

The well itself is set into a bank, its waters flowing into a small pool in a beautifully hidden spot, overhung by trees. Mr Howells cleared out the site, which was being threatened by straying cattle.

He also found the well's metal gate, and has replaced it. His love for the site ensures its survival.

opposite,
clockwise from top left:

The so-called **Ffynnon Teilo / St Teilo's Well** [12.3 / SS 118 992] on the green below the Abbey Hotel, and outside its outer walls, is well-hidden today in bushes and secured with an unattractive metal gate;

the ruins of St Deiniol's Chapel, Penally;

The third wellspring site at Penally, the nicely-landscaped **Ffynnon 'Tŷ' / 'House' Well** [12.4 / SS 118 993], is a large, circular brick-lined basin full of clear water, protected by a recently-constructed aluminium gate;

American pilgrims at St Deiniol's Well, May 2018 (left to right: Herb Nichols, Annette Nichols, Constance Pepin)

right:
Port Clew chapel ruins;
Ffynnon Porth Lliw, Freshwater East

the living wells of wales

12.6 the voice of the wells

Ffynhonnau Sain Gofan / St Govan's Wells
nr Bosherston,
Pembrokeshire
SR 967 929

Set within the Pembrokeshire Coast National Park, on the Wales Coast Path, the great wellspring jewel in this area is St Govan's Chapel. Squeezed into a cleft in the cliff walls, it is thought to have been built sometime between 1300 and 1500, based upon Govan's original plan. It is accessed by a flight of steep stone steps, the number of which is said to vary – as often seems to be the case at these special sites – depending on whether you are going up or down!

St Govan may have been the sixth century Gobham, Abbot of Dairinis in County Wexford, or perhaps even Gawain of Arthurian fame, retiring here after his king's death.

If the former, then he was an Irish abbot who choose to live out his last years here as a hermit, building the first chapel, and dying in the year 586. But, no one really knows. It is even suggested that 'he' was Covan, the widow of an Irish king who chose to spend her final days in contemplation at this isolated spot.

opposite:
Sid Howells
at Ffynnon Porth Lliw

right:
St Govan's Chapel

the living wells of wales

One tale tells of Govan being chased by pirates and a cleft opening in the cliff face to hide him where his chapel now stands, and closing until his pursuers had gone. Others claimed that he was a reformed thief. Some say that hand prints in the rock floor of the cave behind the chapel's altar – used perhaps as a rough shelter before the chapel was built – are those of the saint himself. Others believe that his body is still buried beneath the altar here.

There are actually two wells at St Govan's: one with its arched stone well-housing below the chapel towards the sea, famed once for its ability to cure lameness, and now sadly dry; and the other set into the floor of the chapel itself, just to the left of the upper door, which it was claimed relieved eye complaints, skin diseases and rheumatism.

right:
St Govan's (two) Wells

opposite:
the antechamber and altar
inside St Govan's Chapel, 2008
(the cross and wheel decorations
are now largely gone)

sir benfro / pembrokeshire

What is certain, however, is that this isolated setting, hidden between rocks and the sea with only birds, fish and seals for company, would have provided a perfect hermitage for the devote believer:

St Govan, he built him a cell
By the side of the Pembroke sea,
And there, as the crannied sea-gulls
  dwell,
In a tiny, secret citadel
He sighed for eternity.

St Govan, he built him a cell
Between the wild sky and the sea,
Where the sunsets redden the rolling
  swell
And brooding splendour has thrown
  her spell
On valley and moorland lea.

St Govan still lies in his cell,
But his soul, long since, is free,
And one may wonder –
  and who can tell –
If good St Govan likes Heaven
  as well
As his cell by that sounding sea?

AG Prys-Jones

the living wells of wales

Poets, painters and composers – as well as writers and photographers like myself – have all drawn inspiration from places like St Govan's.

An exciting new project, *The Voice of the Wells*, based upon our wellspring cultures, is being developed by St Davids' resident Jo MacGregor and her partner, Dan. Here are some of her thoughts:

There is voice in everything; it's just a case of tuning in long enough to decipher it.

'The Voice of the Wells' is a phrase coined by author Sharon Blackie in her exceptional book If Women Rose Rooted. *The phrase stuck with me and its seed has been pushing up shoots, gradually manifesting a musical project.*

I have always sung in sea caves and rocky crevices, chapel ruins and wells. The stony parameters of these spaces give a raw resonance to the human voice ... and something more.

In any space, natural or otherwise, if you sing one note at a time, you will find some that jar and have dissonance, and some that resonate and feel totally fluid. In these rocky spaces near the edges of Celtic lands, I have found that there is a point somewhere in these notes where the space almost sings back.

It feels to me as though the very walls of a cave, or stones of an arched well, are joining in and beginning to sing their story, their sorrow, their joy into the notes.

For me, as a singer, this is a small way that I can say 'our lands are important, they have stories locked inside them'. These places have names which are written deep in our bones, which we would do well to remember, and give attention to.

Jo and her team are planning to create an album of music, a song for each of the selected spaces, "*as an offering to those who are waking up and seeking a re-connection with the land, and themselves*".

above and opposite near:

local musicians,
Jo and Dan MacGregor
at St Govan's Chapel
and wells

opposite, far:

Bletherston Church

sir benfro / pembrokeshire

12.7 pooling resources

**Ffynnon Drefelen /
Bletherston Church Well**
nr Narbeth,
Pembrokeshire
SN 0645 2175

The impressive stone basin and extensive pool of Bletherston Holy Well is located a little to the north of St Mary's (originally St Keyne's) Church in Bletherston, though access is easiest from the road.

The waters here were said to have been used for baptisms in the church, as well as in the relief of children's ailments.

This beautiful, though little-known site deserves to be more regularly visited and much better cared for (no locals knew of its existence except the farmer).

12.8 a reliable source

**Ffynnon Leonard /
St Leonard's Well**
Crundale Rath, Rudbaxton,
Pembrokeshire
SM 9856 1890

Situated high up on the northeastern slope of an Iron Age hillfort on Crundale Rath, the presence of a pure and reliable source of water was undoubtedly one of the main reasons for developing a settlement here, though the well is now dry.

The Christianised St Leonard's Well specialised in eye cures. A medieval chapel or hospice dedicated to the saint once stood nearby, but nothing of it now remains. Even the well, it seems, is slowly being swallowed by vegetation.

sir benfro / pembrokeshire

opposite far:
Bletherston Church Well

opposite near:
The letters carved above St Leonard's Well read *'Fons Sti Leonardi'*, probably added during the site's restoration in 1915;

the interior of St Leonard's Well

left:
St Leonard's Well on Crundale Rath

the living wells of wales

12.9 a sort of vanity fair

**Ffynnon Garadoc /
St Caradoc's Well**
Haverfordwest,
Pembrokeshire
SM 942 143

St Caradoc's Well isn't always easy to find, set as it is into the northern bank of Merlin's Brook, dropping down from the path to the river, but it certainly rewards perseverance in the search.

Caradoc is believed to have lived at nearby Haroldston. A native of Brecknockshire, he was, in his early years, harpist at the court of Rhys, the Prince of South Wales, until after a mishap with his master's favourite dogs, he was sacked, broke his lance and turned to God via Llandaff, Gower, Barry Island, and eventually Pembrokeshire, at which point his contact with this well began.

Ffynnon Garadoc was said to have been a favourite haunt of this hermit saint, and was also visited by lovers on Easter Monday morning, when *"a sort of vanity Fair, where cakes were sold and country Games celebrated"*. It was believed that a young woman could see the face of her future husband in this well if, on Easter Monday, she threw three pins into the water. It is reported that one disappointed soul though saw *"the evil face of a hairy monster"*!

left:
the shrine of St Caradoc at St David's Cathedral;

St Caradoc's Well, Haverfordwest

opposite:
St Bride's Inn and Well, Little Haven

12.10 hot dragons and cool beer

Ffynnon Tafarn Sain Ffraid / St Bride's Inn Well
Little Haven, nr Haverfordwest, Pembrokeshire
SM 942 143

Although this is one of Pembrokeshire's most interesting and unusual wells – situated in a room off the bar of St Bride's Inn at Little Haven – little is known of its origins or usage ... despite the presence of red and green inflatable dragons and the hotel's St Bride naming.

A black and white photograph in the bar shows the small room full of barrels, in order to keep the beer cool ... but that's about it.

the living wells of wales

12.11 aidan's enclosure ?

**Ffynnon Gastell Llawhaden /
Llawhaden Castle Well**
Llawhaden, nr Haverfordwest,
Pembrokeshire
SN 074 174

Llawhaden Castle was built as one of the several impressive residences by and for the bishops of St Davids. Its construction began as early as 1115, though what can be seen today

is largely from the late fourteenth century. Llawhaden is an anglicised form of the Welsh Llanhuadain, meaning the monastic enclosure of St Aidan, the Irish monk who founded his church here on the banks of the Eastern Cleddau in the sixth century.

above:
St Bride's Inn Well,
Little Haven

right top to bottom:
Llawhaden Castle;
St Aidan's Church,
Llawhaden

opposite:
Llawhaden Castle Well

sir benfro / pembrokeshire

the living wells of wales

12.12 portals to the underworld

Pistyll Sanctaidd Castell Henllys / Castell Henllys sacred spring
nr Nevern, Pembrokeshire
SN 115 393

Castell Henllys is unique. It is the only location in Britain where accurately reconstructed roundhouses and other buildings stand on the exact site of their originals, dating back to as far as 300 BC. The reconstructions here include a sacred spring, recognising

the importance of such sites within the spiritual world-view of our earliest ancestors:

Iron Age people believed water was a meeting place of the world of the gods and the world of the people. Villagers left precious offerings for the gods to thank them for all that nature gave them and to protect them against dangers. Places such as springs, lakes, rivers and swamps were revered as they were seen as portals to the underworld.

from the *Castell Henllys Guidebook*

sir benfro / pembrokeshire

opposite, left to right:
reconstructed roundhouse;
Castell Henllys sacred spring

above:
images from the
Castell Henllys site

12.13 faith in the well

**Ffynnon yr Ychen /
St Teilo's Well**
nr Llangolman,
nr Pembroke
SN 101 270

... the faith in the well continues in a measure intact, when the walls of the church have fallen into utter decay. Such is the great persistence of some ancient beliefs; and in this particular instance we have a succession which seems to point unmistakably to an ancient priesthood of this spring of water.

from *Sacred Wells in Wales*
by John Rhŷs and TE Morris
writing about St Teilo's Well
in *Folk-Lore*, Volume 4 (1893)

At the strange series of stone-walled pools near the village of Llangolman that make up St Teilo's Well, the saint's skull was used in the healing process, clearly a christianised adaptation of the Celtic Cult of the Head. Those who drank water from it here, it was said, would be cured of all illnesses of the chest, and particularly whooping-cough. To receive the full benefit from the waters, however, the skull had to be handed to the sufferer by the senior living member of the local Melchior family.

The story is told of a carriage full of invalids from the Gower Peninsula coming to take the waters here, but returning home no better for their long trip. On being told of the drinking protocol, however, they returned, sought the use of the saint's skull and all *"departed in excellent health"*. Only the top of the skull survives and it is now in the care of Llandaff Cathedral. However, as the saint is said to have triplicated himself after death (in order to satisfy the competing demands for relics of Llandaff Cathedral, Llandeilo Fawr and Penally Abbey), it is not clear from which of the three this one comes. It has even been suggested that the bone is that of a young woman, not an old man (which Teilo would have been at the time of his death).

Today – in a sad contradiction of Rhŷs and Morris' *"faith in the well"* – cows and sheep graze freely here (appropriate, perhaps, as one of its alternative names is the 'Oxen Well'). This is seriously damaging the stones, and – combined with its unkempt, overgrown and often-waterlogged nature – makes it almost impossible to fully appreciate the site, let alone get near to feeling anything of its spirit and significance for those who once considered it a healing and holy place.

the living wells of wales

above:
St Teilo's Well

12.14 rags, crosses, beads and flowers

**Ffynnon Gapan /
Llanllawer Sainted Well**
nr Llanychaer, nr Fishguard,
Pembrokeshire
SM 9872 3601

Local tradition suggested that the water from the finely built, stone-vaulted Llanllawer Sainted (or Holy) Well granted wishes both good and bad depending on whether the proffered pin was straight or bent. Situated above the Gwaun Valley, it is sometimes known as Ffynnon Gapan or the 'Lintel Well'. Richard Fenton described it as a healing well in 1810 (*A Historical Tour through Pembrokeshire*), especially efficacious for treating eyes.

The adjacent church – now in great distress – was rebuilt in the mid nineteenth century, incorporating ninth and tenth century elements. It lies within an elliptical enclosure suggesting the Christian adoption of an originally-pagan site.

On previous visits to Ffynnon Gapan, the waters have bubbled and flowed freely and 'clouties' and other offerings were abundant; on my most recent visit it was dry, reflecting perhaps the state of the church above it, although rags, crosses, beads and flowers were still being left here.

above:
Ffynnon Gapan,
nr Llanychaer

the living wells of wales

sir benfro / pembrokeshire

opposite, top to bottom:

the dry interior of
Ffynnon Gapan,
nr Llanychaer;

Two seventh century stone wheel crosses on either side of the gate to Llanllawer church may have been erected to prevent the entrance of evil spirits.

St David's Church
at Llanllawer,
locked and rapidly
decaying

12.15 no fishing

Ffynnon Wnda / St Wnda's Well
Llanwnda, nr Fishguard,
Pembrokeshire
SM 9318 3954

St Gwyndaf, *"an irascible Breton"*, was a sixth century associate of St Aidan ... until they fell out. It was reported that Gwyndaf, after a quarrel with his sainted colleague, cursed the stream he was crossing not far from Fishguard.

right:
St Gwyndaf's Church,
Llanwnda and its
cross-marked early Christian
stones set into its walls,
discovered during restoration work
in 1881. It was here that
Trevor Silverman's
funeral service was held
in January 2018
[see 12.1].

It seems that Gwyndaf had been thrown from his horse and broken his leg when a fish suddenly leapt from the water. The stream, it is said, never again supported fish.

left:

the path to Llanwnda Holy Well
This was another site cared for by the late Trevor and Chris Silverman, displaying another of his simple signs, recycling broken slate tiles from the roof of Gumfreston Church [12.1].

sir benfro / pembrokeshire

right :
Trevor and
Chris Silverman
at Ffynnon Wnda,
nr Fishguard

Ffynnon Wnda and Llanwnda near Fishguard, the well and the church dedicated to the petulant saint, were major resting places on the pilgrim road to Saint Davids, particularly for those arriving by boat from Ireland.

St Gwyndaf eventually retired to Bardsey Island, where he died.

right :
Ffynnon Wnda

12.16 a narrow path

**Ffynnon Nicolas /
St Nicholas' Well**
St Nicholas, nr Fishguard,
Pembrokeshire
SM 901 356

This is a wonderful site ... if you can find it. There are no signs and the well housing is hidden in dense and often boggy ancient woodland. Stand with your back to the community centre at St Nicholas and walk straight across the grass towards a single telegraph pole, this will lead you to the path into the trees. When two paths cross, go straight ahead and follow the narrow curving overgrown path to the well. It's a fine structure with its clear waters feeding several large irregular pools at a site with a powerful primitive atmosphere.

To add to the blessings here, there are three fifth to sixth century inscribed stones inside its church at St Nicholas. The first, known as the 'Tuncetace Stone', is set into one of the chancel walls and was once incorporated within a nearby stile. It is inscribed in Latin: *Tuncetace uxsor daari hic iacet* ('Here lies Tuncetace, the wife of Daarus'). The other two are located close to the second chancel arch and were once used as gateposts in a nearby farm (like those at Llanllawer [12.14]). One is decorated with a small cross and the name *Paani*.

left, and opposite left:
Ffynnon Nicolas /
St Nicholas' Well

opposite right:
the interior of
St Nicholas Church
and two of its
ancient stones

sir benfro / pembrokeshire

the living wells of wales

And, so to the St Davids Peninsula, the final destination. Although hidden away at its south-western extremity, this is the spiritual heart of Wales. *The Mabinogion* called it *"gwlad hud a lledrith"*, the 'land of magic and enchantment'.

12.17 giving birth to a new idea

Ffynnon Santes Non / St Non's Well
nr St Davids, Pembrokeshire
SM 7510 2438

This already magical area of pagan circles and standing stones was the place where Nonnita, Nonna, Nun, Nonni or as she has come to be more generally known St Non is said to have given birth to David around the year 589 AD. There are almost as many versions of her story as there are of her name. One claims that she was the grand-daughter of the powerful chieftain, Brychan Brycheiniog, whose twelve sons and twelve daughters played such a major role in spreading Christianity throughout South Wales, and a relative of the legendary Uthyr Pendragon; another that she was an Irish princess. In one tale she was married to Sanddé or Sant, the King of Ceredigion; in another Sanddé had taken her against the birth of her son, who was to become the patron saint of the Welsh, occurred, appropriately perhaps, during a violent thunderstorm which protected her from his anger. In a further story, her powerful birth pangs cracked the rock upon which her church was to be built. All agree, though, that at the moment of David's birth, the spring that was to bear her name burst forth from the ground.

After its latest extensive renovation, the well was re-dedicated in July 1951 and is now the destination of regular pilgrimages, situated as it is on its cliff-top location beside the Pembrokeshire Coastal Path, a little to the south of St Davids. Above the well and the chapel ruins is a small new Catholic chapel dedicated to Our Lady and St Non, with fine stained glass windows of the saints Bridget, Catherine, Margaret and Non, all believed to be aspects of the Mother Goddess.

sir benfro / pembrokeshire

opposite, left to right:

Ted Harrison is an artist based in Wales and in Shetland. He visited thirty-five holy well sites throughout Wales, and painted them using the water from each well. ("*I still have 35 labeled plastic bottles of holy water at home!*") His work was exhibited in St David's Cathedral. This is his response to Ffynnon Non;

stained glass images of Non in the chapel above St Non's Well

above:
the interior and exterior of St Non's Well

sir benfro / pembrokeshire

12.18 elvis is in the house *

**Ffynnon Ddewi /
St David's Well**
Porthclais,
nr St Davids,
Pembrokeshire
SM 739 242

*hidden beneath a dense growth
of brambles /
The location of the well was an area
of impenetrable woodland that was
fenced off and inaccessible.*

sundry field notes on visits to
Ffynnon Ddewi, 1921 and 2011

Ffynnon Ddewi is another site liberated from its covering of trees, earth and decades of overgrowth and then cared for by the late Trevor Silverman, complete with another of his signature slate-tile signs.

It tells the next chapter in St David's story as it is thought that this was the location of his baptism, conducted by St Elvi, Ailbhe, Aelbyw or Elvis, Bishop of Munster (although that service is also claimed to have taken place at his own **St Elvi's Well** [SM 813 240] near Solva).

* And if more proof was needed the St Elvis Well looks towards the Preseli Mountains!

opposite:
Of St Non's Well, Browne Willis
writing in the early eighteenth century reported that
*"Some old simple People go still to visit this Saint …
expecially upon St Non's Day, which they keep holy,
and offer Pins, Pebbles, Etc."*
And R Fenton writing in 1903 said that
"the bottom of the well shone with votive brass".

top image, left to right:
American holy well pilgrims at St Non's Chapel,
May 2018 (top image, left to right: Steve Damas,
Nancy Damas, Hywel Roberts, Louisa Keleher,
Kathy Keleher, Tom Kurz, Greg Tromiczak,
Herb Nichols, Annette Nichols, Constance Pepin)

the living wells of wales

Browne Willis, writing in 1715 reported that Ffynnon Ddewi had a spring or water spout running under a chapel here *"into a cistern at ye east under ye pinion or gable of ye building"*. No remains of this chapel have yet been found. And this is Nona Rees, writing in the 1950s: *"the waters ran from a cowl-shaped well head through a little stone channel into a stone basin"*.

Porthclais was the main port for St Davids, and the only really safe haven on the peninsula. It is easy to imagine the early saints and later pilgrim visitors arriving here and paying their first respects at Dewi's well before their short journey to his shrine.

opposite left:
Porthclais estuary and harbour

opposite right:
Ffynnon Ddewi / St David's Well, Porthclais

above:
the late Trefor Silverman at the entrance to the Porthclais holy well;

American pilgrims visiting Ffynnon Ddewi (left to right: Nancy Damas, Steve Damas, Constance Pepin, Greg Tromiczak)

right:
St David's Cathedral

12.19 in the footsteps of 'dewi ddyfrwr'

Pistyll Dewi / St David's Spring
St David's Cathedral,
Pembrokeshire
SM 739 242

He took bread and watercress,
The water of rivers,
Horsehair as his only dress,
Penitent at the fountain's edge.

Lewis Glyn Cothi (1420-1490), on St David

Although there are a few interesting wellspring sites in St Davids city itself (**Whitewell** [12.49]; **Ffynnon-y-Cwcwll** [12.43]), sadly, nothing today remains of Dewi Ddyfrwr (or David 'the Water Drinker')'s famous **Pistyll Dewi**, although we do have a good idea where it might have been.

Situated in the grounds to the east end of St David's Cathedral, it is said to have been created at a time of drought when St David himself prayed for a new water supply. On occasion, it even ran with wine and with milk.

the living wells of wales

far left:
the probable site of Pistyll Dewi

left:
icons of David and Non on the newly-renovated St David's Shrine in St David's Cathedral

opposite, near:
the interior of St David's Cathedral

opposite far:
St Teilo's Well, 2012, before clearance

sir benfro / pembrokeshire

12.20 st teilo's friends

**Ffynnon Sant Teilo /
St Teilo's Well**
Llandeloy, nr St Davids,
Pembrokeshire
SM 857 267

This holy well is dedicated to St Teilo, already encountered at Llandeilo [6.18], Penally [12.3] and near Llangolman [12.13]. Situated to the south of Llandeloy church, and surrounded by a low ring of stones, it is sometimes difficult to locate amongst an overgrown mass of vegetation and nettles. On my last trip, however, a green path had been mowed to it, and its stones and waters cleaned (probably by the organisation that now cares for its church).

The appropriately named Friends of Friendless Churches exists to save historic places of worship from demolition or decay. These are the words of Ivor Bulmer-Thomas at the time when he set up the organisation in 1957: *"An ancient and beautiful church fulfills its primary function merely by existing. It is, in itself, and irrespective of the numbers using it, an act of worship ... their message is delivered not for half an hour on Sundays, but every hour of every day of every year, and not merely to those who enter, but to all who pass by"*, a powerful sentiment that could be equally applied to our sacred spring and holy well sites.

Still a consecrated building though no longer used for regular worship, the Arts and Crafts designed church of

St Teilo here in Llandeloy (from its twelfth century origins, and roofless at the beginning of the twentieth century) is a real joy. Its intricate and beautifully carved screen, spiral stair, rood loft, altar and reredos, were all constructed between 1925 and 1926.

the living wells of wales

sir benfro / pembrokeshire

12.21 benefits culture

Ffynnon Faiddog (Maedog) / St Aidan's Well
Whitesands Bay,
nr St Davids,
Pembrokeshire
SM 7384 2720

There is an enormous mismatch between the currently unimpressive remains of St Maedog's Well beside the narrow road down to Whitesands Bay near St Davids ... and the tales it can still tell.

St Aidan (or Maedog in Welsh) of Ferns in County Wexford – born in 558 and died c.623 – is not to be confused with the St Aidan of Lindisfarne fame. Uncertainty about our Aidan's origins, though – his wide-ranging activities in both Ireland and Wales, and the alternative dates recorded for his death – have suggested to some that he is, in fact, the conflation of two saints, one Irish and one British ... or maybe he just used his time on this earth to the greatest effect.

The name Aidan means 'fire' and is related to the god of the underworld in Irish mythology, and he certainly did have a very special range of powers. He was said to have floated across a lake on a stone for his baptism; he both cured the sick and dying as well as sometimes reversing a cure, considering sickness to be *"good for the soul"*; he was a great curser; and defeated a whole Saxon army by rolling stones onto them.

He was also known for his great benevolence, on one occasion permitting beef to be eaten during Lent with the explanation that the meat was merely *"milk and vegetables in condensed form"*. He repaired a broken beer jug he had dropped that he was taking to give to his fellow monks by making the sign of the cross over it; and made roads appear through inpenetrable bogland.

He also brought drowned boys back to life; and was famed for taking hives of bees from Wales to Ireland where, apparently, they were scarce at the time.

opposite:
St Teilo's Well, 2018, after clearance

left:
the font and altar at St Teilo's Church, Llandeloy

above:
Luke Rowlands at Parc y Capel, above Whitesands Bay, nr St Davids
The sixth century St Patrick's Chapel ruin is near to the spot where St Faiddog's boat is said to have landed, and where, some say, St David received some of his education. (I received mine from Luke.)

Ffynnon Faiddog overlooks the hills of Carn Llidl along the coast to the north and the popular beach of Whitesands to the west. Its current unattractive state is due to 1960s road widening that drained the well. Jacki Sime, who lives at Ffynnon Faiddog, the cottage across the lane from the well, is a published photographer and writer with a background in marine environmental protection and is a founder member of the St Davids Eco Group. She has plans as significant and potentially miraculous as any of those attributed to St Aidan:

I have made it my mission to remove litter from around the coast, predominantly focusing on rubbish that accumulates on the more inaccessible coves and beaches. The accumulation of intact plastic and small plastic pieces on and above the strand line has escalated over the last few years. Interestingly, top of the discarded rubbish list is plastic water bottles, followed by water bottle tops, fishing tackle, and plastic milk bottles.

So, I plan to launch a scheme throughout the peninsula, encouraging both locals and visitors to cease buying water in plastic bottles and introduce for sale the peninsula's own, not-for-profit reusable stainless steel water bottles.

There would be no better way of putting this concept into action than to have spring water accessible for consumption again from Ffynnon Faiddog. Not only would it be amazing to have spring water available locally and free, but also the well, together with the bottles, have the potential to be utilised as an imaginative educational tool, making the St Davids Peninsula a flagship model for freeing Wales of plastic bottles.

This is an inspiring example of the kind of response to the neglect and decay of so many once-important well-spring sites, responses that suit the needs of today and, in the process, help create a more responsible and healthy tomorrow for both its human and animal occupants.

sir benfro / pembrokeshire

opposite:

Jacki Sime
at Ffynnon Faiddog;
and what remains today
of her well beside the path
to Whitesands Bay

left:

the view of Carn Llidl
from Ffynnon Faiddog

12.22 a last resting place

Naw Ffynnon / Nine Wells
nr Solva,
Pembrokeshire
SM 786 24

Nine Wells, near Solva, was the 'last resting place' for pilgrims before arriving at their main destination, the shrine of the patron saint of Wales at St Davids. One can imagine the scene here as prayers were chanted, mass celebrated, candles lit, rosaries dipped in the various waters, food and drink served, water bottles filled, horses fed, watered and rested, and sick and weary pilgrims bathed in ecstatic anticipation of the final leg of their spiritual journey.

Historically, Nine Wells was the sister well to St Non's [12.17], with each affording half the cure during the heyday of pilgrimage during the Middle Ages. And the waters here were also used to wash the Cathedral's holy relics.

A little way west of the Nine Wells site, in a field beside the main road, sits an old water tower, above some hidden, very impressive underground reservoirs into which the waters of the Nine Wells were once pumped (uphill) to feed St Davids for a period of some sixty years. There is currently a campaign to protect this historic site from demolition, important as it is within the Nine Wells Pembrokeshire story. (see: www.nine-wells.org.uk).

The Nine Wells valley has at least three well sites: the (nine) Holy Wells on the road side of the busy A487 to St Davids; the well below The Pink House (possibly for the farm and now in urgent need of repair); and the small well by the cove (possibly for animals). The valley also has a number of other benefits, including a sculpture within an old quarry beside the path, the remains of a mill near the sea, and two mill ponds. The most appealing aspect, however, is the walk itself, from the main Nine Wells site to the beach and the sea, via these many attractions.

And just as at Ffynnon Faiddog [12.21], local resident Elizabeth Daniels has plans for her Nine(+) Wells area. Elizabeth, who teaches mindfulness, moved here nearly four decades ago. In 2012, she started a group called The Wellspring, *"with the intention of clearing and maintaining and honouring the wells both here and beyond"*. She has already developed accommodation for up to twelve people at Nine Wells for spiritual and creative retreats and holidays, inspired by the proximity to the Nine Wells valley, the wellspring sites and their history. She also has ambitious plans for both the restoration and interpretation of the wellsprings, the involvement of local schools, and the further stimulation of other creative responses (through sculpture, painting, poetry and music).

sir benfro / pembrokeshire

opposite:

the green Nine Wells Valley path
to the sea

above, clockwise from top left:
one of the small hidden wells down the Nine Wells Valley;
the only surviving well-housing at the Nine Wells main site;
the Nine Wells Valley site revealed by Elizabeth Daniels;
a closer view of the well below Elizabeth's house;
the interior of Nine Wells' surviving housing;
Elizabeth beside the well below her house

the living wells of wales

below:
American pilgrims at the only remaining well-housing at Nine Well
(left to right: Herb Nichols, Annette Nichols, Steve Damas, Tom Kurz, Louisa Keleher, Greg Tromiczak, Kathy Keleher, Constance Pepin, Nancy Damas);
and three of the capped wells

sir benfro / pembrokeshire

12.23 the force that drives the water *

Ffynnon Tregroes / Tregroes well
Whitchurch,
nr St Davids,
Pembrokeshire
SM 8049 2556

This is a superb site, easily accessible, with a fine dome-shaped stone structure, and pools dropping down through picturesque woods to the river Solva, its mill and, eventually, to the sea.

left:
the two-toned staining of the stones at Ffynnon Tregroes

One of its most intriguing aspects – along with its cocooning of trees – is the staining red of the tops of the stones in the streams which flow from the well (presumably rich with iron), leaving the parts buried in the sandy soil unpainted, unaffected by the flow. This is a truly liminal place which, like most wellspring sites, when visited adds colour to our lives.

the living wells of wales

Water, seemingly the softest and most malleable of substances, actually has a massive power to quietly effect change, both in the landscape as well as, if we let it, in us. This is Dylan Thomas' 1934 poem, *The force that through the green fuse drives the flower*.

The force that through the green fuse drives the flower
Drives my green age; that blasts the roots of trees
Is my destroyer.
And I am dumb to tell the crooked rose
My youth is bent by the same wintry fever.
The force that drives the water through the rocks *
Drives my red blood; that dries the mouthing streams
Turns mine to wax.
And I am dumb to mouth unto my veins
How at the mountain spring the same mouth sucks.
The hand that whirls the water in the pool
Stirs the quicksand; that ropes the blowing wind
Hauls my shroud sail.
And I am dumb to tell the hanging man
How of my clay is made the hangman's lime.
The lips of time leech to the fountain head;
Love drips and gathers, but the fallen blood
Shall calm her sores.
And I am dumb to tell a weather's wind
How time has ticked a heaven round the stars.
And I am dumb to tell the lover's tomb
How at my sheet goes the same crooked worm.

What we are being offered at the living wells of Pembrokeshire, Wales and elsewhere is a re-positioning within our lives of these once sacred places that are today on the neglected margins of most people's experience.

And in revisiting their full-of-wonder tales in a world that needs more than ever a degree of re-connection with the imagination, and with the natural and with the true, we may take a few steps nearer, perhaps, to Thomas' still sparking *"green fuse"*.

the living wells of wales

and ...

12.24: Ffynnon Fair / St Mary's Well
Warren, Castlemartin
SR 932 975
The church here dates back to Norman times but – in recent danger of collapse – was renovated in 1988 by an ecumenical trust, as a symbol of German / British reconciliation after World War Two. It has a restored chamber organ inside, reputedly owned by the German composer, Mendelssohn, and a simple cross designed by Eric Gill in its graveyard.

12.26: Ffynnon y Stryd Fawr / Main Street well
Pembroke Town
SM 986 014

12.27: Yr Hen Ddyfrffos / The Old Conduit
Monkton
SM 979 014
the 1864 village well, at the junction of the main road from Pembroke and Watery Lane, nr the impressive rebuild of St Nicholas' Priory (now the Priory & Parish Church of St Nicholas & St John), and its adjacent historic ruins

12.25: ffynnon pentref / village well
Well Hill, Pembroke Town
SM 990 014

12.28: Ffynnon a chafn ymyl y ffordd / roadside well and trough
nr Stackpole
SN 987 967

sir benfro / pembrokeshire

12.29: Ffynnon Sant Ioan / St John's Well
Tenby
SN 130 008
Once the main source of water for the town of Tenby, today, often overgrown with ivy, it is easy to miss, despite the presence of its rather dull plaque.

12.33: Ffynnon Fair / Lady Well
Haverfordwest
SM 9548 1522
occupied today by a modern drain and remembered only by a street sign ('Fountain Row')

12.30: Ffynnon bedydd mynwent eglwys Santes Fair Burton / Burton St Mary's churchyard baptismal well
Burton, nr Neyland
SM 9853 0561
in a consistently poor state of repair on all of my many visits over the years since its sanitised restoration / reconstruction between 1985 and 1986

12.34: Ffynnon Madoc / St Madoc's Well
Great Rudbaxton Farm, Rudbaxton
SM 961 206
There has been considerable debate about the exact location of this once-important well, including at a plot within the graveyard of the thirteenth century St Michael's Church (formerly known as St Madoc's), across from this site I now believe to be the most likely one within woodland on Great Rudbaxton Farm, adjacent to the church car park.

12.31: Ffynnon Nicolas / St Nicholas' Well
Watery Lane, Monkton, nr Pembroke
SM 976 010
Access is denied today by head high vegetation, aggressive fences wrapped in barbed wire, and 'Private Property' signs.

12.32: Ffynnon Marged / (St?) Margaret's Well
nr Narbeth
SN 111 119
down a narrow, well-kept path to the left of Maes-y-Ffynnon house, off West Lane in Templeton

12.35: Ffynnon Leonard / St Leonard's Well
Rosemarket
SM 9553 0807

319

the living wells of wales

12.36: Ffynnon Higgon / Higgon's Well
Haverfordwest
SM 9618 15071
Lying on the 'Fortune's Frolic' walk, along the east bank of the Cleddau Wen, the former well is a significant structure, similar in design to that at Maendu [6.8], in Brecon. Reputedly once imbibed by pilgrims on their way to St Davids, today Higgon's Well's waters are piped across the Cleddau for bottling and distribution by Alderwicks Ltd (est. 1921). Now difficult to visit, it is set within the garden of a private house, only visible obliquely and at a distance (though a drinking fountain has been provided on the footpath below, being used here by the author's mother and late father here).

12.37: ffynnon pentref / village well
Walton West, nr Little Haven, nr Haverfordwest
SM 867 128

12.38: Ffynnon Fair / Mary's Well
Maenclochog, nr Fishguard
SN 0753 2706

12.39: Ffynnon pentref ymyl y ffordd / roadside village well
Dinas Cross, nr Newport
SN 011 388

12.40: Ffynnon Shan Shillan / Shan Shillan Well
Letterston, nr Fishguard
SM 9384 2961
dedicated to St Silin / Sulien, a local sixth century prince

12.41: Ffynnon Buarth Brynach / St Brynach's Well
Bernard's Farm, nr Maenclochog
SN 054 280
Once boasting a stone-built arch surrounded by a cut-stone wall with a medieval chapel nearby, it is today in a very poor state.

pen llŷn / the llŷn peninsula

12.42: Ffynnon Llonwen
Llangolman,
Llandilo,
nr Maenclochog
SN 1049 2726
a disappointing site, today used as a rubbish tip

12.43: Ffynnon-y-Cwcwll / Quickwell
off Nun's Lane, St Davids
SM 7534 2550
Hidden in shrubbery within the garden wall of 4 Ty Nancy, it is mainly known now in the name of the adjacent car park! This is a large beehive-shaped structure with a new locked wooden doorway, and a well-hidden plaque reading: *'This well was restored by subscription AD 1813'.*

12.44: Ffynnon Dogfael / St Dogmael's Well
nr Wolfs Castle,
nr Fishguard
SM 9690 2792
The well is in the beautifully landscaped private gardens of St Dogwell's Church vicarage (where the water was pumped until 1974).

12.45: Ffynnon y Cei, Solfach / Solva Quayside Well
nr St Davids
SM 799 241
with a toilet and shower block inappropriately-sited next door
I am glad to report that the size and nature of the signs of late have been diminished, the showers moved, and the back of the well lime-washed.
(2007 / 2017)
enjoyed by American pilgrims after a long walk, May 2018

12.46: Ffynnon Pen-Arthur / King Arthur's Well
nr St Davids
SM 7508 2656
This crudely-capped well supplies water to the house of the same name (and at which three inscribed stones were found, including Mesur y Dorth, now in St David's Cathedral).
Luke Rowlands, my guide to Ffynnon Pen-Arthur

the living wells of wales

12.47: Ffynnon
Drenewydd /
Trenewydd Well
Trenewydd Farmhouse,
nr Llanwnda,
nr Fishguard
SM 913 396

12.48: Ffynnon
Justinian /
St Justinian's Well
above Porthstinian,
nr St Davids
SM 724 252
padlocked and
unimpressive,
but with views of the
nature reserve of
Ramsey Island
(to which the saint
walked, despite losing
his head); and his fine
sixth century chapel

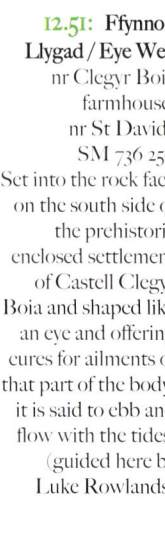

12.49: Ffynnon
Wen / Whitewell
St Davids
SM 7509 2514

12.51: Ffynnon
Llygad / Eye Well
nr Clegyr Boia
farmhouse,
nr St Davids
SM 736 250
Set into the rock face
on the south side of
the prehistoric
enclosed settlement
of Castell Clegyr
Boia and shaped like
an eye and offering
cures for ailments of
that part of the body,
it is said to ebb and
flow with the tides.
(guided here by
Luke Rowlands)

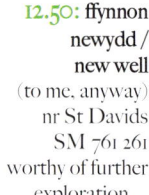

12.50: ffynnon
newydd /
new well
(to me, anyway)
nr St Davids
SM 761 261
worthy of further
exploration ...

pen llŷn / the llŷn peninsula

DEFENDING THE FOUNTAIN
a few last words

Let me get it right. What if we got it wrong?
What if we weakened ourselves getting strong?
What if our wanting more was making less?
And what if all of this wasn't progress?

from Lemn Sissay's poem, 'What if?'

We must keep our well clear of the beast's dirt.

Waldo Williams, from his 1946 poem, 'Preseli' – written as a protest against the Ministry of Defense's plans to use the Preseli Mountains in Pembrokeshire as a firing range

We are bleeding at the roots, because we are cut off from the earth and sun and stars, and love is a grinning mockery, because, poor blossom, we plucked it from its stem on the tree of Life, and expected it to keep on blooming in our civilised vase on the table.

DH Lawrence, 1928

Unless thou canst defend the fountain thou canst not defend thy dominions.

from *The Mabinigion*: 'The Lady of the Fountain' (trans. Gwyn Jones & Thomas Jones, 1949)

cartoon by Moz / Matthew English (from *Private Eye* magazine no.1487, 11-24 January 2019)

Many of the 'living wells' of Wales are in fact ... dead. While some of our once important sacred springs, holy wells, therapeutic spas, abbey, church and castle wells, and drinking fountains, spouts and troughs are still visible and, though much less commonly, in daily use, the title of this book – *The Living Wells of Wales* – is more of an aspiration than a description ... an entreaty, a call to action even.

As you will have read and seen in the once treasured wellspring sites featured here, many have now been abandoned, some buried beneath piles of rubble, some completely destroyed, ploughed up by farmers frustrated with having to swerve their tractors around another pile of old stones, lost to drainage, to road-widening schemes or built over by a new bridge or housing development, often without a second thought. This, sadly, is a main theme in the story of our wellspring sites into the twenty-first century. And the new experiments in fracking in Britain could pose the greatest threat of all, injecting highly-pressured water and a toxic soup of chemicals and sand into a well – disturbing and polluting its water courses – in order to open up fissures in the rock to release natural gas to burn.

Brian Fagan in his *Elixir: a human history of water* (2011) describes its three ages:

In the first, water was so scarce that it became sacred in almost every culture. By the time of the Industrial Revolution, human ingenuity had brought water and life to even the most arid landscapes. This was the second age: water as commodity. Soon enough even desert regions like Las Vegas and the Gulf States glimmered with swimming pools and golf courses.

Today we are entering the third age of water. As the global population nears nine billion and ancient aquifers run dry, we must once again learn to treat the elixir of life with reverence. We may even need to adopt the water ethos of our ancestors if we are to solve the water crises of the future.

The ways in which we are treating our wellspring sites are a perfect litmus test of our progress, or lack of it. We can laugh, perhaps, at the stories of spirits in rocks and in trees, in mountains and rivers, in sacred springs and holy wells, but whose mythology is destroying the world and creating huge inequalities of health, wealth and opportunity?

Climate change is the product of the hegemony of a particular set of myths which argues for perpetual growth through the exploitation of the earth's finite body, firmly stuck within Fagan's 'second age of water'. We need to ask ourselves: Who today has the most useful response to our planet's survival: the homogenising materialism of market economics or that of so-called 'primitive' people with their reverence for the land and its creatures? Perhaps we should be revisiting their sacred geography of respect and reciprocity which prioritised guardianship over greed.

liquid assets

While the sacred springs and holy wells of Wales offer a rich though sometimes contradictory diversity of constructions and of meanings, what is unchanging and certain is the fact that, in our privileged part of the world, we often take water for granted and complain bitterly on the very rare occasions when there is not enough to feed our lawns or wash our cars. It almost always flows easily at the turn of a tap for us, while more than a billion people worldwide lack a regular and safe supply, and two and a half billion don't have access to adequate sanitation. And – according to WaterAid – every 15 seconds a child dies from water-related diseases.

The following are the words of Segueda Zouga, a woman from Burkina Faso in West Africa:

As soon as the sun rises at 6am, we go to fetch water. We take whatever containers we have down to the dry river bed and dig for water, there. It can take three hours to dig deep enough to reach water and we have to go three times a day.

I have had six children and yet only two of them have survived. My only choice is to give them water which is not safe to drink, or no water at all. I worry about the water I give them constantly. All of us get ill often. My children and I get fevers, stomach cramps, and diarrhoea.

Water is the overwhelming problem in my life and in the lives of the other families in this village. All day, I think about nothing else. At night, I go to sleep worrying about fetching water …. All of us go, old women, young women, pregnant women – even the children. We all have to do our bit. I know the children should go to school but what choice do we have? What use is education if I can't give my children enough water to drink?"

Running alongside this desperate necessity, each year in Britain alone we spend more than half a billion pounds on bottled water and some eight million on its advertising. Water's growing scarcity is becoming an ever greater attraction for big business, seeking big profits both in the UK as well as throughout the world, aided and abetted by Western governments, including our own. The result is rising water prices and disconnections, further damaging the poor, and an almost total failure to re-invest, any profits made being returned to the already rich.

These new / old struggles for water rights will in the very near future, in the view of many commentators, eclipse the wars for oil we are currently engaged in, as a pure water source becomes the new global battleground in a world where population is increasing rapidlt while the water supply remains the same.

This is film-maker Peter Swanson (of Global Visions) writing in 2008:

"By the year 2020, nearly fifty nations will suffer severe water shortages. By 2025, more than a dozen nations will need water from rivers controlled by hostile neighbours. By 2030, many cities that have existed for centuries will simply dry up."

And here is part of Maura Dooley's fine long poem, 'The Source', in which she asks: *"What does it mean when a well runs dry?":*

We've taken too much,
pumped up, poured out
more than we need and now
in Venice, Bangkok, London,
we are the slippery, subsiding
  places
of the earth and must learn to
  manage
what has been given.

What does it mean when a well
  runs dry?

Here at my door a window
  cleaner
wants to refill his bucket of water,

I will carry the pail
like that most precious phial,
a twist of glass that held the tears
that washed the feet of Christ.
I will swing open my ordinary
  faucet,

spill the slops of everyday life
down the drain, out to the sewers,
swill the blood from the sink,
the stains from the sheet,
and call on those saints
Brigid, Anne, Winifred,
whose faith was as knowledge,
an awakening, a promise,

a splash of cold water to the face

drawing new water from our wells

A 2018 announcement by Vice Media's 'creative' agency Virtue argued that commercial brands could fill the spiritual void left by the decline of organised religion. Aimed in particular at the young, it proposed offering *"the tools and resources they need to nurture their soul and wellbeing"* (Julie Arbit, Vice) through the substitution, I assume, of Versace for the Virgin Mary and Jimmy Choo for Jesus Christ at the United Church of Calvin Klein!

RS Thomas also recognised this need to fill a god-shaped hole (although he probably wouldn't have approved of Vice Media's alternative proposals):

> In cities that
> have outgrown their promise
> people
> are becoming pilgrims
> again, if not to this place,
> then to the recreation of it
> in their own spirits.

(from 'The Moon in Lleyn')

The rediscovery of interest in sacred spring and holy well sites has increased during the last few years, born perhaps out of this spiritual vacuum, as well as a growing concern about the way we are treating our planet. The polarisation of people and of ideas, the increasingly unsatisfactory benefits of consumerisation, the ever present threat (and reality for many) of war, alongside the squandering of our natural resources has led to a search for alternative ways to live and the imagining of different futures. All of these issues are leading us to seek a purer reality and a simpler explanation for what it means to be human. And despite the apparent history of amnesia, of neglect and sometimes even willful destruction, the good news is that wellsprings' essential contract is still on offer: look after us and we will look after you!

So if, in creating this book, I can introduce one person to the joys of wellspring exploration, change one person's mind about how important it is for us to preserve and cherish these places, and encourage one person to begin working to protect a wellspring site, my efforts here exploring, recording and writing about these wonderful places will all have been … a complete waste of time! What we need is a revolution, a mass movement of understanding, respect and most importantly action, a seismic transformation (and not through fracking) to change the physical, intellectual and emotional landscape around our sacred spring and holy well sites throughout Wales and beyond.

the deluge of time

Out of monuments, names, words, proverbs, traditions, private records and evidences, fragments of stories, passages of books and the like; we doe save and recover somewhat of the deluge of time.

Francis Bacon (1561-1626)
from 'Advancement of Learning', 1605

The Living Wells of Wales, like most works which touch upon the past, looks both forward and back. In exploring, bemoaning and celebrating the often contradictory though nearly always captivating narratives of our wellspring cultures throughout time, we can begin to make from the complexities of the past something of relevance to our lives today and our survival into the future.

LP Hartley famously wrote that *"The past is a foreign country; they do things differently there"*, but perhaps through this brief package tour into our yesterdays, we can bring home some illuminating souvenirs for ourselves, and for those generations who will live in the world we have created for them.

The first words in this book were taken from a poem, so a poem ends it, too.

It's called 'An Tobar' ('The Well'), by Cathal Ó Searcaigh, an Irish poet, writing in the Ulster dialect of the Irish language (translated here by Frank Sewell). It speaks of the need to remember the many and diverse levels of gifts that the pure water from a natural spring provides, particularly in hard times like these, and the need to stay near to the source, both of water, as well as of the real things, the deep things, the things that have, or at least should have, real meaning and real value in our lives.

'It'll set you up for life',
said old Bríd, fire in her eyes,
handing me a bowl of well-water,
the cleanest in all Gleann an Atha
from a well kept by her people's
people, a family heirloom
tucked away in a secluded spot
with a ditch like a moat around it
and a flagstone for a lid.

When I was coming into my own
back in the early sixties here,
there wasn't a house around
without the same sort of well;
everyone was all chuffed then
about how clean and healthy
theirs was kept and wouldn't let
a speck of dust cloud its silver
lining; and if a hint of red-rust
was found, they bailed it out
right away using a tin bucket;
then to keep their well sweet,
freshened it regularly with kiln-lime.

From our family well sprang
bright clearwater full of life.
With tins and crocks, they dipped
  into it
day after day, and any time their
  throats
were parched by summer's heat,
it slaked and soothed them in fields
and bogs – a true pick-me-up
that set them hop, skip and jumping
for joy, cleansing them all their lives.

For a long time now, running water
snakes towards us from distant hills
and in every kitchen, both sides
of the glen, water spits from a tap,
drab lackluster water that leaves
a bad taste in the mouth while
among my people the real thing
is forgotten about. Brid once said,
'it's hard to find a well these days',
as she filled up another bowl.
'They're hidden in bulrushes and
  grass,
choked by weeds and green scum
but for all the neglect, they've lost
not a drop of their true essence.
Find your own well, my lad,
for the arid times to come.
They dry up who steer clear of
  sources.'

bibliography & suggested further reading

The Holy Wells of Wales, Francis Jones (University of Wales Press, 1954)

Holy Wells in Britain: a Guide, Janet Bord (Heart of Albion, 2008)

Sacred Waters: Holy Wells and Water Lore in Britain and Ireland, Janet & Colin Bord (Harper Collins, 1985)

Cures and Curses: Ritual and Cult at Holy Wells, Janet Bord (Heart of Albion, 2006)

Sacred Springs; in search of the Holy Wells of Wales, Paul Davis (Blorenge Books, 2003)

Ffynhonnau Cymru: Ffynnonau Brycheiniog, Ceredigion, Maldwyn, Maesyfed a Meirion, Eirlys Gruffydd (Gwasg Carreg Gwalch, 1997)

Ffynhonnau Cymru: Ffynnonau Caernarfon, Dinbych, Y Fflint a Môn, Eirlys & Ken Lloyd Gruffydd (Gwasg , 1999)

Spas and Springs of Wales, Audrey Doughty (Gwasg Carreg Gwalch, 2001)

The Ancient Wells of Llŷn, Roland Bond (Llygad Gwalch, 2017)

The Living Stream: Holy Wells in Historical Context, James Rattue (Boydell Press, 1995)

The Magic and Mystery of Holy Wells, Edna Whelan (Capall Bann Publishing, 2002)

The Water of Life: springs & wells of mainland Britain, Ian & Frances Thompson (Llanerch Press, 2004)

Holy Wells: A pilgrim's prayer companion and guide, Brendan O'Malley (Canterbury Press Norwich, 2014)

Holy Wells Cornwall: a photographic journey, Phil Cope (Seren 2010)

The Dancing Pilgrimage of Water: writings on the rivers, lakes and reservoirs of Wales, Phil Cope [with Dewi Roberts] (Gwasg Carreg Gwalch, 2010)

Borderlands: new photographs and old tales of the sacred springs, holy wells and spas of the Wales - England borders, Phil Cope (Seren 2013)

Holy Wells Scotland, , Phil Cope (Seren 2015)

Sacred North: travelling in the footsteps of the earliest Christian missionaries to Cumbria, Northumberland, Scotland and beyond, Phil Cope [with Fr John Musther] (2018)

The Physicians of Myddfai: cures and remedies of the mediaeval world, Terry Breverton (Cambria Books, 2012)

Magic and Medicine: the story of the Physicians of Myddfai, Arblaster, Swan & Bernays (Dinefwr Press, 2002)

Myddfai: Its Land and Peoples, David B. James (1991)

Unholy Water? Ffynnon Elian 'The Cursing Well', Jane Dryhurst Beckerman (2017)

St Winefride, Her Holy Well and the Jesuit Mission, C.650-1930, TW Pritchard (Bridge Books, 2009)

A Historical Tour through Pembrokeshire, Richard Fenton (Davies & Co., 1811)

Saints and Stones: a guide to the pilgrim ways of Pembrokeshire, Damian Walford Davies & Anne Eastham (Gomer, 2002)

bibliography & suggested further reading

St Davids Peninsula: A Journey In Time, Jacki Sime (Shore Light Press, 2017)

In Pursuit of Saint David, patron saint of Wales, Gerald Morgan (Y Lolfa, 2017)

Pilgrimage: A Welsh Perspective, Nona Rees & Terry John (Gomer, 2002)

Celtic Sacred Landscapes, Nigel Pennick (Thames & Hudson, 1996)

A Tour in Wales (2 vols.), Thomas Pennant (Henry Hughes, 1778, 1783)

Lives of the Welsh Saints, Gilbert H Doble (University of Wales Press, 1971)

Saint's Cults in the Celtic World, Boardman & Reuben Davies [edit.] (Woodbridge, 2009)

Lives of the British Saints, Baring-Gould & Fisher (1907)

Religion, Language and Nationality in Wales, Glanmor Williams (Cardiff, 1979)

The Hidden Messages in Water, Masaru Emoto *(Beyond Words Pub., 2004)*

Elixir: a human history of water, Brian Fagan (Bloomsbury, 2012)

Saving Churches: The Friends of Friendless Churches: the first 50 years, Matthew Saunders (Frances Lincoln, 2010)

The Wayfinders: Why Ancient Wisdom Matters in the Modern Word, Wade Davis (House of Anansi Press, 2009)

reports, blogs, websites

Arolwg i Gyflwr Ffynhonnau Pen Llŷn yn yr Ardal o Harddwch Naturiol Eithriadol ('Survey to the Condition of Wells in Pen Llŷn in the Area of Outstanding Natural Beauty') 2005, Elfed Gruffyd (via AHNE Pen Llŷn AONB: ahnellynaonb@gwynedd.gov.uk)

Cadw Scheduling Enhancement: Holy Wells, Iwan Parry, George Smith & David Hopewell (Gwynedd Archaeological Trust No.2156 / Report No.931 / March 2011)

Clwyd-Powys Archaeological Trusts' Historic Settlements in the former Brecknock Borough (CPAT Report No.1056) and *Medieval and Early Post-Medieval Monastic and Ecclesiastical Sites in East and North-East Wales* (CPAT Report No.1090)

Medieval and Early Post-Medieval Holy Wells: A Threat-Related Assessment, Mike Ings, Dyfed Archaeological Trust for Cadw, 2011

Medieval and Early Post-Medieval Holy Wells: a Threat-Related Assessment, Additional Sites, Dyfed Archaeological Trust, 2012

The Pembrokeshire Cemeteries Project: excavations at Porthclew Chapel, Freshwater East, Pembrokeshire, 2009, Dyfed Archaeological Trust / Second Interim Report

Penally Abbey Hotel, Pembrokeshire: Archaeological Watching Brief, 2016, Dyfed Archaeological Trust

Pilgrims trail to St Davids: consulting and defining the route, 2012, Andrew Dugmore,

Ian Taylor / Wellhopper: *www.wellhopper.wales*

Friends of Friendless Churches: *www.friendsoffriendlesschurches.org.uk*

WaterAid: *www.wateraid.org/uk*

the living wells of wales

index of wellspring sites

Abbey Well, Strata Florida	144
All Saints Well, Gresford	126
Amphitheatre well, Plas Glyn-y-Weddw	81
Balineae Silures (Castell Collen)	135, 148
'Beast' trough, nr Abergavenny	186
Bishop Gower's Well, Llanddew	164, 188
Bletherstone Church Well, nr Narbeth	283-84
Box Tree Well, nr Cwmyoy	188
Bride's Inn well, Little Haven	287
Bronllys Castle Well	157
Bronant well	158
Burton St Mary baptismal well	319
Caerphilly Castle well	233
Caerleon Roman Baths	193-94
Caernarfon Castle wells	46
Caerwent Roman Baths	195
Caldicot Castle well	199-200
Canton drinking fountain, Cardiff	239
Cardiff Castle well	243
Cardiff Civic Centre drinking fountain	244
Carreg Cennen Castle well	175-76
Castell Coch well, nr Cardiff	244
Castell Henllys sacred spring	290-91
Castle Well, nr Cwmyoy	185
Catbrook village well	210
Chepstow Castle wells	201-02
Corntown well and baptismal pond	233
Cowbridge village pump	243
Criccieth Castle well	91
Dairy Well, Llandaff Cathedral	240
David Watkins animal trough, Hay-on-Wye	186
Dinas Cross roadside well, Pembrokeshire	320
Dolycoed Spa, Llanwrtyd Wells	153-56
Dwlch i Dduw, nr Llanon	267
Eye Well, Brecon	185
Eye Well, Hay	188
Eye Well, Llandrindod	149
Eye Well, nr St Davids	322
Felin Uchaf well-house, Pen Llŷn	91
Ffynnon Aelhaearn, Llanaelhaearn	89
Ffynnon Aelrhiw, Plas yn Rhiw	72-74, 330-31
Ffynnon Allgo, Llanallgo	41
Ffynnon Angaeron, nr Goytre	162-63
Ffynnon Arian, Mynytho	69
Ffynnon Baglau, Ynys Enlli	86
Ffynnon Barfau, Ynys Enlli	86
Ffynnon Beris, nr Llanberis	53-55
Ffynnon Beuno, Clynnog Fawr	65-67
Ffynnon Beuno, Gwyddelwern	126
Ffynnon Beuno, Tremeirchion	110-11, 164, 238
Ffynnon Capel Begawdin, Porthyrhyd	263, 264-265
Ffynnon Capel Erbach, Porthyrhyd	263-64
Ffynnon Carreg, Ynys Enlli	90
Ffynnon Ceinwen, Cerrigceinwen	41
Ffynnon Corn, Uwchmynydd	89
Ffynnon Corn, Ynys Enlli	88
Ffynnon Cristin, Ynys Enlli	90
Ffynnon Cybi, Llangybi	142
Ffynnon Degla, Llandegla	112-13
Ffynnon Ddewi, Porthclais	303-05
Ffynnon Ddoged, Llanddoged	126
Ffynnon Ddrewllyd, Cwm-Twrch Isaf	227-28
Ffynnon Dolysgwydd, Ynys Enlli	87
Ffynnon Drewi, nr Bronant	131, 132-33
Ffynnon Dwynwen, Llanddwyn Island	32-33
Ffynnon Dyffryn Tawel, Strata Florida	143, 145
Ffynnon Dyfnog, Llanrhaeadr	93, 114-16
Ffynnon Dyno Goch, Ynys Enlli	90
Ffynnon Eidda, nr Blaenau Ffestiniog	57
Ffynnon Eilian, Llaneilian	36-37, 39
Ffynnon Eilian, Llanelian yn Rhos	37, 99-102
Ffynnon Eluned, Llechfaen	164, 167
Ffynnon Enddwyn, nr Dyffryn Ardudwy	43, 56
Ffynnon Engan, Llanengan	79, 82
Ffynnon Fach, Crimea Pass	126
Ffynnon Faelog, nr Llowes	186
Ffynnon Faglan, Llanfaglan	50, 51
Ffynnon Faiddog, Whitesands Bay	180, 309-11, 312
Ffynnon Fair, Bryncroes	88
Ffynnon Fair, Haverfordwest	319
Ffynnon Fair, Llanfair Caereinion	158
Ffynnon Fair, Llanrhos	127
Ffynnon Fair, Maenclochog	320
Ffynnon Fair, Maentwrog	48, 49
Ffynnon Fair, Mynytho	71
Ffynnon Fair, Nefyn	88
Ffynnon Fair, Penrhys	214-18
Ffynnon Fair, Pilleth	157
Ffynnon Fair, nr Trefnant	97-99, 127, 259, 266
Ffynnon Fair, Uwchymynydd	83-85
Ffynnon Fawr, Nottage	225-26
Ffynnon Felin Bach, Pwllheli	88
Ffynnon Fyw (or Dduw), Mynytho	68, 69
Ffynnon Gadfan, Llangadfan	158
Ffynnon Gapan, nr Llanllawer	293-94, 297
Ffynnon Gofer, Llanover Estate	186, 259
Ffynnon Gybi, Clorach Fawr	19, 41, 142
Ffynnon Gybi, Llangybi, Ceredigion	142
Ffynnon Gybi, Llangybi, Gwent	204-05
Ffynnon Gybi, Llangybi, Llŷn	59, 61-64
Ffynnon Gynfran, Llysfaen	127
Ffynnon Gynidr, Glasbury	157
Ffynnon Gwyfil, Plas Brondanw	50
Ffynnon Gwynhoedl, Ynys Enlli	88
Ffynnon Hafod Newydd, Strata Florida	145
Ffynnon Llandennis, Cardiff	245
Ffynnon Llanfihangel Dinsylwy, nr Llanddona	38
Ffynnon Llawddog, Cenarth	138
Ffynnon Lletyr Fadoc, Llandudno	127
Ffynnon Lleuddad, Botwnnog	89
Ffynnon Llonwen, Llangolman	321
Ffynnon Mair, Margam	221, 223
Ffynnon Oer, Swyddffynnon	157
Ffynnon Owain Roland, Ynys Enlli	90
Ffynnon Pant, Plas yn Rhiw	77
Ffynnon Pen-Arthur, nr St Davids	321
Ffynnon Pen-y-Groes, Pen Cilan	79-80
Ffynnon Plas Bach, Ynys Enlli	90
Ffynnon Plas yn Rhiw	78
Ffynnon Porth Ysgaden, nr Tudweiliog	89
Ffynnon Rhufeinig, nr Criccieth	88
Ffynnon Sadwrn, Llandudno	127
Ffynnon Saint, Plas yn Rhiw	75-76
Ffynnon Sanctaidd, Pistyll	89
Ffynnon Sant Ffraid, nr Swyddffynnon	136-37
Ffynnon Sara, nr Derwen	117-18
Ffynnon Sarff, Mynytho	70-71
Ffynnon Shan Shillan, Letterston	320
Ffynnon Tregroes, Whitchurch	315-17
Ffynnon Trwy'r Nant, Llanbedrog	90
Ffynnon Tŵdno, Llandudno	127
Ffynnon Tyn-y-Garreg, Strata Florida	146
Ffynnon Ty Pilla, Ynys Enlli	90
Ffynnon West End, Trefor	89
Ffynnon Wnda, Llanwnda	295-96
Ffynnon-y-Capel, nr Dolgellau	57
Ffynnon yn Ddragau, Bancyfelin	267
Ffynnon y Saint, nr Aberdaron	79
Free Chalybeate Spring, Llandrindod	149, 159
'Garrison Well', Machynlledd	158
Grange Gardens drinking fountain, Cardiff	244
'Grotto of Hygrea', Llanarthne	267
Gumfreston Holy Wells, nr Tenby	270, 271-75
Ham Cross well, Llantwit Major	243
Harlech Castle wells	47
Harlech horse trough	57
Hendre roadside trough	211
Higgon's Well, Haverfordwest	320
Holy Well, Abergavenny	185
Holy Well, Reynoldston, Gower	256
'House' Well, Penally	276
Kithen Well, nr Parkmill	256
Lithia Saline well, Llandrindod Wells	149

index of wellspring sites

Llandaff City roadside well, Cardiff	239
Llandaff Fields drinking fountain, Cardiff	244
Llanddewi Brefi village pump	157
Llandrindod pump room other well	149
Llanfair Discoed village well	205
Llanfyllin bridge well	140
Llangammarch Wells	152
Llangybi's other well	89
Llanover roadside trough 1	186
Llanover roadside trough 2	186
Llanrhos Church drinking fountain	127
Llawhaden Castle well	288-89
Llysworney well	243
Llywelyn's Well, Cilmeri	158
Llwyn-yr-eos Farm well, St Fagans	241
Logan's Well, nr Myddfai	187
Lord Boston's Sulphur Well, Penrhoslligwy	40
Lord Penrhyn's Well, Ysbyty Ifan	126
Maendu Well, Brecon	136, 161, 177-79
Margaret's Well, nr Narbeth	319
Mary Magdelene's Well, Cerrigydrudion	127
Mary Short memorial fountain, St Asaph	128
Mary's Well, nr Rhuddlan	127
Mill Well, Parkmill, Gower	256
Monks' Bath-house, Margam Park	221-22
Monmouth Victorian well	211
Murton Green village well	251
New Inn Well House, Cross Ash	179
Nine Wells, nr Solva	312-14
North Crickhowell drinking fountain	188
Ogmore Down Well, St Bride's Major	233
Old Conduit, Monkton	318
Patrick's Spring, Govilon	185
Pembroke Town Main Street well	318
Pembroke Town village well	318
Penarth Fawr medieval well	91
Pen yr Allt Rocks Well, Machynlledd	157
Physicians of Myddfai Well	168-69
Pistyll Dewi, St David's Cathedral	305-06
Port Clew Holy Well, Freshwater East	277-78
Prestatyn Roman Bath-house	128
Priory Well, Brecon	185
Quickwell, St Davids	305, 321
Raglan Castle wells	191, 196-98
Rees Goring Thomas fountain, Llanon	267
roadside fountain, nr Llanelli	267
roadside trough, nr Llanelli	267
Rock Park well, Llandrindod	147, 149, 150-51
St Anne's Well, Llanmihangel	238
St Anne's Well, Trefecca	187
St Anthony's Well, Llansteffan	258, 260-61
St Beuno's Well, Holywell	128
St Bride's Inn Well, Little Haven, Pembs	287-88
St Bride's Major village well and pond	243
St Brynach's Well, nr Maenclochog	320
St Cadoc's Well, Pentyrch	244
St Canna's Well, Hay-on-Wye	181-82
St Caradoc's Well, Haverfordwest	286
St Celer's Well, Llangeler	261-62
St Celynin's Well, Llangelynin	44, 102, 104
St Cenedlon's Well, Rockfield	210
St Cenydd's Well, Llangennith	251-52
St Ciwg Well, nr Pontardawe	233
St Collwyn's Well, Pyle	224
St Cyngar's Well, Llangefni	41
St Cynhafal's Well, Llangynhafal	128
St Davids 'new' well	322
St David's Well, Nottage	233
St Deiniol's Well, Penally	276
St Dogmael's Well, nr Fishguard	321
St Dyfan's Well, Llandyfan	174
St Eluned's 'Penginger' Well, Brecon	164, 165, 188
St Fagan's Holy Well, St Fagans	241
St Genau's Well, Llangenny	188
St Govan's Wells, nr Bosherston	269, 270, 279-83
St Gwenfaen's Well, nr Rhoscolyn	34-35, 37
St Gwladys' Well, Basseleg	210
St Helen's Well, Dolwyddelan	105-07
St Illtyd's Well, Llanrhidian	253-54, 257
St Issui's Well, Partrishow	171-73
St John's or Castle Well, Hay	187
St John's Well, Tenby	319
St Justinian's Well, nr St Davids	322
St Leonard's Well, Rosemarket	319
St Leonard's Well, Rudbaxton	284-85
St Madoc's Well, Rudbaxton	319
St Mary's Well, Hay	187
St Mary's Well, Warren	318
St Myllin's Well, Llanfyllin	140
St Nicholas Church pump	243
St Nicholas' Well, Monkton	319
St Nicholas' Well, St Nicholas, Pembs	297-99
St Non's Well, Eglwysfach	139
St Non's Well, nr St Davids	270, 300-02
St Oswald's Well, nr Holywell	126
St Padarn's Well, Aberystwyth	158
St Patrick's Well, Llanbadrig	39-40
St Peter's Well, Caswell Bay	247, 249-51
St Sannan's Well, Bedwellty	203
St Seiriol's Well, Penmon, nr Rhosybol	29, 30
St Teilo's Church Well, Llandeilo	185, 307
St Teilo's Well, Llandaff Cathedral	240
St Teilo's Well, Llandeloy	307-09
St Teilo's Well, Llangolman	174, 291-92, 307
St Teilo's Well, Penally	276, 307
St Tewdric's Well, Mathern	211
St Trillo's Holy Chapel Well, Rhos on Sea	108-09
St Winefride's Well, Holywell	65, 81, 97, 110, 119-25, 153, 164
Salmon's Wells, Penllyn	235, 236-37
Sandford's Well, Newton	233
Scotch Baptism Well, Harlech	57
Segontium Roman Fort wells, Caernarfon	44-45
Sir Charles Morgan Well, Brecon	188
Skenfrith memorial well	211
Skenfrith roadside trough	211
Skirrid Mountain Well, nr Abergavenny	187
Solva Quayside Well, nr St Davids	321
Stackpole roadside well and trough	318
Swansea Castle well	248-49
Swan Well, Hay	183
Sweetwells, Pont-y-Rhyl, Garw Valley	229-30
Taff's Well, nr Cardiff	231
Tarren Deusant, nr Llantrisant	212, 219-21
Town Well, Hay	187
Tredunnock village well	211
Trefriw Wells and Spa	94-97, 147, 259
Trenewydd Well, nr Llanwnda	332
Trinity Well / St Cenydd's Well, Ilstone	256
Usk Castle well	210
Valle Crucis Abbey well, nr Llangollen	128
Valle Crucis Farm well, nr Llangollen	128
Victoria Park drinking fountain, Cardiff	244
Victoria Wells, nr Llanwrtyd Wells	158
Virtuous Well, Trellech	81, 206-09, 238
Walton West village well, Pembs	320
Well of Arthur's Kitchen, Llanddeiniolen	57, 153
Wharf (or Walk Well), Hay	184
White Castle well	210
Whitewell, St Davids	305, 322
Wilcrick wishing well	210
Witches Well, Holyhead	41
Y Ffynnon ym Mhentre Llandre	140-41